The Growth Of English Education
1348–1648

THE GROWTH OF ENGLISH EDUCATION 1348–1648

A Social and Cultural History

Michael Van Cleave Alexander

The Pennsylvania State University Press
University Park and London

Library of Congress Cataloging-in-Publication Data

Alexander, Michael Van Cleave, 1937-
    The growth of English education, 1348-1648 : a social and
cultural history / by Michael Van Cleave Alexander.
        p.   cm.
    Includes bibliographical references.
    ISBN 0-271-00687-0
    1. Education—England—History.   2. Education, Medieval—
England.   3. England—Social conditions.   4. England—Civilization.
I.   Title.
LA631.A47   1990
370'.942—dc20   89-37531

For Ann and Cissie,
Mischa and Peter

Contents

Introduction

This book grew out of a general interest in the educational and
cultural developments of the Elizabethan and early Stuart periods,
England's greatest cultural flowering. Since World War II, if not
before, there has been a steady interest in those developments,
and scholarly work of a high order has often resulted. But too
often the contributions made between 1558 and 1642 have been
portrayed as revolutionary in nature and impact—as totally new
occurrences without precedents or harbingers during earlier
eras.[1] As I read and reflected on the surviving evidence, it
became increasingly apparent that the movements that came to
full maturity during the reigns of Elizabeth I and James I could
be traced back to the time of the Black Death and the Hundred
Years War. In short, there had been a gradual buildup of interest in the provision of better education for England's youth,
with a variety of interlocking factors providing the necessary
momentum. As a consequence, what seemed to have been an
"educational revolution" after 1558 was in fact the culmination
of an evolutionary process already more than two centuries old.

At the same time I was groping my way towards that conclusion, I was perplexed by the findings of David Cressy, and
especially by his book *Literacy and the Social Order: Reading
and Writing in Tudor and Stuart England* (1980). According to
Dr. Cressy, who made an exhaustive study of surviving wills
and whether they had been signed or not, *illiteracy* remained
the common characteristic of the English people during the
sixteenth and seventeenth centuries. In his view, less than 18
percent of all adult males could read and write, whereas the
proportion of adult women who were literate was even lower,
never rising above four or five percent.[2] If there had actually

been a growing interest in education since the mid-fourteenth century, with scores of new schools and colleges being founded and educational opportunity becoming appreciably wider, how was such restricted literacy still possible? In view of the way so much was being done to help poor children attend school for a time and to assist able boys without means to undertake advanced studies at Oxford or Cambridge, was it not likely that education and literacy were far more prevalent among the English people? Moreover, was it accurate or even appropriate for Dr. Cressy to compare Elizabethan England, a basically free society, with certain districts of Poland and eastern Europe, where serfdom was still entrenched and there had been no comparable increase of educational institutions? These are among the most important questions I sought to answer in this book; and partly because of the narrative format I adopted and the essentially literary nature of the evidence I considered, I came to fundamentally different conclusions from those offered by Dr. Cressy. The individual reader can of course decide for himself between our rival interpretations.

In the pages that follow I also attempt to show how developments in one educational sphere affected what took place in others. Excellent monographs on single aspects of the long period 1348–1648 have appeared from time to time. But usually they concentrate on individual grammar schools or on the endowed schools of a particular district or region; on separate Oxford and Cambridge colleges or the changing role of the universities in general; on the rising educational qualifications of the parish clergy, the lawyers, or some similar group; or finally, on the establishment of the printing industry and the growth of popular literacy. To make such specialized studies is only the first step towards real historical understanding, since developments in one sphere often triggered changes in others. For example, the establishment of the tutorial system at the universities had an eventual impact on the instructional methods used in both the grammar schools and the Inns of Court. Although there are obvious pitfalls in any comprehensive undertaking of this sort, I think it is possible to relate within a single book the main developments that occurred in all those areas during the period under review and to compare what happened in one sector to what was taking place elsewhere.

During the research for this book, I became increasingly impressed by the way women encouraged the educational developments of the period. Female donors made unusually generous contributions in light of the limited funds they commanded. Moreover, because women were unable to profit in any direct way from the new schools, colleges, and scholarships of the period, it would not have been surprising had they withheld all support from an educational system that operated almost exclusively for males. Yet female donors were just as convinced as their male counterparts that improved education was necessary for the further spread of the Christian message. So they played a major part in the steady expansion of educational institutions that occurred, and one of the truly significant contributors of the period was a woman—Lady Margaret Beaufort, the mother of Henry VII.

The educational activities of the clergy, especially before the Reformation, came as much less of a surprise. Between the 1350s and the 1530s the bishops and archbishops enjoyed almost princely incomes and seldom had family obligations to consider. As a result the prelates were more generous than any comparable group in supporting the schools and colleges of the realm, their donations eclipsing those of the aristocracy or the middle class. Once the Reformation began and the hierarchy's income was halved through unfair land exchanges required of them by the crown, the scale of their educational philanthropy declined significantly, although it still remained substantial. Indeed, during the reigns of Elizabeth I and James I, the prelates continued to be active on the educational front, founding new grammar schools and graduate fellowships in record numbers and donating valuable books and manuscripts to university, college, and cathedral libraries. However, they were no longer in a position to found new academic societies at Oxford and Cambridge, like the many they had established between the 1350s and the 1530s.

If the hierarchy played a less significant role from the mid-sixteenth century, the lesser clergy emerged about that time as important educational patrons. Between the 1540s and the 1620s the archdeacons, rectors, and vicars of rural England made a collective contribution of no slight significance. Thus, even though the laity derived the greatest benefit from the expansion of educational opportunity during those years, the clergy deserve considerable credit for creating that expansion in the first place.

Because of the comprehensive nature of my subject, I have inevitably drawn on the work of innumerable scholars in the

United States, Canada, Australia, and of course the British Isles. From the notes it should be apparent to whose writings I am principally indebted. At this point I wish to single out for special thanks only those authorities whose books and articles were especially helpful in the preparation of this study.

Among the larger works that shaped my interpretation were volumes written or edited by Lawrence Stone, Kenneth Charlton, John Lawson, Nicholas Orme, A. F. Leach, Mark Curtis, Joan Simon, Margaret Aston, Margaret Deanesly, Felicity Heal, Rosemary O'Day, H. C. Porter, C. E. Dent, Wilfrid Prest, Sears Jayne, Foster Watson, Neil Ker, Hugh Kearney, H. S. Bennett, James McConica, Mordechai Feingold, A. B. Cobban, Jo Ann Moran, Maria Dowling, J. J. Scarisbrick, A. G. Dickens, David Knowles, Robert Weiss, and W. K. Jordan. Among the older studies that proved indispensable were the classic histories of the two universities by C. E. Mallet and J. B. Mullinger and the various monographs published over a long period by J. A. Venn. Equally important for the grammar schools was the comprehensive account written as long ago as 1818 by Nicholas Carlisle.

I also depended heavily on learned articles in such academic journals as *Past and Present, History of Education, The British Journal of Educational Studies,* and *The Library.* Occasional pieces in *The Journal of the History of Ideas, The History of Education Quarterly,* and *Studies in Philology* also proved helpful. It would be impossible to extend thanks to the authors of all those fine studies, or to those who wrote essays for various *festschrifts* and other collections, which I found to be equally informative. But I feel I should call special attention to the several excellent accounts of pre-Reformation lawyers by E. W. Ives and to Malcolm Parkes's indispensable essay, "The Literacy of the Laity in the Middle Ages."

As I grow older I am increasingly convinced of the dual nature of historical study. On the one hand, every historian builds on the contributions of earlier generations as well as the findings of contemporary scholars, in a sort of vast collective enterprise. But on the other hand, historical investigation is a rather solitary endeavor, since in the final analysis all interpretations are essentially personal. As Paul Johnson writes in his fine *History of the Jews,* the account he gives " ... is a personal interpretation of Jewish history." In the same fashion my study of educational and cultural developments in late medieval and early modern England is my own unique view of those happenings, why they occurred and how they were significant.

Another scholar writing on the same subject would probably select different factors to stress and other points to emphasize. This is inevitably the case because, as Daniel Boorstin has observed, historians are creators as well as discoverers, and creative ability varies tremendously from individual to individual. I only hope that most readers see a purpose to my choice of topics included in this book and that I have not misrepresented the views of any scholars from whom I have borrowed. Final responsibility for the overall interpretation advanced in these pages is of course completely my own.

Note on Money

During the period covered by this book, the pound sterling (£) contained 240 pennies, and not just 100 as today. These 240 pennies (240*d.*) were grouped in twenty shillings (20*s.*) of twelve each. Hence, £1 = 20*s.* = 240*d.*

Although pounds, shillings, and pennies were the main coins and monetary units of the time, there were many others. Probably the most important of the others were: (1) the mark, which was equal to two-thirds of a pound, or 13*s.* 4*d.;* and (2) the noble, which was half of a mark, or 6*s.* 8*d.*

How to determine the value of fifteenth- and sixteenth-century money in relation to today's prices is an almost impossible economic problem. Suffice it to say that a skilled artisan rarely made over 3*s.* a week, or £7 16*s.* a year. A student at one of the universities could usually manage on £3 annually, while a parish priest who had a stipend of £8 or more considered himself fortunate. Of course, prices rose steadily over the period, and by 1575 some observers believed that a stipend of £30 annually was necessary to attract a parson who was a university graduate. Country gentlemen had incomes of anywhere between £100 and £700 a year. At the end of the fifteenth century the richest peer in the kingdom, the duke of Buckingham, had a total income of approximately £5,000. By the first decades of the seventeenth century, the wealth of important landowners had risen dramatically, the earl of Newcastle deriving rents of almost £23,000 yearly from his many estates during the 1620s and 1630s.

1

The Black Death
and the
Crisis in Clerical Education

For more than a century before the Black Death of 1348–49, a concern about the quality of clerical education had been evident in England. Vicars and curates of small rural parishes, who seldom made over £6 a year, had long been known to be poorly trained, with almost no knowledge of theology and only the most basic educational skills. One of the first leaders to call attention to the problem was Stephen Langton, archbishop of Canterbury during the first quarter of the thirteenth century. That conscientious prelate, one of the framers of Magna Carta, had characterized most of the lower clergy of the realm as "dumb dogs" without sufficient understanding to perform masses and other religious services properly. Some years after Archbishop Langton's time, the famous Constitutions issued by Archbishop Peckham in 1281 stated that "the ignorance of the priests casteth the people into the ditch of error; and the folly or unlearning of the clergy, who are bidden to instruct the faithful in the Catholic faith, sometimes tendeth rather to error than to sound doctrine." Despite the growing realization that clerical training needed to be improved, little was done before the middle of the fourteenth century to strengthen priestly education. In fact it took the catastrophe of the Black Death, and the crisis atmosphere that resulted from that tragic occurrence, to prompt several rich bishops to give generous aid to a cause from which they had previously remained aloof.

Striking England sometime between May and July 1348, the Black Death acquired its name from the dark blue patches that disfigured the skins of most victims of the disease, which consisted of three separate but related strains of plague—bubonic, pneumonic, and septiacemic. Those who contracted the bubonic variety had at best a 35 percent chance of survival, whereas those who became infected with either of the other two forms almost never recovered. Indeed, the septiacemic strain was so lethal that death often occurred within a day of the onset of the disease, before any outward symptoms had time to become apparent.

Because the mortality rate increased almost tenfold during the epidemic, some 35 to 40 percent of England's total population of approximately 6,000,000 died in less than a year. As a consequence the wool trade and most agricultural pursuits suffered extreme dislocations; traditional social bonds were undermined if not altogether destroyed; regular religious observances came to a halt in many localities; and effective government and administration were briefly paralyzed. As in all predominantly peasant societies, recovery from such a debilitating blow was comparatively rapid, so that the most obvious effects of the pestilence had vanished within a decade. But as the survivors failed to realize at the time, plague had become endemic throughout the land, with the result that later outbreaks occurred in 1361-62, 1368-69, 1371, 1390-91, 1405, and in subsequent years as late as 1665. Admittedly, most of the later outbreaks were more regional than national in character, although the plague of 1390-91 was so long and severe as to be considered almost comparable to the Black Death itself. Yet it was the first great epidemic that made an ineradicable impression on men's minds, since it struck without warning or precedent and initiated a period that lasted for several centuries.

Because of the bishops' registers of the period, there is considerably more evidence about the mortality rate among the secular clergy than for any other group in society.* Studies of individual dioceses indicate that approximately 45 percent of

---

*The secular clergy, as opposed to the regular or monastic clergy, lived in the everyday world and served as priests (rectors, vicars, and curates), deans, archdeacons, and bishops or archbishops.

all parish priests died during the Black Death, while in a few sections another 15 to 20 percent fled in order to escape infection. In percentage terms the greatest number of clerical deaths occurred in the sees of Norwich, Exeter, and Winchester, where almost 49 percent of all holders of benefices seem to have perished. At Ely the rate was only a fraction lower, at 48.5 percent; while at Lichfield and Coventry, which was probably the least afflicted bishopric, the mortality rate was approximately 39 percent.

In contrast to the parochial clergy, the bishops and archbishops suffered considerably less from the contagion, only a few of them becoming victims. The elderly bishop of Worcester, Wulstan de Bransford, died of the disease in August 1349, although he had sought safety on a remote country estate. Aside from Bishop de Bransford, the only prelates who succumbed after definitely being infected were John Offord, who died as archbishop of Canterbury in May 1349, and Offord's short-lived successor Thomas Bradwardine, who died at Lambeth the following August.

If most of the prelates survived the catastrophe, the Black Death added immeasurably to their burdens. Villeins and other tenants of episcopal estates suffered as grievously as the general population; so crops were neither planted nor harvested, livestock often went untended, and rents and tithes fell into arrears. Almost as worrisome, several of the bishops saw virtually all their administrative aides perish, with the result that few qualified men remained to serve them in any capacity. The prelates' greatest concern, however, was that divine worship would be interrupted and perhaps halted altogether. This was certainly not the time for the sacraments to be unavailable to the faithful; but in many districts so many priests had died or fled that mass could not be celebrated, confessions heard, or funerals conducted properly. Accordingly most of the bishops filled vacant benefices without delay and ordained almost any man who happened to be at hand.

Because of the speed with which most vacant livings were filled, the quality of those in holy orders declined from its already low level. An important chronicler of the period, Henry Knighton of Leicester Abbey, observed in fact that:

> ... there was everywhere so great a scarcity of priests that many churches were left destitute, without divine service, masses, matins, vespers, or sacraments. . . . Within a little time, however, vast numbers of men

> whose wives had died in the pestilence flocked to take
> orders, many of whom were illiterate . . . save as far as
> they could read a little, although without understanding.[1]

Not only were inadequately trained men often entrusted with
the performance of important religious duties, but in at least
one instance a man of obvious criminal tendencies became a
priest. After snatching the purse of a woman of Waltham,
Essex, this man was speedily arrested and hanged, causing him
to be remembered less than fondly as "William the one-day
priest."

Perhaps the prelates should have striven to keep such a
potentially dangerous situation for the church from developing.
But the ecclesiastical hierarchy was too concerned about pressing
immediate needs to allow the ranks of the priesthood to remain
depleted, and this explains why so many plural and irregular
ordinations occurred. William Edington, for example, who was
bishop of Winchester from 1346 until 1366, presided at twelve
exceptionally large ordinations in 1349 and 1350, at each of
which numerous candidates were presented in the interests of
time. In addition he conducted a number of quasi-private
ordinations of one or two candidates each, which were technically
illegal since they occurred without papal or archiepiscopal
dispensation. Another bishop who bent the rules repeatedly for
the same reason was John Gynewell of Lincoln. During and
immediately after the Black Death, Bishop Gynewell held several
massive ordinations in his stricken diocese, with its nearly
1,900 parish churches. Between 1 June and 1 September 1349,
Bishop Gynewell filled over 600 vacant benefices; while at a
Christmas service in the following December, he ordained 76
deacons and 60 subdeacons, so they, too, could be instituted to
empty livings. By March 1350 this overworked bishop's sense of
urgency had caused him to appoint to 1,350 livings in all.

The irregular practices that began in 1348–49 with the Black
Death continued in later years when other epidemics occurred.
During subsequent visitations the clergy suffered less severely
than during the first great infestation, but their ranks were
severely thinned nonetheless. In Leicestershire in 1361, 43
priests perished when the disease reappeared, and so too did
the dean and seven of the canons of the collegiate church at
Newark. The parochial clergy of Essex suffered comparable
losses during the epidemic of 1361–62, when the mortality rate
rose to seven times the normal figure, causing that outbreak to

become known as the *Secunda Pestis*. The many clerical deaths in Essex are sufficient to explain the plural ordinations conducted by Simon Sudbury, bishop of London, within whose jurisdiction Essex lay. At Chelmsford on a June day in 1362, Bishop Sudbury ordained fourteen candidates to the priesthood and fifty-five others to minor orders, including the first tonsure. Immediately after ordaining these sixty-nine candidates, Bishop Sudbury presented seventeen of them—five priests, four deacons, and eight subdeacons—to vacant livings, which is evidence in itself of another growing irregularity of the period: the practice of allowing men in only minor orders to hold benefices.

Because of the increasingly serious problems associated with the priesthood, the bishops and archbishops had good reason to worry about the low level of clerical education. Unless steps were taken to improve the training and thus the image of the parish clergy, the church as a whole would fall into disrepute. Yet it would be an error to assume that no action was taken until the Black Death made the need for reform absolutely essential. During the decade before the disease struck, the obvious need to raise clerical standards had led to the establishment of two new colleges at the universities. The first of these was Queen's College, Oxford, which was founded in 1341 by Robert Eglesfield, chaplain to Edward III's wife Philippa. Queen's College was intended to increase the number of learned priests in Cumberland, Eglesfield's native county, and also in Westmorland, where he held both a benefice and the manor of Renwick, which went to form the new society's endowment. Queen's College received support not only from Eglesfield but also from the royal couple and several courtiers. However, it seldom comprised more than six fellows and twelve undergraduate students during its first century of existence, although the statutes called for the maintenance of twice as many.

The second college to be established just before the Black Death was Gonville Hall, Cambridge. This society was founded by Edward Gonville, who was vicar-general of the diocese of Ely as well as rector of Terrington, Norfolk. Most of Gonville's wealth came from a rich inheritance, however; and for Edward III's campaign against France in 1346, he was assessed the sum of 300 marks, the same amount required of the bishop of Hereford and the prior of Norwich. In March 1347 Gonville began to purchase lands in Cambridge as a site for his intended society, and on 28 January 1348 he obtained the king's assent for a college to consist of a master, four fellows, and twelve undergraduates, all of whom were to prepare for clerical careers by studying theology and dialectics. Although Gonville Hall soon came into being, its founder did not complete all the necessary legal provisions for the endowment, nor issue statutes to govern its affairs, before he died in 1351. As a consequence it briefly looked as if his foundation might collapse and disappear.

These few, meager efforts to improve clerical education were but a prelude to the many important steps taken during the century after the Black Death. Between 1350 and 1450, ten new colleges were established at the universities in either direct or indirect response to the pestilence. In this way the system of higher education in late medieval England received an unexpected boost from the worst catastrophe ever to befall the English people.*

The first bishop to respond energetically to the crisis caused by the Black Death was William Bateman, bishop of Norwich between 1344 and 1356. Bateman's diocese had suffered extremely cruel losses during the pestilence, and even his own brother died from the disease. A distinguished canon lawyer who had resided for several years at the papal curia, Bateman made several important contributions to higher education during the last decade of his life. In 1346 or 1347 he established a fund of £100 from which poor Cambridge students could borrow sums of up to £4, which was more than sufficient to finance a year's study at that time. After the death of his friend Edmund Gonville, he gave needed aid to Gonville Hall, which, as previously noted, had been founded during the first months of 1348.

---

*Seven of the ten colleges founded between 1350 and 1450 concentrated on training men for the secular clergy. These were: Trinity Hall, Cambridge (1350); Corpus Christi College, Cambridge (1352); New College, Oxford (1379); Lincoln College, Oxford (1427); All Souls, Oxford (1438); King's College, Cambridge (1441); and the Cambridge society of 1446 that eventually became known as Queens' College. In addition, an eighth college of the era, Canterbury Hall, Oxford (1362), was originally intended for both aspiring parish priests and student monks of the Benedictine order, although it was soon restricted to the latter element. The two other academic societies founded before 1450 were: St. Bernard's College, Oxford (1437), which catered only to student monks of the Cistercian order, and Godshouse, Cambridge (1439), which specialized in training men to serve as teachers in the country's grammar schools, many schoolmasters having perished during the epidemics of the time.

However, after its founder's demise in 1351, that society saw much of its endowment, and thus its ability to survive, vanish. As the chief executor of Gonville's will, Bateman soon made handsome provision for the fledgling institution, granting it the manor of Triplow and the tithes of three different rectories. In addition he donated many of his own books to form a college library and provided clerical vestments and silver cups for use in the chapel. Finally, in September 1353, he issued statutes for the college that remained in effect until 1558.

Bateman made his most significant educational contribution a short time before going to the rescue of Gonville Hall. Between 1350 and 1352 he established a Cambridge society of his own, Trinity Hall, to educate priests who would specialize in civil and canon law as preparation for eventual high-level service in both church and state. It is possible that he conceived this project a few years earlier; but as the historian of that college contends, "the shortage of clergy following the pestilence of May–September 1349 probably confirmed and ripened his intention."[2] Whatever the case, Bateman issued the foundation deed for Trinity Hall on 15 January 1350, and five days later the bishop of Ely, in whose diocese Cambridge was situated, extended his formal approval. Late the next month Edward III granted permission for the new college to acquire lands and presentations to parish churches worth up to 100 marks a year. Almost at once Bateman pledged the nucleus of his personal collection to serve as a college library, and within a short time he donated 92 works on theology and civil and canon law. By the time he issued governing statutes for the society in December 1352, it possessed a site and buildings purchased from the prior of Ely and also a small endowment that included the advowsons of six parish churches. Planned for a principal or master, twenty fellows, and a large but unspecified number of undergraduates, Trinity Hall consisted of only the principal, three fellows, and three undergraduate scholars when Bishop Bateman died in January 1356. Thereafter the society grew slowly, with only four additional fellowships (all for priests and future canon lawyers) being established by later benefactors before the reign of Henry VIII.

Although Trinity Hall was a considerably smaller society than its founder envisaged, doubtless because of the way Gonville Hall competed for valuable resources, the college soon became known for the liberal support it provided its members. Fellows of nearby Peterhouse and of the oldest comparable institution at Oxford, Merton College, received yearly payments of £2 10s. each; but the apprentice lawyers of Trinity Hall were granted stipends ranging between £3 16s. and £4 11s. 4d. per year, with occasional bonuses on festival days. As a distinguished historian of the medieval universities noted some years ago, "Clearly Bishop Bateman . . . did not intend his fellows to be either paupers or ascetics."[3] Because Trinity Hall was always his favorite project, Bateman bequeathed all the vestments, plate, and jewels he had not already bestowed on Gonville Hall to the society of his own foundation.

At the same time Trinity Hall was coming into existence, another new Cambridge college—Corpus Christi—was being founded in response to the ravages of the Black Death. Several trade guilds had observed that, owing to the shortage of priests after the plague, it had become far more costly to have masses performed for the souls of departed members, relatives, and friends. Should one or more guilds establish a new college, they ought to be able to rely on its clerical members to celebrate masses at the traditional price. The initiative in this enterprise was taken by the guild of Corpus Christi, a flourishing association of meat and grain dealers. During the early 1350s this guild formed a union with the smaller Guild of the Virgin Mary, the resulting body becoming known as the Guild of the Precious Body of Jesus Christ and the Glorious Virgin Mary. The new association then opened negotiations with Bishop Bateman, who suggested several land transfers as a way of rounding off the sites of Trinity and Gonville Halls. By surrendering several scattered tracts desired by the bishop, a composite site was obtained for the new society, which was officially named the College of Corpus Christi and the Blessed Mary; and sometime during the winter of 1351–52 it came into being.

The guild's next move was to elect Henry the Good, duke of Lancaster and England's greatest peer, as its honorary head. A victim of the plague in 1361, Henry was widely known for his personal piety and his book of devotions, *Mercy, Grand Mercy.* With the duke's assistance, the guild obtained a royal licence in November 1352 for the establishment of a collegiate society to consist of a master and two graduate fellows. The duke also secured authorization for the college to acquire the advowson of St. Benedict's (or more popularly St. Bene't's) Church in Cambridge. Almost immediately the college began to hold worship services in that church, and it accordingly became known in the popular mind as Bene't College, which it was often called until the Victorian period.

Statutes for Corpus Christi were issued in 1356 on the pattern of those of Michaelhouse, a small college established a generation earlier. The first master of Corpus Christi, Thomas Eltestle, lived until 1376 and left the society in a flourishing condition. He bequeathed all his own books and plate to the college and was active in canvassing gifts from others. Henry Tangmer, a prominent guild member, gave the institution eighteen houses in Cambridge as well as 85 acres of pasture outside the town walls. William Horwood granted it eight cottages and five messuages; and through the generosity of Sir John de Cambridge, the college was able to establish two additional fellowships before the end of the fourteenth century.

After the establishment of Corpus Christi, a decade elapsed before another new college — Canterbury Hall, Oxford — came into being at either university. The founder of Canterbury Hall, which was functioning by December 1362, was Simon Islip, archbishop of Canterbury for nearly twenty years. Once Islip succeeded to the throne of St. Augustine in September 1349, he proved to be a remarkably forceful primate, occasionally berating Edward III for violating the rights of the church, although the king had earlier found him to be a cooperative Lord Privy Seal. In addition the archbishop was a severe critic of priestly misconduct and frequently denounced the avarice and laziness of clerics who had survived the Black Death. In Islip's own archiepiscopal see, the ranks of the secular clergy were so depleted by the epidemics of 1348-49 and 1361-62 that divine worship was often conducted improperly, the new priests being men of little education. On one occasion Islip even complained:

> Those who are truly learned and accomplished in every kind of learning have been largely exterminated in the epidemics, and ... because of the lack of opportunity, very few are coming forward at present to carry on such studies.[4]

In an effort to rectify such deficiencies, the archbishop decided to found a new college at Oxford, where he had taken a doctorate in civil and canon law forty years before.

Although Islip's new college was designed to train better qualified parish ministers, it was given a second task as well:

the provision of accommodations for student monks from the great monastery of Christ Church, Canterbury, which the archbishop maintained was lax about securing advanced training for its members. Thus as originally constituted, Canterbury Hall consisted of a warden and three monks from Christ Church along with eight scholars who came from the ranks of the secular clergy. Islip's idea of combining seculars with regulars on the same collegiate foundation may have been sound in theory, but it failed in practice, as serious bickering between the two groups occurred. By the end of 1365, Islip was willing to acknowledge his experiment a failure; and in December of that year he dismissed the first warden, Henry Woodhall, and replaced the three monastic fellows with secular priests, thereby converting the college into a wholly secular foundation. As the new warden he appointed the learned theologian John Wyclif, who had recently resigned the mastership of Balliol College upon accepting a benefice worth more than that society's statutes permitted.

Within four months of making these changes, the archbishop died, without obtaining Edward III's assent to them. Consequently it was an easy matter for Islip's successor, Simon Langham, who was abbot of Westminster at the time of his elevation to the primacy, to reverse his predecessor's action. On 22 April 1367, Archbishop Langham reinstated Woodhall to the wardenship of Canterbury Hall and expelled Wyclif and all the seculars, who were thereupon replaced with monks. Although their cause was hopeless from the start, Wyclif and his aggrieved associates waged a fierce struggle, even appealing to the pope for reinstatement. However, in 1370 a final decision in the case went against them; and from then until the late 1530s, when Henry VIII dissolved all the monasteries and their dependent colleges, Canterbury Hall was rightly considered a daughter house of Christ Church, Canterbury.

Although Archbishops Islip and Langham can be criticized for giving only nominal support to Canterbury Hall, such a charge cannot be leveled against the next college founder of the period, William of Wykeham. Over time William of Wykeham became passionately devoted to the cause of clerical education, and he gave unusually generous aid to the two institutions he founded.

One of the preeminent bishops of the late Middle Ages, William of Wykeham occupied the great see of Winchester from 1366 until his death in 1404. Even before his elevation to that rich bishopric, which was rated for tax purposes at £2,977 a year, he began to receive lesser positions in the church, which included an archdeaconry worth £350 annually. In addition he held fifteen canonries, thirteen prebends, and numerous other appointments with a collective worth of nearly £525 a year. Thus Wykeham was one of the greatest pluralists of the age with a total yearly income of more than £3,850, a vast sum for the period. This made it possible for him to indulge his tastes on a grand scale. He paid to have the majestic nave of Winchester Cathedral remodeled in the late Gothic style; and he also financed the rebuilding of the chapel and cloisters of the large collegiate church of St. Martin-le-Grand, of which he was the dean from 1360.

Possibly because St. Martin-le-Grand was one of the three London churches of the age that operated a school,* Wykeham's interest turned increasingly to educational matters; and on several occasions he remarked, "Though I am not a scholar myself, I will be the means of making more scholars than any other scholar in England." By establishing new educational institutions, Wykeham also hoped, like Bateman and Islip earlier, to "make good the wastage of educated clerks following the Black Death." As the diocesan of a rich and important bishopric from 1366, he cannot have failed to know how poorly trained the average parish priest still was, particularly since he himself ordained nearly 4,000 men during his thirty-eight years as bishop.

As early as 1369 Wykeham began to buy land in Oxford, where he hoped in time to found a college on the pattern of Merton, oldest and largest of the university's academic societies. Wykeham was impressed by the general arrangements made a century before for Merton and also by the way its founder, Walter de Merton, had established an associated grammar school that sent its better graduates on to the college for further work. Although clearly the most important, Merton was not the only foundation that may have inspired Wykeham. In 1314 Walter de Stapledon, bishop of Exeter, had established Stapledon Hall, which subsequently evolved into Exeter College, for twelve students from Cornish and Devonshire families. In addition Stapledon had founded a grammar school adjacent to Exeter Cathedral to prepare boys for admission to his newly-established Oxford society. The same sort of dual arrangements had been

*The other two were St. Paul's and St. Mary le Bow.

made by Robert Eglesfield in 1341 when he established Queen's College, Oxford and a large "feeder school" in Cumberland. Thus Wykeham had several models to guide him in the important work of founding a new college along with an associated grammar school that would send its better students on for university training.

Exactly when Wykeham committed himself to such an extensive enterprise cannot be determined with complete certainty. But on 1 September 1373 he made a ten-year agreement with a Hampshire schoolmaster, Richard of Herton, who pledged to teach grammar to four boys at Winchester "whom the bishop maintains and will assist at his own cost . . . and would take no others to be taught without leave of the said father." Within three more years Wykeham was also paying the main expenses of seventy poor students at Oxford, who were lodged at various places in the town under the general supervision of Richard Tunworth, a fellow of Merton.

During the mid 1370s, Wykeham was preoccupied with the political and administrative problems stemming from the declining health and ultimate death of Edward III. As a consequence he was unable to take steps to convert his two *ad hoc* institutions into permanent societies until after the accession of Richard II in 1377. He began the process the next year by obtaining a papal bull that authorized him to appropriate a rich Wiltshire rectory for the endowment of a college of seventy schoolboys at Winchester. Yet before doing anything more for that institution, he redirected his gaze to Oxford and obtained a royal license to found an academic society there on 20 June 1379. Five months later he issued an official charter for "Saint Marie College of Winchester in Oxenford," which soon became known simply as New College; and at the same time he replaced the temporary warden, Richard Tunworth, with his own nephew, Nicholas Wykeham. In March 1380 the original buildings of New College, which were patterned on those he had earlier constructed for Edward III at Windsor, were begun.

Before the original quadrangle of New College was completed in April 1386, Wykeham turned his attention back to the grammar school at Winchester, for the support of which he bought two Hampshire manors in 1380. Two years later he obtained letters patent authorizing him to establish "Saint Marie College of Winchester"; and on 20 October 1382 he executed the foundation charter for the grammar school during a ceremony in his chapel at Southwark. On that occasion he formally admitted the seventy original students and named as their first warden Thomas of Cranley, who was currently a fellow of Merton.

In the statutes for his two institutions, Wykeham decreed that no one should be admitted to study who suffered from deafness or any other bodily defect that might prevent him from taking holy orders. In addition he offered a possible bonus of £2 to all graduates of New College who entered the priesthood. Because of this, A. F. Leach was undoubtedly correct in maintaining some years ago that Wykeham's goal was "to provide educated clergy . . . to fill up the gaps caused by the Black Death" and that "the plague was in sober truth the proximate cause of the foundation of Winchester College."[5] Recently a distinguished medievalist has advanced a somewhat different explanation of Wykeham's objectives. In the words of R. L. Storey, he intended his Oxford society at least as:

> . . . a spectacular memorial to a spectacular career . . . in his mind its fundamental purpose was as a great chantry to make intercession for the repose of his soul. He provided for the services of the chapel by ten chaplains, three clerks and sixteen choristers, and he ordered that they alone were to be retained if the college's income failed.[6]

There is certainly some truth in Mr. Storey's observations; but Wykeham almost had to make the arrangements he did in order to ensure the permanence of New College, with ability to withstand possible financial setbacks in the future. Even if all the other members had to be discharged during a period of hardship, the institution might still survive, provided a staff of priests and choristers remained in being. Moreover, it was as an educational foundation and not as a great chantry that the establishment of New College set an important precedent for the future.

Although modeled on existing institutions, Wykeham's twin societies were nevertheless of crucial significance for educational developments during the next two centuries. In the first place, they were established on a scale that surpassed all previous foundations of their kind. At Winchester there were 103 paid members of the society in all, making it eight times larger than the grammar schools affiliated with Merton and Queen's Colleges. As for New College, it was also an unusually large institution for the era, with some seventy fellows, or far more than were attached to any existing foundation. At the seven older Oxford colleges, there were a total of sixty-three fellows, almost half of which were affiliated with Merton. Regarding the Cambridge colleges of the period, the largest by far was The King's Hall, with thirty-two fellows; but the average society at the eastern university had no more than five or six. Thus by establishing a college for seventy fellows, Wykeham founded a collegiate institution of unprecedented size.

Being one of the country's leading book-collectors, Wykeham was able to provide from his own holdings so that the scholars of New College would have an impressive library to use. In 1382 or 1383 he donated 240 well-chosen volumes; and within another year, 52 additional tracts, including 37 on medicine, were given by William Rede, bishop of Chichester since 1369. Bishop Rede was probably Wykeham's closest associate on the episcopal bench, and he had assembled one of the largest collections of the era, having some 370 books in all. At his death in 1385, Rede left 100 more books to New College and an equal number to Merton, where he had studied as a young man. During that age the average academic society in England had only 40 to 50 books, and most were guilty of keeping their holdings rather haphazardly in wooden chests placed in a corner of the hall or the refectory. Wykeham refused to countenance such makeshift arrangements and had a handsome library chamber some seventy feet long constructed at New College. This was the first real library facility erected by an English academic body and an important pointer towards the future, when every collegiate society would have an extensive collection of books.

Probably because he knew he was surpassing the work of all previous educationalists, Wykeham made unusually generous financial arrangements for his two foundations. At Winchester the original lands set aside for the endowment produced annual revenues of £307, an exceptionally large sum for the period. By the time of his death in 1404, he had conveyed additional properties to the school, thereby increasing its income to £450 yearly. As for New College, Wykeham created an even larger endowment for its support, since its permanent revenues exceeded those of the seven older Oxford colleges combined. In addition to a number of small, scattered tracts, Wykeham granted twenty-one entire manors to New College, and of those more than a dozen were accompanied by the advowson to the local parish church. Located mainly in Buckinghamshire, Wiltshire, Essex, and Kent, the endowment was largely complete by 1397, when it produced a total income of £627 12*s*. 9*d*.

Regarding the relationship that existed between Winchester and New College, only a few points need to be stressed here. Wykeham clearly expected the best graduates of the grammar school to continue their studies at the Oxford society. Indeed, he restricted admissions to New College to boys who had previously been enrolled at Winchester. At the same time he granted the warden and fellows of New College the right to elect the warden of Winchester, who was required to be a past or current fellow of New College. Despite this last provision, Winchester was a fully autonomous corporation, and its status as a self-governing body was "far superior to that enjoyed by any other existing school."[7] Because the warden of New College received a yearly stipend of £40, which was twice that of his counterpart at Winchester, the former was clearly felt to be superior to the latter, and there was never a time when a man was moved from the higher to the lower position. But on several occasions a particularly capable warden of Winchester was promoted to the headship of the Oxford society. This happened for the first time while Wykeham was still alive. In 1389 the first warden of Winchester, Thomas of Cranley, was elected to the same post at New College, although he departed within a few years for Ireland, where he soon became archbishop of Dublin.

Despite the importance of the various arrangements made for them, the real significance of Wykeham's two colleges lies in the provisions he made for the inclusion of students from all social classes and their instruction. At Winchester, which was of course a society of schoolboys, the teaching of Latin grammar was naturally stressed above all else.* A practical educationalist, Wykeham knew that a thorough grounding in Latin grammar was a prerequisite for successful university work: hence his emphasis on a student's total mastery of that subject before he proceeded on to New College. Students at Winchester were normally expected to be between eight and twelve years of age at the time of entry, although any boy under seventeen might be elected to a fellowship provided he showed "great promise of being sufficiently learned in grammar by the time he was

---

*Because there were three chaplains and three chapel clerks on the foundation, Winchester doubled as a collegiate church, but the emphasis on worship was always subordinate to that on education.

eighteen." The average student was expected to be from a humble background and would therefore be a paid member of the foundation; but Wykeham also provided for the inclusion of up to ten *extranei commensales,* or "sons of noble and influential persons, special friends of the said college." These students were required to pay all their own expenses but would receive the same instruction as the other boys in grammar and any additional subjects that were taught. As E. F. Jacob once noted, this statutory provision for lay students "who had not previously frequented the grammar schools" was an important pointer towards the future, since it "invited a new element to participate in the life of the society."[8] Because of this it is hard not to regard Winchester as an early forerunner of the later public schools, which catered primarily to the sons of the gentry.

At Winchester the students were actually instructed by a master and an usher, whose yearly stipends were £10 and £3 6s. 8d., respectively. In addition the older boys were required to assist and encourage the younger ones, for which reason Wykeham adopted the prefect system that had been pioneered at Merton and Oriel Colleges. In each bedchamber, shared by up to eleven students, there were to be three senior boys who were obligated by the statutes to:

> ... superintend the studies of their chamber-fellows, and diligently oversee them, and from time to time when called upon, truly to certify and inform the Warden, Sub-Warden, and Master Teacher of their morals, behaviour, and advancement in learning ... so that such scholars who are under any defects in morals or are lazy in their studies may receive due and sufficient chastisement, correction, and punishment according to their faults.[9]

This system, which almost invited abuse by the older boys, evidently worked quite well at first. By the last years of Henry IV, the fame of Winchester was widespread, and there was mounting pressure on the part of rich parents to enroll their sons there. In 1412 Henry Beaufort, Wykeham's successor as bishop of Winchester, learned that there were as many as 100 *extranei commensales* at the school; and he demanded a return to the ten who were legally permitted by the statutes.

As for New College, it was particularly important as the prototype of those later English colleges that consisted of students at all levels—from beginning undergraduates to scholars who had already finished their master's degrees and doctorates. The earliest societies at Oxford and Cambridge had consisted entirely of graduate members, although at The King's Hall, which Edward II had founded at the eastern university in 1317, undergraduates had been accepted at first as integral members of the foundation. However, during the years since 1317, the number of under-graduate students at The King's Hall had declined as the graduate component expanded. As a consequence there were still only a dozen or so undergraduates among the 100-odd paid members of all the endowed colleges together as late as the mid-1370s. Nearly all the undergraduates then in residence at the universities lived in private hostels or unendowed halls that averaged fewer than 25 members each. But with the establishment of New College in 1379, a new pattern was set for the future. William of Wykeham fully intended for undergraduates to be integral members of his academic society, and in 1384 they held 29 of the 70 fellowships provided by the college. Thereafter the number of undergraduates associated with the other colleges began to increase. By 1438 their numbers had risen to 200, and by 1552 to almost 450.

Because Wykeham was willing for boys as young as fifteen to be elected to fellowships at New College, he made special provision for the instruction of younger students in their initial years of residence. He in fact adopted the same prefect system he decreed for Winchester, although he required only one senior student to sleep in each bedchamber, so as to be available to assist the younger pupils. In addition he appointed five aca-demic deans as general supervisors of studies. But his principal contribution lay in establishing the germ of the later tutorial system, which in time became a leading characteristic of the English universities.

During their first years at New College, students were expected not only to attend the university lectures and disputations but also to take instruction from certain designated fellows of the college itself, chosen by the academic deans and known as *magistri informatores*. Precursors of the later and more famous tutors, the *magistri informatores* received special payments from the college for their work—in theory 5s. a year for each pupil they taught but in practice considerably less, since Wykeham decreed that no more than 100s. of the college's yearly revenues should be used for that purpose. Evidence from the year 1399 indicates that the system was firmly in place by that juncture and working smoothly. At that time the sub-warden and three of the five *magistri informatores* were supervising the work of thirty-three students enrolled in the A.B. program.

For over a century the *magistri informatores* took no part in managing the personal finances of the boys assigned to their care, which was to be a prime feature of the mature tutorial system. That feature took several generations to develop, and only after 1550 did it become typical of all the colleges at the universities. Peterhouse, Cambridge, for instance, did not adopt the fully developed tutorial system until 1581. However, once a rudimentary tutorial system began to operate at New College during the 1380s and 1390s, it gradually spread to neighboring societies. By the second quarter of the fifteenth century, it had taken hold at University College, Oxford and also at The King's Hall, Cambridge; and within a few more years it would be adopted at the large new society known as King's College, which Henry VI established at the eastern university in 1441.

Because the primitive tutorial system spread even faster during later years, it was usual by the 1520s for entering students to be routinely assigned to a tutor. When in September 1521 the eighteen-year-old Matthew Parker enrolled at Corpus Christi College, Cambridge, he was entrusted to the care of Robert Cowper, a respected scholar and future royal chaplain. By that juncture many parents and relatives were anxious to secure capable tutors for young boys about to enroll at the universities. In 1529 Thomas Cromwell arranged for his son Gregory and his nephew Christopher Wellyfed to be tutored by a leading Greek scholar at Cambridge, John Cheke of St. John's College. Only two years later a learned monk of Evesham Abbey, Robert Joseph, sent a revealing letter to Robert Tailer of St. Alban Hall, Oxford.

> I wrote to you nearly a year ago . . . about my young kinsman, whom I wanted to be your pupil, and you agreed most handsomely. But it came to nothing, because my cousin's father refused the prescribed payment, and preferred to pay 40s. a year to a friar to teach his son to wander, rather than spend a little more and have him taught polite manners at Oxford. Now he is wise after the event, and is indignant at the friar's craftiness. At last I have persuaded him to make an annual allowance of four marks (£2 13s. 4d.). If this is enough for his keep, please enrol him among your pupils. . . . If your house . . . requires a larger outlay, please find him another Hall (*diversorium*) and a severe and grave tutor, who

will keep him from excess and rouse him to letters. I promised his parents to find him such a tutor, so that they can rest assured about his education.[10]

Within a few more years the tutorial system received *de facto* recognition from the crown as an integral feature of university life. When in the spring of 1548 Edward VI decreed an official visitation of Cambridge, he included among his instructions to the commissioners two provisions that related directly to the work of college tutors.

Tutors are diligently to instruct their pupils, are to correct them in proper manner, and are not to permit them to wander about loosely into the town.

Tutors are to receive annually from their pupils, if they are scholars of the college, not more than six shillings and eight pence, but if they are sizars [poor work-study students], not more than three shillings and four pence.[11]

Although it took almost 175 years for the mature tutorial system to develop and become entrenched at both universities, it is indisputable that the impetus for the system emanated from New College and the wise educational ideas of William of Wykeham.

Subsequent generations for decades to come felt a deep sense of gratitude to the great and generous bishop of Winchester, who had made such notable contributions to the educational life of his countrymen. Graduates of his two colleges played leading roles in church and state for the remainder of the middle ages; and those who followed in his path by founding educational institutions of their own invariably modeled them on Winchester and New College, which were such obvious successes. Wykeham's disciples soon became known as Wykehamists; and through their work an understanding of his innovations spread more quickly throughout the realm than would have been the case otherwise. Moreover, the Wykehamist movement helped prepare the way for the reception of humanism, a continental development that also stressed the need for higher levels of education. Although humanism did not become established in England until the latter part of the fifteenth century, it gave powerful reinforcement to the educational movements that began in southern and central England during the aftermath of the Black Death.

Most important of all, because of the many contributions of Wykeham and his disciples, who included such outstanding figures as Henry Chichele (archbishop of Canterbury, 1414-43), Thomas Bekynton (bishop of Bath and Wells, 1443-65), and William Waynflete (bishop of Winchester, 1447-86), the ongoing campaign to raise the educational level of men of the cloth enjoyed considerable success. By the 1450s if not sooner, the priesthood as a whole was a more learned and distinguished group than ever before. The bishops and archbishops were almost invariably university graduates by that juncture. Indeed, of the 131 men elevated to the episcopal bench between 1399 and 1499, 119 (or approximately 91 percent of the total) are known to have taken degrees at Oxford or Cambridge;[12] and it is entirely possible that several others studied at foreign universities. The prelates of fifteenth-century England were also unusually active book-collectors. Archbishop Arundel of Canterbury (d. 1414) and John, Cardinal Kemp (d. 1454) both left valuable libraries of several hundred books. On his death in 1478 William Gray, bishop of Ely, bequeathed scores of important humanist tracts to Balliol College, Oxford. But the most outstanding episcopal library of the era was probably the one assembled by Bishop Waynflete of Winchester. In 1481 Waynflete donated 800 volumes to Magdalen College, Oxford, which he had established in the mid 1450s by enlarging his earlier foundation of Magdalen Hall.[13]

During these same years the educational standards of the lower clergy were advancing also, although at a slower and less uniform rate. A majority of the vicars and curates who occupied small rural churches continued to have inadequate training; and as late as Queen Elizabeth's reign there were still a few men on the scene like the Nottinghamshire vicar of the 1580s who was reputedly so ignorant that he could not distinguish between "Jesus" and "Judas." If the English church harbored such clerics for generations to come, the situation nevertheless showed considerable improvement during the last century of the medieval period. Between 1400 and 1500, as dozens of new schools appeared throughout the realm, the qualifications of even those near the bottom of the clerical ladder grew stronger. In the words of J. R. Lander, rural vicars and curates "became sufficiently literate to conduct the services without error, which was a modest enough development but at least a considerable improvement on the standards of earlier centuries."[14] More-over, priests who occupied benefices in their own right were increasingly urged to study at Oxford or Cambridge. One prelate who was tireless in promoting education throughout his diocese was Thomas Bekynton of Bath and Wells. Of the 671 men Bishop Bekynton admitted to livings between 1445 and 1465, eighty-nine already possessed academic degrees at the time of their institution, and most of those subsequently received authorization to attend a university for additional work. As a consequence of Bekynton's policy, which may well have been adopted by other prelates, there were many more rural priests on the scene like Robert Scoles, who held a doctorate in divinity from Cambridge. Between 1444 and 1470 Scoles was rector-in-residence of the small Suffolk parish of Reydon. After his death in 1470 that same country church was served for more than thirty years by John Hopton, who in 1479 completed an advanced degree in canon law at the eastern university.[15]

Naturally such men as Scoles and Hopton were far from typical of the late-medieval priesthood. But there were dozens of men in parish churches whose qualifications were comparable to those of Hugh Pavy, whose rich father sent him first to Winchester and then to New College, where he graduated in 1450. Instituted three years later to a Devonshire benefice, Pavy was eventually named to two other rectories in the west country as well as to prebends at Wells and Salisbury cathedrals. Another well-educated cleric of this sort was John Barneby, holder of a Cambridge M.A. In 1466 Barneby was presented to the Lincoln-shire living of Leadenham and, five years later, to the Staffordshire rectory of Hanbury-by-Tutbury.[16]

Not only did scores of individual parishes witness a dramatic rise in the academic qualifications of their resident clerics, but so did whole dioceses, counties, and sections. During the fifteenth century the proportion of clerics in Lincoln diocese with university degrees increased from 14 percent to over 30 percent; while in Norwich diocese the improvement was even more dramatic, the proportion of university graduates rising from only 8 percent during the years 1370–1449 to nearly 42 percent for the period 1500–1532. In Surrey by the 1520s approximately 35 percent of all identifiable holders of benefices were Oxford or Cambridge graduates, while many others may have studied at the universities without taking degrees. In addition, a growing number of parish priests, including over 30 percent in the west midlands and border counties, now had their own private libraries and often listed a dozen or more books in their wills. Rather interestingly, the largest gift of books to the Cambridge University Library before Elizabeth's reign was made not by a nobleman or a prelate but by a London priest—Walter Crome, rector of St. Benet's Sherehog, who shortly before his death in 1452 presented ninety-three volumes to the appreciative university authorities. In addition, Father Crome donated seven works to Gonville Hall, where he had been a fellow during the 1420s.[17]

All this strongly suggests that by the eve of the Reformation, both the lower and the higher clergy were considerably better trained than their predecessors of earlier centuries had been. If such was actually the case, much of the credit must be assigned to Wykeham, Bateman, and the other far-sighted survivors of the Black Death. They recognized the dire need to improve clerical education and, at considerable personal expense, took the steps they deemed essential.

2

Education and Literacy
Among the Laity

The increasing stress on clerical education during the century after the Black Death helped to create a similar movement among the laity. After the priesthood, the most important professional group of the era were the lawyers, whose educational progress was equally rapid and sustained. Indeed, between 1400 and 1450 the Inns of Court in London, which trained young men to practice before the royal courts, entered their golden age, which lasted for nearly two centuries and during which they discharged an important educational function. Although the Inns had existed for several generations before 1400, they did not assume a serious educational role until that juncture, or perhaps a few decades earlier. By 1450 their instructional mission had developed to such an extent and become so formalized that it is possible to speak of an "educational revolution" at the Inns during the first half of the fifteenth century.

Because of the high cost of legal training at the Inns, the students were almost invariably drawn from aristocratic families and the professional and merchant elite. At a typical Oxford college during the period, an undergraduate could manage on as little as £2 a year, although this rose by the 1490s to approximately £2 10s. At the Inns, however, the cost of a year's stay was at least six times as great. In his famous description of those

four important institutions, Sir John Fortescue asserted in a
book he completed in 1468 that:

> ... no student could be maintained [in an Inn] on less
> than £13 6s. 8d. a year, and if he has servants to himself
> alone, as the majority have, then he will by so much
> more bear expenses. Because of this costliness, there
> are not many who learn the laws except the sons of
> nobles. For poor and common people cannot bear so
> much cost for the maintenance of their sons.[1]

Fortescue seems to have exaggerated the aristocratic nature of
the Inns, however, since the surviving records reveal the admission of only an occasional peer's son. For example, Lincoln's
Inn accepted the son and heir of the earl of Pembroke in 1468;
but seventeen years elapsed before that Inn admitted another
boy of comparable status, George Dinham, who succeeded to
his father's barony in 1501. Both those young men came from
richer and more prominent families than the average law student of the time, who was from a gentle background, not a
noble one.

A somewhat snobbish attitude pervades all of Fortescue's
comments about the Inns, since they were included in a book
written for the instruction of Prince Edward of Lancaster
(d. 1471), the only child of Henry VI and Margaret of Anjou. But
the very snobbishness expressed by Fortescue helps us to understand why rich fathers willingly assumed the burden of sending
their sons to study at the Inns. In an age when 1,000 bricks
could be purchased for 4s., there was no chance a young gentleman of the Inns would have to share a bedchamber or otherwise fraternize with the offspring of yeoman farmers or day
laborers, as might well have happened at the universities. There
were other reasons as well why affluent families preferred to
send their sons to the Inns rather than to Oxford and Cambridge.
While attending classes in the capital, impressionable young
boys—Lord Pembroke's heir was thirteen when he entered
Lincoln's Inn—would be safe from the seductive appeal of theology and thus could not be induced to become priests or, even
worse, to join a monastic or mendicant order. Of equal importance, while attending an Inn a well-born student could acquire
enough knowledge of the law, even if he did not intend to
become a barrister, to be able to defend the financial interests of
his family and its estates. And finally, during the period before

the triumph of the tutorial system at Oxford and Cambridge, the Inns' students generally received closer academic and moral instruction than their counterparts at the universities, which may have swayed some fathers.

Whatever the specific reasons fifteenth-century parents sent their sons to study at the Inns, those institutions were too expensive to become very large before the end of the medieval period. Fortescue believed they had a total membership of approximately 1,800 men: some 800 in the four greater Inns and another 1,000 in the ten lesser Inns, the so-called Inns of Chancery, which served as a preparatory division for the greater Inns.[2] Although Fortescue's figures have been accepted by many legal historians, including Michael Birks and Sir William Holdsworth, recent research has convincingly shown them to be too high. The most careful student of the legal profession and of legal education before the Reformation is E. W. Ives, who contends that they did not become as large as Fortescue believed until the last years of Queen Elizabeth. In Mr. Ives's opinion, all fourteen of the Inns at the time Fortescue described them in 1468 had no more than 400 professional members, although as many as 300 boys may have been affiliated with them as students.[3] If Mr. Ives's calculations are correct, and doubtless they are, it would appear that only 70 to 75 new students entered the fourteen Inns together during an average year of the fifteenth century.

This is not the place for a detailed account of the system of legal training at the Inns during the late medieval period. For our purposes it is sufficient to note that a student preparing to become a barrister participated in three major activities. First, he witnessed the deliberations of the royal courts at Westminster whenever they were in session; second, he participated in the moots or mock trials that the Inns themselves sponsored throughout the year; and third, he attended the sixteen-session lecture cycles known as Readings, which were conducted every year during Lent and August by senior members of each major Inn. This system of training was well-devised to teach aspiring lawyers the principles of the common law as well as the most effective techniques of pleading. Boys hoping for an eventual call to the bar usually spent six or more years engaged in such activities.

Most of the students stayed for somewhat shorter periods, however—perhaps two or three years on average. These students had no intention of becoming professionals but, by occasionally engaging in the formal activities of their houses, acquired whatever legal proficiency they wished to obtain. In addition they participated in other kinds of study intended to give them and the aspiring barristers alike a smattering of liberal education. A knowledge of both history and religion was encouraged; and there was also instruction in music and dancing, so the students would appreciate the main social graces. Fortescue in fact maintained that the Inns were:

> ... like a school of all the manners that nobles learn. There they learn to sing and exercise themselves in every kind of harmony. They also practice dancing and all the games proper to noblemen, just as those in the king's household are accustomed to practice them.[4]

Amusements like dice and cards were expressly forbidden, however, and at Lincoln's Inn members found guilty of engaging in such recreations were fined 10s. for each offense. The students were also subject to heavy fines and possible expulsion if they bundled women into their rooms. Yet all the members were expected to participate in the Christmas revels, which were elaborate occasions by the mid-fifteenth century. A taste for drama was also strong at the Inns, and both ancient and contemporary plays were performed at regular intervals for the members' enjoyment. Over the years the Inns developed their own libraries and acquired substantial book collections. Probably the earliest such library existed at Lincoln's Inn, where in 1475 the governing board granted 30s. to Roger Townshend for taking care of the books. There was a similar library at the Inner Temple by 1506 but not one at the Middle Temple or at Gray's Inn until the 1550s.[5]

By the last decades of the fifteenth century, the lawyers were a more literate group than ever before, and many had acquired relatively large numbers of books, at least by contemporary standards. In 1468 Sir Humphrey Starkey, a prominent Cheshire attorney, made arrangements for the disposition of a Bible, a psalter, a mass-book, and a dozen or more legal tracts. Another lawyer of the period, Sir Roger Townshend, who died in 1493 and was no doubt the same man mentioned in the previous section, had a larger collection, it appears. In 1500 his several descendants owned at least twenty volumes between them, which they had inherited on his death. Probably the foremost book-collector among the lawyers of the age was Thomas Kebell, a Leicestershireman who had studied at the Inner Temple and died in 1500 after representing the prominent Hastings family for many years. According to a recent analysis of his holdings, Kebell owned thirty-six volumes in all, only two of which were religious service-books. He naturally owned that most-esteemed of contemporary legal tracts, Thomas Littleton's *Tenures*, which had first appeared in 1481; but he also had several important works of literature, including a copy of Boccaccio's *Decameron* in a French translation. A man of wide interests, Kebell possessed about three times as many books as the average university scholar of the period.[6]

In comparison to the lawyers' holdings, those of the gentry tended to be rather small. In 1423 a Cheshire landowner, Roger Jodrell, bequeathed a dozen or so books to his heir; while thirteen years later another Cheshire gentleman, Richard Fitton, left only five volumes to his eldest son. A more respectable collection belonged to the military captain Sir John Fastolf (d. 1459), who lived at Caister Castle, in Norfolk. Fastolf owned nearly forty books, including a Bible, various chronicles in French and English, a "book of Julius Caesar," and copies of the *Romaunce de la Rose* and the *Usages de l'arte de chevalerie*.

The only book collectors among the laity whose libraries rivaled those of the clerical hierarchy were wealthy members of the royal family and high aristocracy. John Plantagenet, duke of Bedford (a younger son of Henry IV), owned what was unquestionably the most valuable private library that ever existed in late medieval England. During the early 1430s, while regent of France for his nephew Henry VI, Duke John paid over £2,300 for 850 choice works that the French kings had acquired over time at enormous expense. On Duke John's death in 1435, many of his books seem to have passed to his younger brother Humphrey, the scholarly duke of Gloucester, who had studied at Balliol College, Oxford for a year and was a serious bibliophile in his own right. During the 1420s and early 1430s, Duke Humphrey assembled a well-chosen library of between 500 and 600 volumes, more than half of which he eventually donated to the Cobham Library at Oxford. These included works by such outstanding classical authors as Plato, Aristotle, Seneca, Cicero, Quintilian, Apuleius, and Aulus Gellius.

During the decades after Duke Humphrey's death in 1447, the leading aristocratic collector was probably John Tiptoft, whose father received a barony after serving as speaker of the

House of Commons on several occasions. Because of his own unswerving support of Henry VI, the younger Tiptoft was made earl of Worcester in 1449; and during the next twenty years he bought books at a steady rate. He soon developed an impressive collection that included scores of the new humanistic works that were already popular on the continent. Before his death in 1470 he followed Duke Humphrey's example and presented many important items, valued at over £330, to the Cobham Library at Oxford.

Among the other noblemen of the era who acquired large numbers of books was John, Lord Howard (d. 1485), who took at least a dozen volumes with him on the naval and military campaign of 1482 against James III of Scotland. Lord Howard's books included manuals on chess and dice as well as tracts on history and chivalry. John de Vere, thirteenth earl of Oxford is known to have acquired at least seventy books by the time he died in 1509; while several members of the wealthy Stafford family spent large sums for books during the early sixteenth century. In 1516, for instance, Edward Stafford, third duke of Buckingham (d. 1521), purchased thirteen different volumes for himself and his son Henry, which included expensive works on history, chivalry, and religion.

The nobles of the period are unlikely to have developed such a taste for books had their class not already begun to pursue higher education. During the first decades of the fifteenth century, scions of great aristocratic families like the Hollands and Greys, Nevilles, Dudleys, and Courtenays, began to arrive at both Winchester and Eton for a few years' study. As noted in chapter 1, there were as many as 100 *extranei commensales*, or rich students who paid for their own room and board, at Winchester by the year 1412.* After several years of study at these large new grammar schools, a few aristocratic boys proceeded on to Oxford and Cambridge for a year or longer. In almost every case these aristocratic youth, who were initially designated as sojourners by the universities, had no desire to complete the requirements for an academic degree. They merely wanted a grounding in the arts and letters, a veneer of polish and education, which might prove useful when they later became suitors in the capital for lands and offices.

A good example of this new kind of university student

*See above, page 16.

was Robert Hungerford, heir to a rich barony. Beginning in 1437 young Hungerford was a prominent and highly esteemed sojourner at University College, Oxford. Shortly after his departure a year later, that same Oxford society accepted John Tiptoft, who, as we have seen, eventually became one of the leading book collectors of the period. Young Tiptoft remained at the university from 1440 until 1443, when his father died and he, as second Baron Tiptoft, assumed responsibility for managing the family estates. One last example of this new sort of aristocratic student must suffice. During the same period John Tiptoft was at Oxford, young Henry Holland, whose father was duke of Exeter and a cousin of Henry VI himself, was loosely associated with The King's Hall, Cambridge. Within the precincts of that fashionable academic society, young Holland maintained a private household in association with his half-brothers John and William, all three boys being attended by a large staff of personal servants.

As this trickle of boys from rich families began, the universities assumed a function they had never discharged before. In previous times the colleges and halls had concentrated almost exclusively on training young men who aspired to take holy orders and become clerical officials. But as young aristocrats arrived to study for a few terms, Oxford and Cambridge sensed the possibility of future gifts and bequests, and they accordingly gave considerable attention to the instruction of privileged youths who had no intention of entering the church. It is important to note, however, that while this movement began during the fifteenth century, it did not triumph until the Elizabethan and Jacobean periods.

Of course, as a few boys with aristocratic connections appeared at the universities, this served as an example to legal and gentle families of means. One of the first legal families to send a son or two to either university were the Hankfords of Devonshire. In 1411 or 1412 young Richard Hankford arrived at New College, Oxford after a previous stay at Winchester, where he had been a student since 1408. Hankford remained at Oxford until 1415, when his grandfather, Sir William Hankford, Chief Justice of the King's Bench, decided he should "assume the role of a youth of his expectations." During that same year young Hankford accompanied Henry V on the celebrated Agincourt campaign against Charles VI of France; and in 1423 he represented his native county in parliament. A family of similar status that adopted the same course for its older sons were the Pastons of

Norfolk, who will be considered in another context later in this chapter. During the last years before the Reformation, several other legal and gentle families followed in the footsteps pioneered by the Hankfords. Between 1475 and 1525 a number of boys from the prominent Wallop family of Hampshire studied for a time at New College, Oxford. In 1497 another rich landowner, Sir Thomas Markenfield, left instructions in his will for his son Ninian to attend one of the Oxford colleges for a period of three years; while in 1501 Robert Constable arranged for his son Marmaduke to study at Cambridge for a similar period.

Because of the growing stress on education, Charles Sisson has rightly observed that a minimal degree of literacy was now commonly regarded as a "qualification for gentry or respectability."[7] That all children of landed families of some wealth were now expected to be able to read is supported by a short document in a fifteenth-century hand which is among the prized muniments of Coughton Court, Warwickshire. The author of this document was probably a local cleric or perhaps the chaplain of a land-owning family of some status. Addressed to a specific but unnamed individual, who may have been the head of the Throckmorton family, this document contained such revealing precepts as:

> When you dine, and also after dinner, say grace standing.
> Let the book [the Bible] be brought to the table as readily
>   as the Bread.
> And lest the tongue speak vain or hurtful things, let there
>   be [Bible] reading, now by one, now by another, and by
>   your children as soon as they can read.[8]

Despite the patchiness of the surviving evidence, it seems likely that boys from landed families of no great wealth learned little more than how to read, write, and keep simple accounts during the fifteenth and early sixteenth centuries. Certainly it would be several generations more before they profited from the type of formal, classical training with an emphasis on ancient languages that prevailed during the period after 1550.

Paradoxically, one of the main reasons for the growth of education and literacy during the late middle ages was the Hundred Years War, which lasted from 1337 until 1453. In actuality the Hundred Years War was a series of conflicts between England and France, since there was little if any fighting during the years 1347–52, 1360–69, 1389–1413, and 1444–49. Despite all those intervals of peace, the war caused bitter anti-French feelings to develop in England just as a violent hatred of the English took hold among the French. But as an intense dislike of French manners and customs became characteristic of the English people, a more rapid spread of education and literacy occurred, owing to greater dependence on the English language.

English had suffered a sharp reverse during the aftermath of the Norman Conquest and the emergence of an Anglo-Norman nobility wedded to the use of French. English cóntinued to be employed for purposes of religious instruction and for a few literary works, such as the famous poem "The Owl and the Nightingale." But the growing strength of monasticism, which was a prime feature of the Anglo-Norman period, caused English to be displaced as the preferred medium for virtually all other works. After King John's loss of Normandy in 1204, the upper classes gradually reverted to the native language in informal situations, so that by the end of the thirteenth century manuals offering instruction in French as a foreign language were appearing. However, French continued to be employed alongside Latin by the government, the church, and families with any claim to gentility, a dependence on English alone being considered a sure sign of "rusticity."

The outbreak of the Hundred Years War in 1337 and the intensity of the anti-French feeling that resulted soon led to the re-emergence of English as a wholly acceptable means of self-expression. Indeed, patriotism almost required the upper classes to employ it once and for all in place of the language of the national enemy. A powerful example was set by the monarch himself. During the 1340s Edward III not only fought with a shield decorated with two lines of English verse but also slept on a campaign bed adorned with an English motto. Partly as a result of this lead from on high, an important cultural transformation took place by the 1390s.

The earliest surviving petition in English rather than in French or Latin dates from 1344; and about that time a Yorkshireman, Richard Rolle (d. 1349), produced the first English-language version of the psalter. During the next decade two Oxford schoolmasters, John Cornwall and Richard Penrich, required their pupils to construe their Latin not into French as in the past but directly into their own native tongue. Once Cornwall and Penrich led the way, other teachers followed suit, with the result that most schoolboys lost their ability to speak French. In

1385 the learned vicar of Berkeley, John Trevisa, complained that the country's youth " 'knew no more French than their left heels.' "9 The earliest surviving English deed dates from 1376 and the first English will from 1387. The oldest extant letter in the vernacular, one sent from Milan by the famous soldier of fortune, Sir John Hawkwood, was written in 1392 or 1393. Although few other English letters were apparently written before 1400, they became increasingly common during the next half-century.

During those same years English was increasingly used for works of original literature, by such famous writers as John Gower, William Langland, and of course the incomparable Geoffrey Chaucer. Their poetry established a flourishing vernacular tradition for the first time since the Norman Conquest, although Richard Bailey rightly reminds us that there had been an "increasing output of English material" during the thirteenth century.10 While the writers of late medieval England did not create a completely new tradition of vernacular literature, they did produce works of greater power, originality, and expressiveness than their predecessors; and they thereby inaugurated the period of "modern English," even if the language continued to develop until it reached a new level of expressiveness between 1575 and 1600. In fact, until the last years of the sixteenth century, most intellectuals scorned English as a primitive and graceless tongue, lacking the eloquence, suppleness, and refinement of the three biblical languages. Accordingly, there was spirited opposition when efforts were made to translate the scriptures from Latin into English, which many considered too crude a medium to convey the all-important message of the Old and New Testaments.

The first prominent figure to call for an English-language Bible was John Wyclif (ca. 1328–84), an Oxford theologian of advanced views. According to Wyclif's famous doctrine of dominion by grace, each individual stands in a direct relationship with God and is therefore directly responsible to Him and obliged to obey all His laws as revealed in the Bible. But if every person must accept and follow the scriptures in all things, he must have a way of knowing what he is required to obey. Hence the Old and New Testaments must be accessible to the laity in an easily intelligible form.

Because of poor health and attacks from conservative theologians, Wyclif himself took little part in the arduous work of translating the Bible. Among his followers who undertook the task were Nicholas Hereford, Philip Repingdon, and John Aston, all of whom were ardent partisans of Wycliffite teachings at late fourteenth-century Oxford. Another contributor to the enterprise was Henry Whitfield, who as a consequence was soon ejected from the headship of Queen's College. It is also possible that William James of nearby Merton was involved in the project. In 1382 James openly defended Wyclif's controversial views about the Eucharist, and during later years his name was periodically linked with "the Lollards," as Wyclif's rather amorphous group of followers soon became known.*

By 1381 or 1382 a translation of the New Testament seems to have been ready, and within several more years an English version of the Old Testament was finished. The whole Bible then began to circulate throughout the realm in manuscript, although the entire work required six volumes or more. Prepared in haste, this first English Bible was stiff, unidiomatic, and completely literal in style and approach. The translators even attempted to preserve the basic patterns of Latin syntax, although this often caused them to sacrifice meaning and intelligibility. Consequently, a freer, more idiomatic translation was soon demanded, the work of revision being undertaken by John Purvey, Wyclif's secretary and closest associate during the last years of his life.

After Wyclif's death in December 1384, Purvey settled in the vicinity of Bristol, where he seems to have contacted John Trevisa (1326–1412), vicar of nearby Berkeley and the leading translator of the age. Among the important Latin works Trevisa rendered into an exuberant English style were Ranulf Higden's *Polychronicon*, a pioneering history of the world to 1360, and Bartholomew Glavill's *De Proprietatibus Rerum*, a systematic attempt to summarize the whole realm of knowledge. Trevisa was doubtless known, at least by reputation, to Purvey: at an earlier time the former had lost his fellowship at Queen's College, for upholding Lollard views. Although there is no clear evidence, Trevisa may well have given aid and encouragement to Purvey. Whether he did or not, a freer, more idiomatic version of the Bible, one with real literary merit, was produced during the years 1388–95.

---

*The term Lollard, which denoted someone who mumbled or spoke indistinctly, was derived from the name of a rebellious sect in the Low Countries.

The superiority of the revised Lollard Bible was obvious to contemporaries as soon as it appeared. Even a noted bishop like Reginald Pecock (d. 1457), a capable Latinist with extensive knowledge of the Vulgate, resorted to it whenever he wished to cite a passage from scripture. That many other clerics in addition to Pecock did so is proof of the great popularity of the revised version, which soon attracted a wide circle of users, who included the Bridgettine nuns of Syon and the Dominican friars of Cambridge. As a consequence, more than 215 copies of Purvey's translation survive to this day, whereas fewer than 25 copies of the first Lollard Bible are still extant.[11]

That the second Lollard Bible was so popular with English readers was owing not just to its considerable literary merit. During the late Middle Ages there was a hunger for more scriptural knowledge on the part of the average layman. Yet the clerical hierarchy adamantly opposed Bible-reading as a devotional exercise by the laity, on the grounds that each individual would develop his own idiosyncratic interpretations. That the prelates' fears were not exaggerated is proved by the subsequent actions of the more radical Lollards, who refused to bow to crucifixes, denounced pilgrimages as a useless form of penance, and assailed the parochial clergy as lazy, quarrelsome, and greedy. In southwestern England several particularly radical congregations adopted Wyclif's view that only the offices of deacon and presbyter had existed during early Christian times. In an effort to restore the church to its ancient purity, they accordingly chose and instituted their own leaders, in complete violation of the bishops' right of ordination.

Hoping to regain control of the situation, the clerical hierarchy met at Oxford in 1408 and adopted the Constitutions suggested by Archbishop Arundel. In this way they erected legal barriers to the use of English Bibles by all readers except those who were known for their orthodox views. Even more important, the Constitutions of Arundel forbade further attempts to translate the scriptures into the vernacular without episcopal permission. Henceforth anyone who attempted to evade that prohibition would be subject to trial and execution for heresy. The new regulations even forbade the reading of translated passages from the Bible during regular worship services. Not until 1538, four years after the completion of Henry VIII's break from Rome, was permission extended for a gospel excerpt to be read aloud in English before the sermon.

Because most adults of the era felt so deprived of scriptural knowledge, many made extreme sacrifices in order to obtain copies of the revised Lollard Bible. In most instances the equivalent of an artisan's yearly wages, sometimes far more, was paid for a single copy. During the reign of Henry IV (1399–1413), an East Anglian man is known to have purchased an English New Testament for 56s. 8d.; while a reliable writer of the mid-sixteenth century held that " . . . some gave a load of hay for a few chapters of St. James or of St. Paul in English." Occasionally humble families banded together to buy copies that they could not afford individually, making small contributions to a common fund until sufficient money was on hand.

The widespread use of English Bibles by poor families suggests that literacy was growing among all classes during the late Middle Ages. Because of the upsurge of educational institutions and the strong desire of most adults to be able to read the scriptures for themselves, even peasants and artisans were making determined efforts to learn how to read. However, it is far easier to suggest an advancing literacy rate than it is to prove such a phenomenon conclusively. Aside from the widespread use of English Bibles, only scattered references exist to support the notion that such a development actually occurred. Yet the literary evidence that survives from that age is of a compelling nature, and only someone predisposed to believe it was an era of mass illiteracy would attempt to refute it. For example, the Abstract Book of the Brewers' Company of London for the year 1422 contains an important passage that explains why the company's directors had recently decided to keep their records in English rather than in French or Latin, as in the past. According to that passage, " ' . . . there are many of our craft of Brewers who have the knowledge of writing in the said English idiom; but in others, to wit Latin and French, before these times used, they do not in any wise understand.' "[12] Equally significant is the tradition that had developed at Norwich by 1424, where the municipal officials posted regular notices in the vernacular on the town gates. These notices conveyed useful information to the country folk who were coming into the town for the weekly market; so the local authorities must have assumed an ability to read on the part of some percentage of those who often arrived from the outlying areas.[13]

Although Sir Thomas More's estimate of the literacy rate during his lifetime dates from over a century later, it is worth recalling at this point. In his celebrated "Apology" of 1533,

More implied that literacy among his contemporaries was between 50 and 60 percent, holding that " ' . . . more than foure partes of all the whole [population] divided into tenn could never reade english yet.' "[14] To be sure, More's estimate must be rejected as too high, since he never traveled more than fifty miles beyond London, the best-educated part of the realm. But there are still good reasons to believe that by the eve of the Reformation, some 25 to 30 percent of England's adults could read, albeit not to write, since the latter skill was considered a specialized one and fewer individuals attained a mastery of it. A fundamental premise of the present study is that, as educational institutions grew in number and educational opportunity widened, a steady growth of literacy occurred, since all students at the grammar-school level or beyond were potential reading teachers, at least among their own relatives and acquaintances.

Most authorities on the period support this proposition about advancing literacy. Margaret Aston holds in fact that, "The fifteenth century was a time of generally increasing literacy and of growing opportunity for lay people to learn how to read and write." Malcolm Parkes is just as convinced and believes that even many poor peasants could understand simple vernacular instructions addressed to them by their employers. In addition, Mr. Parkes cites a twelfth-century monastic figure, Walter Map, who had complained about the way the peasantry of his own time was pursuing education for purely utilitarian reasons. As the blatantly snobbish Map held, " 'peasants . . . are eager to nourish their baseborn and degenerate children in the arts unfitted to their station, not that they may rise from their rudeness, but that they may revel in richess.' "[15] According to this view, the English peasantry even before the time of Magna Carta regarded education and literacy as important keys to social mobility and were determined to pursue them whenever possible.

That the lower-class attitude in this regard was far from wrong is proved by the case of the Pastons, a poor family of Norfolk husbandmen until the 1390s. During that decade the head of this family, Clement Paston, made strenuous efforts to secure an adequate education for his son and heir William. He even borrowed money from his wife's father in order to send William to study the common law at one of the Inns of Court, probably the Inner Temple. An able and hardworking boy, William distinguished himself and eventually became a steward to the bishop of Norwich. In time he became a functionary of the

Common Pleas and, in 1429, a justice of that court with a handsome yearly salary. Thereafter the Pastons' rise was assured, and within another generation they were comfortably settled among the gentry, assembling a large library and obtaining as much education for their sons as other members of that increasingly important class. Indeed, the founder of the family fortunes, William Paston the judge, sent four of his male offspring to attend Cambridge for at least a year. These naturally included his eventual heir John, who spent a short time at Trinity Hall before transferring to Peterhouse. Later this John Paston—several family members bore that name—proceeded to the Inner Temple, where his father had probably attained his mastery of the law and where he himself was subsequently followed by his brother Edmund. Ultimately John sent his own son Walter to Oxford, while Walter's younger brother William attended Eton, where he was enrolled as a boarding student in 1478.[16]

Once the Black Death and subsequent epidemics of plague caused a significant decline of peasant numbers, which led to a weakening of mandatory labor bonds and the decay of villeinage, it became easier than ever for peasant boys to acquire a modicum of education. However, this development was considered a threat by landowners who did not wish their labor charges to rise even more than they had during the previous half-century, when the pool of cheap peasant labor had suddenly contracted, causing a 50% jump in the wages paid to extra workers at the harvest or at plowtime. So the well-to-do made periodic attempts to keep peasant boys from attending school. In 1388 the landed classes even secured a parliamentary act forbidding children of humble families to leave the manor after their twelfth birthday; while in 1391 a more explicit statute decreed that villeins were not to send their offspring to any kind of school whatever. Such attempts to close the door to educational opportunity were bound to fail in the end; and in 1406 parliament acknowledged this by passing a new Statute of Artificers, which stipulated that " ' . . . every man or woman of what[ever] state or condition that he be, shall be free to send their son or daughter to take learning at any school that pleaseth them within the realm.' "[17]

Even after the enactment of the 1406 legislation, there was lingering resentment against the education of lower-class boys. At Gloucester in 1410, loud protests occurred when local teachers reduced tuition payments from 40*d.* to only 12*d.* per quarter, thereby putting education within easier reach of the poor. During that same year two boys were reported to have left a

Bedfordshire manor to attend school without seeking their lord's permission; while as late as 1465 the jurors on a manor near Leeds were fined for failing to report that a young villein had received instruction in reading without his lord's consent. These efforts by the landed elite to thwart the growing demand of the poor for education grew steadily weaker as time wore on; and in 1541 there was final legal recognition of the right of all boys, regardless of their background, to attend school.[18]

There was no comparable opposition to the education of middle-class boys. In fact, strong pressures existed among the wealthier ranks of the *bourgeoisie* for a greater measure of formal training. Both doctors and lawyers had an obvious need for literacy, and so too did bailiffs and stewards on the great manorial estates of the time. As trade and commerce expanded during the late Middle Ages, more and more merchant families desired their sons to be able to read and keep financial accounts. Families that participated in the international wool trade, such as the Celys of Essex and the Springs of Suffolk, required more than a minimal level of intellectual training, since Latin was still the main business language used throughout Europe. Such Bristol merchants as William Pavy, who traded with western France as well as Ireland and Iceland, provided at least six years of formal education for all their sons. During this period several of the great livery companies of London established precise requirements for the schooling of prospective members. The Goldsmiths, for example, had a rule in force by 1478 which forbade any practitioner of their craft to apprentice a boy who could not read and write. The Skinners must have adopted a similar rule, for two of their apprentices, newly arrived from the countryside in 1496, were directed to attend school until they had mastered the basic educational skills.

Middle-class boys were usually educated in schools operated by chantry priests (which will be discussed in the next chapter) or by local clerics who supplemented their meager incomes by taking occasional pupils for small fees. Sometimes such boys were trained in the cathedral or monastic schools of the time or in the dozens of guild schools that existed for the instruction of small children. Occasionally the sons of prominent merchants continued their education in small academies run by scriveners. The early-fifteenth-century scrivener William Kingsmill ran such an academy in London; and during the year 1415 one of his pupils, a boy of twelve, declared that " . . . in three months in

Kingsmill's hostel school he had learned to read and write, to make up accounts, and to speak French."[19] Whether a boy could have learned that much so quickly in a scrivener school seems doubtful. Besides, those institutions rarely accepted boys without prior training at a lower or petty school, so their pupils could usually read without difficulty at the time they were admitted.

Regardless of the quality of the scrivener schools, affluent members of the middle class were increasingly active as book-collectors. In 1420 a merchant tailor of London, John Brinchley, left his heir a copy of *The Canterbury Tales* as well as English and Latin editions of Boethius's ever-popular *Consolation of Philosophy*. Whether Brinchley's library included other books is unclear, although it seems likely. About the same time a wealthy grocer of the capital, Sir William Chichele, a brother of the archbishop, bequeathed a Bible, a psalter, and a primer to his heirs. In addition Chichele left £20 for the purchase of books to be placed in the new Guildhall Library, which had been established through the efforts of Sir Richard Whittington, Lord Mayor of London on several occasions. John Carpenter, who was Town Clerk of the capital from 1417 until his death in 1438, had an impressive collection of seventy to eighty books during his last years; whereas another mercer of the period, Robert Thorney, possessed almost as many works, several of which eventually found their way to the shelves of Trinity College, Cambridge.

Members of the London *bourgeoisie* frequently purchased books from John Shirley, the most enterprising copyist of the age. Shirley was one of the first men to exploit the new methods of cursive writing that had developed during the previous 200 years; and from his large *scriptorium* he conducted a lucrative trade in the production of books. A work he definitely issued in multiple copies was the famous *Secretum Secretorum*, which was believed to be Aristotle's fatherly advice to the young Alexander the Great but was in actuality a twelfth-century fabrication. Between 1420 and 1450 Shirley's *scriptorium* also functioned as a lending library; and on the fly-leaves of books he lent to clients for small fees, he often penned the gentle reminder:

> But sendenth this boke to me agayne
> Shirley, I meane, which is right fayne
> If ye ther-of have had plesaunce.[20]

One last matter remains to be considered in this chapter: the degree to which literacy and education had spread among women by the late middle ages. To be sure, females had fewer opportunities to acquire education, and considerably less money to spend on books, than men. However, determined and resourceful women almost always learned how to read, while females of high social position often acquired fluency in one or more foreign languages. Some women received instruction in basic educational subjects from their husbands, fathers, or brothers; whereas others studied with the family chaplain, the local parish priest, or the nuns in one of the 135 to 140 convents of the time. Virtually all women who became readers took special care to see that their own daughters mastered the skill also. One who clearly did was Elizabeth Woodville, the wife of Edward IV, who used scores of books to educate the seven children she bore her husband. Included in Elizabeth's collection was an illuminated copy of a French newsletter that contained a summary of events in Constantinople after the death of Sultan Mohammed II in 1481. One of Elizabeth's five daughters, Cecily, who eventually married Lord Welles, is also remembered for the diligent way she instructed her own two daughters. The familiar letters of such merchant families as the Stonors and the Celys offer graphic proof of the spread of literacy among middle-class women. But even among an upwardly mobile family like the Pastons, the females, although clearly able to read, generally relied on men to write any letters they wished to send. Only one Paston woman, Margery, who died in 1495, left any evidence of an ability to sign her name, which she always did in an awkward and halting manner, probably because she had few occasions to write.

Late medieval women were motivated to learn to read by a variety of factors. These included: (1) a wish to use the Bibles, psalters, and other devotional works of the time, which were increasingly plentiful and inexpensive; (2) the need or desire to be able to communicate with friends or relatives who lived at a distance; and (3) an interest in reading the histories, romances, and other literary works of the era for either edification or pleasure. It is also possible that an occasional woman learned how to read in order to make herself more appealing to men. Not all husbands of the period were crude chauvinists who sought to keep their wives ignorant and uninformed. As fifteenth-century Englishmen acquired greater culture, some percentage of them developed a taste for stimulating conversation, which compelled their wives and mistresses to obtain a smattering of education also. That this was the case helps to explain why Sir Thomas More went out of his way to note of Jane Shore, the courtesan whose favors were shared by Edward IV, Lord Hastings, and the marquess of Dorset, that she "could both read well and write."[21]

As literacy and education spread among late medieval women, so did the ownership of books, although at a slower rate than among men. As early as 1395 Lady Alice West bequeathed to her daughter-in-law Joanne a missal "and all the bokes that I have of latyn, englisch, and frensch"; while four years later the dowager duchess of Gloucester left her daughter Anne, countess of Stafford a French work with beautiful illuminations as well as "a book of the psalter, primer, and other devotions . . . which book I have often used." To her son Humphrey this same great lady left a psalter and four books in French; while to another daughter who had taken the veil, she bequeathed two psalters, a collection of decretals, a copy of St. Gregory's pastorals, two works of history, and a Bible bound in two large volumes.[22]

Many more examples of this sort have survived for women of the fifteenth century. In 1422 Lady Peryne Clanbowe left a collection of sermons to a young female relative, who was probably a niece or a granddaughter; and about the same time the countess of Westmorland petitioned the heirs of Henry V for the recovery of a cherished copy of *The Chronicles of Jerusalem*, which the late king had borrowed but never returned. At her death in 1422 Eleanor Purdeley had among her personal effects a collection of sermons as well as two other books of a religious nature. The holdings of Elizabeth d'Arcy and Agnes, Lady Stapledon, numbered over a dozen volumes each; while Elizabeth Sywardby's library in 1468 contained at least eight books, three of which were reputed to be very costly. In 1480 Lady Margaret Beaufort received a valuable bequest of books from her mother-in-law, the dowager duchess of Buckingham. These included "a primer with clasps of silver-gilt, covered with purple velvet" and a French-language edition of the works of Lucan, Sallust, and Suetonius, which had been printed in Paris in 1470. Finally, Lady Cecily Neville, the widow of Richard, duke of York (d. 1460), had a large collection of books that she used in her daily devotions. Lady Cecily's books included such works as Hilton's *Contemplative and Active Life*, an unknown author's *Infancy of the Saviour*, and an English edition of the *Liber Specialis Gratie* by a thirteenth-century German nun, Matilda of Hackeborn.[23]

From at least the 1440s, women gave aid and encouragement to the poets of the era. A prolific writer whose main patrons all came from the female sex was Osbern Bokenham, an Augustinian friar of Stoke Clare, Suffolk. To repay his many obligations to the countess of Oxford, Bokenham composed a poetic account of the legend of St. Elizabeth; while soon afterwards he produced a life of Mary Magdalene at the urging of the countess of Essex. He also completed a biographical study of St. Agatha for one Agatha Legge and undertook a similar sketch of St. Dorothy for Isobel Hunt and her husband John. Perhaps Bokenham's most important work was his long account of St. Katherine's life and career, which extended to more than 1,000 lines of rhyming couplets and resulted from proposals made by Lady Katherine Howard and Lady Katherine Denston.[24]

During the last years of the fifteenth century, Lady Margaret Beaufort, countess of Richmond, was an ardent advocate of Bernard André, "the blind poet of Toulouse"; whereas a rich widow of Yexford, Surrey, Thomasine Hopton, had a similar love for the poetry of Thomas Hoccleve, whose writings she bequeathed in 1493 to a favorite grandchild. However, the woman of the period who had the most lasting impact on literary and cultural developments before the Reformation was Margaret of York, the devoted sister of Edward IV and Richard III. An avid reader from childhood, Margaret became the wife of Duke Charles the Bold of Burgundy in 1468. Shortly after her arrival on the continent, Margaret made the acquaintance of that capable man of affairs, William Caxton, who agreed to procure books and manuscripts for her. In fact, Margaret's insistent demand for reading materials caused Caxton himself to become a translator of foreign books and ultimately to journey to Cologne in order to learn the new techniques of printing by means of interchangeable metal letters. But that important development, and an account of the early English printing industry with its consequences for the further spread of literacy, must await a later chapter.

3

Humanism, Monastic Conditions, and New Educational Institutions

It is now time to consider the role of humanism in the educational and cultural developments of the late medieval period. Humanism was an intellectual movement that appeared first in the city-states of northern Italy and then gradually spread elsewhere, becoming established in England by the end of the fifteenth century. Because humanism appeared relatively late in England, it did not provide the impetus for those changes, already described in the two preceding chapters, which began during the mid-fourteenth century. Yet because of its fundamental stress on education, humanism gave powerful reinforcement to those developments already underway and prolonged the period of growth that might otherwise have ended before the Reformation. In addition, humanism led to a significant increase of popular support for higher education; it promoted an awareness of the need for more rigorous female training; and by stressing such subjects as mathematics, astronomy, history, morals, music, and physical skills, as well as ancient languages, it established the groundwork for what soon became known as "liberal education."

"Humanism" is not an easy term to define, for the movement encompassed a variety of methods and approaches. Yet all humanists were united in the quest for eloquence, which caused them to seek a mastery of both grammar and rhetoric and to reject the emphasis on logic and theology that had prevailed during earlier centuries. Moreover, unlike the medieval schoolmen, humanist teachers put a premium on educating laymen for the public responsibilities that might confront them in later life. Indeed, it has been said that the overriding objective of humanist teachers was to educate "complete citizens" and that they accordingly "created the modern idea of the gentleman, whose nobility is conferred by virtue and learning . . . rather than by birth."[1]

Once humanist ideas came to maturity in northern Italy during the first half of the fifteenth century, they gradually spread into other parts of Europe. Their transmission was accomplished by a variety of means; but in so far as England was concerned, they were transported by two groups of travelers: Italian scholars who journeyed to England in search of patrons, and Englishmen who appeared in Italy on diplomatic business or went there for advanced studies after initial work at Oxford or Cambridge. In addition, humanist ideas percolated into England—or, to be more precise, the ground was prepared for their reception—by means of the many books and manuscripts procured from abroad by such important bibliophiles as Humphrey, duke of Gloucester (d. 1447) and William Gray, bishop of Ely (d. 1478). Finally, after the establishment of printing by mechanical means during the years 1476–1500, a more rapid spread of humanist ideas occurred, since Caxton and all the other early English printers published a large number of humanist tracts within a short period.

Between 1418 and 1450, several leading Italian scholars made prolonged visits to England. These included Piero del Monte, Tito Livio Frulovisi, and, most important of all, Poggio Bracciolini. In 1416 Poggio discovered an authentic copy of the famous *Institutio Oratoria*, the most important educational tract of the Roman writer Quintilian (d. A.D. 95). That event created a sensation in scholarly and literary circles; and in 1418 Henry Beaufort, cardinal-bishop of Winchester, invited Poggio to join his household. The Italian scholar remained in England for four years; but because of his somewhat abrasive manner and Cardinal Beaufort's preoccupation with governmental matters, the former failed to make a permanent contribution to the establishment of humanism in England.

The first foreign-born scholar to exert a lasting influence in this regard was Antonio Beccaria, the most distinguished graduate of the palace school at Mantua that was led for more than two decades by Vittorino da Feltre. Born about 1410, Beccaria arrived in England in 1439 and seems to have remained for eight years. During that period he served as personal secretary to Humphrey, duke of Gloucester, and conducted all his Latin correspondence in such an admirable style that it set a new standard for the future. In addition he translated several Greek and Italian works into Latin, since his patron's linguistic skills were limited to that language, and to English and French.[2]

During the second half of the fifteenth century, so many Italian scholars spent a few years in England that it would be tedious to discuss them all. Yet two humanists were of such clear importance that they must be mentioned, at least in passing. The first of these was Stefano Surigone, a native of Milan, who lectured at Oxford between 1454 and 1471. Surigone was an accomplished Latin poet whose verses were among the best of the period. Consequently, he succeeded in raising the level of Latin studies at Oxford, to which he returned in 1478 after a seven-year interval at Cologne. Meanwhile at Cambridge a similar contribution was being made by the Franciscan scholar Lorenzo da Savona. Both a humanist and a scholastic, Lorenzo had studied at Bologna under the great Francesco della Rovere, later to become Pope Sixtus IV. After lecturing at Bologna and then at Oxford for several terms, Lorenzo migrated to the younger English university, where he taught theology for almost a decade. While at Cambridge he wrote an important humanist tract, the *Nova Rhetorica,* which he had completed by July 1478. Within the next two years, this large work of 362 pages was printed twice, first by Caxton at Westminster and then by the anonymous schoolmaster-printer of St. Albans. Thoroughly Ciceronian in spirit, the *Nova Rhetorica* began by stressing the value of rhetoric in practical affairs and defended the subject as an appropriate one for higher study. After finishing this, his most outstanding work, Lorenzo produced a guidebook to proper letter-writing and composed a long Latin poem that he dedicated to William Waynflete, bishop of Winchester for many years.

At the same time dozens of Italians were pursuing humanist activities in England, almost as many English-born scholars were traveling to the continent and gaining inspiration from the humanist fount itself. One of the first to do so was Andrew Holes, who served the crown in a diplomatic capacity between 1432 and 1444. During those years Holes became a friend of Pope Eugenius IV, and in 1439 he took a doctorate in canon law at Padua. While residing in Florence for nearly five years, he purchased so many books from the famous bookseller Vespasiano da Bisticci that they had to be crated and shipped to England by sea. Holes therefore deserves to be remembered as one of England's pioneering collectors of humanist books. On his death in 1457, his holdings were divided between the libraries of three Oxford colleges and Salisbury Cathedral, of which he had been chancellor for over a decade.[3]

Two somewhat younger Englishmen who were deeply influenced by humanist ideas while in Italy were William Gray and Robert Flemmyng. After taking undergraduate degrees at Oxford, both Gray and Flemmyng studied at Padua during the mid 1440s, and for a time they also attended the famous lectures of Guarino da Verona, professor of rhetoric at Ferrara from 1436 until his death in 1460. In November 1445 Gray was appointed Henry VI's chief proctor at the papal curia. Once he arrived in Rome, Gray wielded a strong influence because of the admiration felt for his wide learning. In 1450 Nicholas V, the founder of the Vatican Library, unsuccessfully solicited the see of Lincoln for him; but four years later the pope did arrange for him to become bishop of Ely. When Gray left Italy in 1454, he already owned a large collection of classical and neoclassical works, including the *Ethics* of Leonardo Bruni, the orations of Guarino and Poggio Bracciolini, and the letters of Petrarch. On his death in 1478, he bequeathed 200 volumes to his Oxford alma mater, Balliol College, thereby doubling its library at a stroke.[4]

Just as Gray substantially enlarged the collection of Balliol College, Robert Flemmyng greatly strengthened the holdings of nearby Lincoln College, which his uncle, Richard Flemmyng, bishop of Lincoln had founded in 1427. The younger Flemmyng was undoubtedly a more dedicated scholar than Gray, and while still at Padua during the 1440s he made a transcription of Cicero's *De Officiis*. Yet Flemmyng's greatest interest was in Greek studies, which he pursued systematically for nearly forty years. From Guarino's lectures he had obtained such a deep knowledge of Greek that he was able to compile a pioneering Graeco-Latin dictionary. Flemmyng was also important because of his great love and extensive knowledge of Latin poetry. He owned all the works of Horace as well as several modern commentaries on them. He also appears to have been the first Englishman to acquire all the comedies of Plautus and the important critique of Terence's plays by Aelius Donatus.[5]

Because Flemmyng worked alone and took no students, a slightly later traveler to Italy, William Sellyng, had a considerably greater impact on the next generation of English scholars. Born about 1430, Sellyng entered the great Benedictine monastery of Christ Church, Canterbury, in 1447 or 1448. Within a few years he was sent by his order to study at Canterbury Hall, Oxford, where he was in residence by 1454. Two years later he became a priest, and on 7 February 1454 he supplicated for the bachelor of divinity degree. Eventually Sellyng developed an interest in humane letters and attended the lectures of Latin eloquence given by Stefano Surigone, who, as noted earlier, taught at Oxford between 1454 and 1471. In 1464 Sellyng obtained permission from his monastery to pursue his studies on the continent for three years, and by 1466 he had completed a doctorate in divinity at Bologna. While at that university he may have studied Greek with the Byzantine refugee Andronicus Callistus. Whether he did or not, he soon gained a mastery of that language by working with the noted Florentine humanist Angelo Poliziano.[6]

Sellyng was back in residence at Canterbury by May 1469 at the latest. In 1471 he was appointed chancellor of Christ Church, and from 1472 until his death in 1494 he was prior of that large institution. Almost from the time he became prior, Sellyng offered instruction in Greek and Latin to interested monks of his house — and also to promising boys of the neighborhood, who included Thomas Linacre, a leading humanist of the next generation. Despite heavy administrative tasks, Sellyng pursued his scholarly interests, collecting manuscripts for the monastic library and preparing a Latin translation of an important tract by St. John Chrysostom. All the while his reputation as an outstanding orator was growing, and in 1487 Henry VII included him on a ten-man delegation to Rome. Although this embassy was nominally headed by the bishops of Durham and Hereford, it fell to Sellyng to extend Henry's formal homage to Pope Innocent VIII in a Latin oration that was hailed for its eloquence. In helping to establish sound classical scholarship in England, Sellyng was important in two principal ways. Not only did he bequeath to his successors a collection of important texts, but through his inspired teaching he also created "a vigorous impetus that was not lost after his death."[7]

Aside from Christ Church during Sellyng's time, humanism seems to have made almost no converts in the other monasteries of the age. Between 1491 and 1500 there was some humanist activity at Reading Abbey, but only because of the presence there of a Greek refugee, Johannes Serbopoulos, who transcribed books for private clients. Somewhat earlier a scholarly abbot of St. Albans, John Whethamstede, had developed a fleeting interest in humanism. Between 1435 and 1440 Whethamstede had been in communication with Piero del Monte, one of the first Italian scholars to journey to England. At the abbot's request, Piero, who served the pope as collector of Peter's Pence, supplied copies of the writings of Dante, Petrarch, Boccaccio, and probably Leonardo Bruni. But despite his wide interests, Whethamstede never became a true humanist. To him Christian dogma was always of paramount importance, and after the publication of Lorenzo Valla's tract proving the forgery of the Donation of Constantine, he made repeated efforts to defend that spurious document, which had long been used to buttress papal claims to power.[8]

Except for these few examples, there is little to suggest that humanism made converts among the regular clergy of the age. Not only did the religious houses fail to respond to the New Learning, as humanism was known at the time, but they also ignored the establishment of printing by mechanical means, which is particularly curious since the monasteries had traditionally been important centers of book production. Once Caxton led the way and opened the first English print shop in 1476, the abbeys and priories remained strangely oblivious to that critical advance, the most important technological innovation of the age. Of the approximately 700 monasteries and friaries that existed during the two generations before their suppression by Henry VIII, only the houses at St. Albans, Tavistock, and Abingdon are known to have had any connection with printing presses, and only at Tavistock did a monk participate in the work itself.[9]

To a degree the intellectual vitality of English monasticism had been sapped by the Black Death and later visitations of plague, from which the regular clergy were slow in recovering. At their zenith in numbers and influence between 1100 and 1345, the religious houses thereafter suffered such grievous setbacks that even the strongest were permanently affected.

Monasteries and convents that had averaged fifty members before the Black Death rarely comprised more than thirty inmates during the period 1485–1535, while a few houses failed to achieve even half their previous size. Glastonbury Abbey, for example, which had usually had about 100 inmates during the reign of Edward I (1272–1307), numbered only 48 men on the eve of the Reformation. Romsey Abbey in Wiltshire suffered an even more debilitating decline, since it never counted over 25 inmates between the 1350s and the 1530s, although it had boasted 90 members in 1333. On the other hand, Westminster Abbey was slightly larger in 1399 than it had been during the mid 1340s; while Whalley Abbey had twenty more members in 1353 than it had had a decade earlier. Even if a few houses grew and prospered after the initial epidemic of plague, it is nonetheless true that the regular clergy never recovered completely from the high mortality of the recurrent visitations of the disease. In 1509, when monastic numbers were greater than at any time since 1347, there were approximately 12,000 monks, nuns, and friars in all the religious houses of the kingdom. This suggests that the pre-Reformation regular clergy was only 70 percent as large as its early fourteenth-century century counterpart, which had consisted of some 14,000 men and 3,500 women.

Because monastic numbers never completely recovered, the religious houses were not the great cultural and educational force after 1348 that they had been during earlier ages. In particular, the smaller monasteries and nunneries, those with fewer than a dozen members and insufficient revenues for their maintenance, witnessed a steady deterioration of conditions, which occasioned much adverse comment. In some instances the smaller religious houses even neglected prayers and mandatory spiritual duties, so it seemed prudent to suppress them altogether. This step was first taken by William Waynflete, who spent twenty years trying to improve the performance of the residents of Selborn Priory, Hampshire. When all his efforts failed, Waynflete secured royal permission late in 1485 to suppress that once-large monastery and add its estates to the endowment of Magdalen College, Oxford.[10] A similar, albeit briefer, case involved the nunnery of St. Rhadegund, in Cambridge. By the mid 1480s that convent had acquired a thoroughly evil reputation, being widely regarded as altogether corrupt and dissolute. In October 1487 the new bishop of Ely, John Alcock, visited the convent and ruled that its eleven nuns were unfit to elect a successor to the late prioress. Thereupon Bishop Alcock appointed the most deserving member of the house to the vacant position. But the new prioress was unable to stem the tide of decay, and by 1495 all but two of the nuns had withdrawn to convents elsewhere. When in the latter year Bishop Alcock visited St. Rhadegund's again, he found the buildings to be "utterly dilapidated and wasted." So he decided to suppress the nunnery once and for all, and in June 1496 he secured a royal licence to use its properties to found a new college. In this way the society known as Jesus College, Cambridge, which initially consisted of a master and several dozen members, came into being.[11]

It would be wrong to conclude from this that English monasticism was a totally spent force by the end of the fifteenth century. Lax and corrupt practices were typical of only the smaller abbeys and priories, whose members often lived in virtual poverty. The larger abbeys were still known for their religious zeal, and their inmates continued to make worthwhile contributions. During the first quarter of the fifteenth century, a Carthusian monk in Yorkshire made an English translation of pseudo-Bonaventure's *Meditations*, which was thereafter one of the most popular books of the age. About 1440 an anonymous friar of King's Lynn completed the *Promptorium Parvulorium*, the first English-to-Latin dictionary, which was reprinted at least six times by 1535. At Ramsey Abbey, which had an excellent library, an unknown monk was knowledgable enough to be able to compile the first Hebrew lexicon. Yet the most prolific writer of the era was undoubtedly the learned monk of Bury St. Edmunds, John Lydgate (d. 1450). Lydgate produced a number of important works, including a popular account of the Trojan Wars and a long life of St. Edmund in English verse, which commemorated a royal visit to Bury in 1433.

As noted earlier in this chapter, Richard Sellyng made Christ Church, Canterbury an important centre of humanist activity between 1472 and 1494. A short while later Richard Kidderminster, abbot of Winchcombe from 1488 until 1527, worked equally hard to make his house a bastion of study and scholarship. Kidderminster himself gave weekly lectures on the *Sentences* of Peter Lombard, while three monks with advanced training in theology led daily discussions on the Bible. At Mount Grace Priory in Yorkshire, important mystical treatises were written by John Norton and Richard Methley; while Henry Bradshaw of Chester Abbey made a study of the writings of John Skelton, the best poet of the early Tudor period; and in 1513 he published a carefully written life of St. Werburgh.

Just as individual abbeys showed continued vitality, the Cistercian order as a whole demonstrated an enhanced commitment to education during this era. In the early 1430s Cistercian houses throughout the realm launched a drive for funds with which to endow an Oxford college for student monks of their order. During earlier ages the Cistercian monasteries of England, Ireland, and Wales had relied on Rewley Abbey to provide lodging for any members they sent to study at the older university, but that small house was now hopelessly decayed. The Cistercians therefore wished to establish a permanent society of their own at Oxford, but their money-raising efforts fell considerably short of the mark. Luckily, their plight soon came to the notice of Henry Chichele, the current archbishop of Canterbury, who sympathized with their goal and agreed to underwrite the project. Within a short time Chichele bought a five-acre tract on the outskirts of Oxford, and in March 1437 he obtained the king's permission to found a college "to the honour of the most glorious Virgin Mary and St. Bernard." At the same time the archbishop paid all the costs of erecting a large T-shaped building, which he deeded over to the grateful monastic order. The resulting society soon became known simply as St. Bernard's College; and it remained in being until the dissolution of all the religious houses and their affiliated colleges by Henry VIII.[12]

Two other religious orders—one of monks and the other of friars—excelled the Cistercians in their commitment to education. Throughout the fifteenth and early sixteenth centuries, the Benedictines maintained three different societies at Oxford for student monks of their order. These were Canterbury Hall and Durham and Gloucester Colleges, all of which were large and healthy institutions. From 1428 there was also a lone Benedictine society at Cambridge, which originated as a cell of Croyland Abbey and was originally known as Monks' Place. However, Henry Stafford, second duke of Buckingham (d. 1483) gave so much assistance to Monks' Place, financing the construction of its first brick buildings and the main fabric of the chapel, that it was popularly known as Buckingham College from the 1490s.

Although less evidence survives for the mendicant than for the monastic orders, it is obvious that the Dominicans were equally active on the educational front during these years. The Dominicans maintained large friaries at both universities for their student members; and they also supported a preparatory school at Langley Regis, where promising young recruits were taught logic and natural philosophy in a two-year course. Further, an official ruling of 1525 held that every Dominican friary in England should keep at least one student at either university at all times.[13]

Since the publication of a papal decree of 1336, monastic houses with fewer than eight members had been expected to maintain 5 percent of their total membership at a university on a recurring basis. Despite the growing concern for higher education, it is far from clear whether the English religious houses faithfully met that obligation, which was bound to cause hardships for abbeys with fewer than twenty inmates. Certainly some houses made no effort to comply; and in 1423 the abbot of St. Werburgh's, Chester, was found to have sent no scholars to either university for twelve years, which prompted a chapter ruling that he should be severely punished. Also in 1423 the officials of Gloucester College, Oxford, complained that seven different abbeys were failing to send their full contingent of student monks to the college. The two worst offenders were Bruton Abbey in Somerset and Evesham Abbey in Worcestershire, neither of which had sent a single monk in three years. Later in the fifteenth century, in 1492, Bishop Goldwell of Norwich noted that his own cathedral priory had a poor record of maintaining student members at the universities.[14]

On the other hand, the great Hertfordshire abbey of St. Albans, one of the kingdom's richest houses, never faltered in its support of higher education. From at least the time of Abbot Thomas de la Mare, who headed that monastery from 1370 until 1396, St. Albans was careful to send several student monks to the older university each year. In addition, Abbot Thomas and his successors had a sincere concern for the well-being of Gloucester College, to which they often sent manuscripts as well as stone and other materials for building purposes. That St. Albans was the pacesetter in regard to education can be seen from a 1529 survey, which revealed that the abbey was then maintaining six students, or just over 11 percent of its total membership, at Oxford.[15] Although smaller and less prosperous than St. Albans, Westminster Abbey was almost as conscientious about securing advanced education for its members. During the long period 1360-1539 there were always two or more full-time monks from Westminster at Oxford. Usually three such monks were enrolled, and, on a few occasions, as many as six.[16]

As the sixteenth century wore on, additional monks also arrived at the eastern university to study for a time, although the monkish element at Cambridge was always smaller than at Oxford. Moreover, because of the dearth of monastic societies at Cambridge, different arrangements had to be made for the lodging of student monks there. Individual monasteries often signed indentures with existing secular colleges, a course Butley Abbey took in 1500 when it contracted with Gonville Hall "for the reservation of a convenient room . . . for their men." Because Gonville Hall was still a small institution with fewer than fifteen members, its master was doubtless pleased to lodge an occasional monk from Butley, which was an easy way to raise funds to help with current operating expenses. During the first decades of the sixteenth century, over a dozen Butley monks resided for a year or two at Gonville and then returned to their Suffolk monastery, usually to share what they had learned with their fellow members. Gonville Hall is also known to have provided lodging to monks from other houses, including Norwich Priory and Castleacre Abbey in Norfolk.[17]

During the years 1500–1540 *hundreds* of student monks were in residence at the universities: so many in fact that the names of 750 such men who studied at Oxford alone have been discovered.[18] Among the other monasteries of the period that were conscientious about securing advanced training for their members were: (1) Hailes Abbey, which normally sent three scholars to Oxford each year; (2) Tavistock Abbey, which had a practice of keeping two or three members at Gloucester College, Oxford; (3) the large priory of St. Pancras, which attempted to keep at least two of its more capable members at Cambridge; and (4) Norwich Cathedral Priory, which, despite Bishop Goldwell's harsh report of 1492, is now believed to have kept between one and four students at the eastern university throughout the fifteenth and early sixteenth centuries.[19]

If the monasteries did a better job of providing advanced training for their members than is commonly believed, how conscientious were they about providing adequate instruction for all their novices? There is no easy answer to this question, since the evidence is inconclusive and poses difficult problems of interpretation. Yet it appears that the larger and richer houses were increasingly active on this front during the late medieval period. The pacesetter, as in so many ways, was St. Albans Abbey. During the early 1430s, the abbot of that rich house took the pioneering step of appointing a grammar master from the outside, one with presumably better qualifications than an inmate, to instruct recruits who had not yet taken irrevocable vows. Gloucester Abbey followed this lead in 1513, when it too engaged an outsider to teach grammar and singing to its younger members. About the same time, Winchcombe Abbey adopted the same practice, and during its last decades of existence Winchcombe often spent £21 a year for that purpose.[20]

Those three houses were large and wealthy institutions, however, and there is little evidence that the smaller and poorer abbeys were doing anything comparable. Even some of the larger monasteries made no systematic provision for their younger members' training as late as the reign of Henry VIII. In 1511 Archbishop Warham visited St. Augustine's, Canterbury, and was distressed by what he saw, since most of the monks attending divine service were "wholly ignorant of what they read to the great scandal and disgrace both of religion and the monastery in particular." The archbishop therefore decreed that St. Augustine's must provide a skilled teacher to instruct the novices in Latin grammar. During the same year and again in 1514, Archbishop Warham made similar visits to St. Peter's Priory, Norwich, where he also noted "the lack of a skilled teacher . . . to teache the novices and other youths grammar." After ignoring gentle hints for over a decade, St. Peter's was finally commanded in 1526 to engage a schoolmaster to teach Latin grammar to its newest members.[21]

Similar problems existed at Westminster Abbey until shortly before this time. An indenture signed in July 1504 by Henry VII and Abbot Islip of that prominent house contains clear references to the low educational attainments of the average inmate of The Abbey, of which the former acknowledged he had long been aware. Hoping to rectify the problem, Henry conveyed lands to Islip and his successors, the income of which was reserved for the support of three additional monks whose chief tasks would be to instruct all future novices in grammar and to celebrate mass in the large new chantry the king intended to erect there.[22] A comparable agreement was made in December 1527 for the benefit of Faversham Abbey, Kent. By that indenture Dr. John Coles, warden of All Souls, Oxford, conveyed estates in four parishes to the abbot and monks of Faversham. All rents derived from those lands were to be used "for the endowment and maintenance of a School, wherein the Novices of the Abbey should be instructed in Grammar."[23]

Just as there was an interest in providing better training for young monks, a few contemporaries were concerned about the even lower educational attainments of the average nun of the era. Of course a presumption had long existed that women needed less instruction than men, and that belief would continue for centuries. Of equal importance, harsh economic realities militated against more than a few nuns receiving anything but the most basic training. During the last years before the Dissolution, some 26 houses for men had revenues in excess of £1,000 annually; but of the 135 to 140 nunneries of the age, only the convents of Syon and Shaftesbury did. Thus considerably more of the poorer religious houses, those with insufficient funds, were convents for women than monasteries or friaries for men. That a majority of the nunneries were miserably poor had two unfortunate consequences for female education. First, fewer than a dozen convents had the financial resources to hire a schoolmaster from the outside to instruct their younger members, as an increasing number of monasteries did after 1500. And second, the libraries of the nunneries were, with few exceptions, considerably smaller than those of the institutions for men. At the large abbeys of Bury St. Edmunds and Christ Church, Canterbury, there were collections of at least 2,000 volumes before the end of the fifteenth century. The cathedral priory at Norwich had holdings of nearly 1,350 volumes, while many others had between 800 and 1,000 books. In contrast, the nunneries' collections tended to be significantly smaller, since only Syon and Shaftesbury had as many as 1,000 volumes. In general, the houses for women had fewer than 100 books each, and most of those books were primers, antiphoners, and devotional works in the vernacular. Consequently, only a few nuns were able to develop their intellectual skills, and virtually none had any fluency in Latin.

Nevertheless, the leading authority on these matters, the late Eileen Power, believed that many nuns could read familiar tracts in Latin as well as popular writings in English. Indeed, Miss Power stressed that all the nuns were required to participate in the daily offices, "for which reading and singing were essential."[24] Whatever the percentage of nuns who could read, a much smaller proportion acquired facility in writing, since the latter skill was not considered an essential one at the time. Rather interestingly, when the Warwickshire convent of Nuneaton surrendered to the crown in September 1539, not one of the twenty-seven nuns who witnessed the event signed the official instrument but merely made an "X" in the margin beside her name as already printed by the scrivener who had prepared the document.[25] There are several possible explanations for why the nuns did not sign their names, however, including a desire on the part of the royal commissioners to hasten unpleasant proceedings; so it would be extraordinarily rash to suggest that all twenty-seven of those nuns were illiterate.

Although the average nun's educational attainments were severely limited, there are reasons to believe that standards were somewhat higher by the 1530s than they had been a century earlier. In 1535 Dr. John ap Rice, one of the royal commissioners who helped to direct the Dissolution, declared that the nuns of Lacock Abbey knew French well and had no trouble interpreting documents in Norman French that pertained to their house. Comments of a similar nature have been made by a modern historian about the nuns of Syon Abbey. According to Professor F. R. Johnson, the sixty-odd members of Syon "were well read in vernacular spiritual literature [but] . . . may not have been so familiar with Latin and may have had difficulty in understanding the liturgy."[26] Because this seems a fair appraisal of the nuns' skills in what was probably the best convent in the land, there was an obvious need for much additional improvement.

The need for further progress was especially urgent because of the nuns' practice of accepting pupils into their midst as a way of raising sorely needed funds. During the century before the Dissolution, scores of female convents boarded young children from wealthy families and occasionally charged as much as 1s. 8d. per week for each boy or girl accepted. Whether the nunneries ever provided anything more than minimal training for their students is doubtful. In the area of instruction the nuns were naturally hampered by their own restricted accomplishments; and there is no proof for Geoffrey Baskerville's assertion that "the young ladies were taught by governesses, just as young gentlemen in abbeys were instructed by schoolmasters."[27]

The clerical hierarchy objected strenuously to the educational activities of the nunneries, not because of their lack of fitness for the work but because individual nuns often became deeply attached to their pupils, on whom they lavished suppressed maternal feelings. Nuns and students slept together in common dorters; they ate, walked, and prayed together; and in the prelates' opinion, such close personal relationships were harmful to the nuns' spiritual life. The hierarchy never succeeded in keeping the convents from accepting pupils, although it did establish a maximum age beyond which they could not retain them. In general boys were required to leave the nunneries by their ninth birthdays, while girls were allowed to stay only until the age of fourteen.[28]

Between 90 and 95 nunneries accepted boarders during the late Middle Ages, and approximately 1,000 children received such educational training every year. Few nunneries admitted more than ten pupils at a time, although an occasional house accepted responsibility for considerably more. At Polesworth Abbey, Warwickshire, there were normally between thirty and forty students—all "gentlemen's children"—during its final years of existence. At St. Mary's, Winchester, in 1536, twenty-six nuns were entrusted with the care and education of twenty-six female students, "all daughters of lords and gentlemen." This explains why that nunnery has long been mistakenly characterized as "a fashionable seminary for young ladies."[29]

In more than a few cases, local or regional feeling was intensely favorable to the schools run by the nunneries. The people of Godstow, Oxfordshire, in a futile attempt to persuade Henry VIII to spare the local priory, even submitted a petition claiming that "most of the gentlewomen of the county were sent there to be bred." Virtually the same argument was used by Robert Aske in 1536, when he sought to rally support for the Pilgrimage of Grace, a northern revolt sparked by the suppression of the smaller abbeys earlier that year. Aske declared to the aroused people of Yorkshire that an especially compelling reason for action was that "in nunneries their daughters were brought up to virtue."[30]

There was almost as much popular support for schools operated by monasteries as for those run by nunneries. Probably not over eighty monastic schools existed throughout the country at the end of the middle ages, but they performed a worthwhile service by providing free education to approximately 1,500 poor boys each year. One such student was Thomas Linacre, who, as already noted, received his earliest training at Christ Church, Canterbury, during the time of William Sellyng. Another student of that sort was John Morton, who eventually rose to become archbishop of Canterbury, a cardinal, and Henry VII's Lord Chancellor for more than a decade. As a boy Morton attended the school operated by Cerne Abbey, Dorset, after which he entered Balliol College, Oxford. Of course, a number of gentlemen's sons also obtained their educational start in these schools. During the 1450s the abbot of Hyde near Winchester had "eight noble boys lodging with him in order to study"; while at Woburn Abbey during the 1490s there were usually at least three young gentlemen among the pupils of the grammar master there. Before his departure for the continent in 1519, Reginald Pole, a son of the earl of Salisbury and a distant cousin of Henry VIII, was a student for some years at the Carthusian monastery of Sheen. Finally, between 1532 and 1536 the stepson of Arthur Plantagenet, Viscount Lisle, studied at Reading Abbey with its distinguished schoolmaster Leonard Cox.[31]

In some of these schools the teaching was still entrusted to a monk of the house, as in earlier periods. But increasingly the abbeys and priories found it convenient to hire an outsider, a recent university graduate who had not yet secured an aristocratic patron. Unfortunately, the monasteries that chose this course seem to have been far from generous to the men they employed to teach their students. Typically they paid stipends of only £2 to £6 annually, although they often provided board, lodging, fuel, and a new gown each year as well. At Forde Abbey, Dorset, the last teacher hired before the Dissolution was William Tyler, a secular priest. Tyler's yearly stipend was £3 6s. 8d., a plebeian wage, although he did receive other benefits. In view of such low remuneration, it might be suspected that the teachers in the monastic schools were poorly qualified for their duties, but such was not always the case. Tyler, who headed the school at Forde Abbey during the 1530s, was a university graduate with an M.A. degree; while at Reading Abbey the last schoolmaster, Leonard Cox, was an excellent grammarian who wrote the preface to an important French textbook by John Palsgrave and in 1532 published a valuable tract of his own, *The Art or Craft of Rhetoric.* Perhaps because of his unusually strong qualifications, Cox received the handsome yearly stipend of £10.[32]

During the century before the Dissolution, a number of schools operated by monasteries disappeared. For example, the monks of Whalley Abbey supported a school in the nearby village of Blackburn from the 1320s until 1514, when it became superfluous owing to the establishment of a nearby grammar school by the earl of Derby. Similarly, the monastic school at Bruton-upon-Trent flourished until 1453, when its main teacher was charged with attempted murder. Because of that unfortunate incident, the monastic school soon faded from view, to the dismay of the local people. By 1524 there were so many complaints about the abbey's failure to provide instruction for the children of the area that the abbot wisely contributed to the establishment of an endowed school within a short distance of the monastery. One last example of this sort must suffice. At the large Benedictine monastery of Evesham, a large school existed for some decades before the 1460s, when the abbot began to pay an annual subsidy of £10 "with meat and drink to a schoolmaster for keeping a free grammar school in the town of Evesham."[33]

The declining number of monastic schools was owing, at least in part, to the establishment of scores of new schools operated by chantries. Chantries were private endowments in land and other kinds of wealth that provided for the performance of masses for the souls of the founder, his or her parents, and any other designated individuals. Chantries were usually established in cathedrals and large collegiate churches, but occasionally a special chapel or parish church was erected to house them. The first chantries had appeared during the twelfth and thirteenth centuries, when their numbers increased rapidly. Apparently there was a lull in such foundations during the first decades of the fourteenth century; but the onset of the Black Death in 1348 triggered a new period of expansion, particularly in the London area. By 1366 St. Paul's Cathedral had as many as sixty-six such endowments, although that number was later reduced through amalgamation. After 1400 there were never as many new chantry foundations as during earlier times, probably because of their increasing cost. Yet chantries were always cheaper to establish than religious houses, so their numbers continued to grow, albeit more slowly; and by the Reformation England had hundreds of them. During the reign of Edward VI, when all the chantries were suppressed, royal commissioners detected 424 in York diocese alone, while more than 2,000 others existed elsewhere in the realm.

The primary duty of chantry priests was to perform masses for the spiritual benefit of certain named individuals, whether living or dead. But the tradition soon developed of linking schools to chantries, the priests being expected to instruct local children on weekdays. According to legend, the first chantry school to be founded came into being at Wotton-under-Edge, Gloucestershire, in 1384. However, a chantry school was clearly in existence at Harlow, Essex, as early as 1324; while the original school of that sort was probably the one that had been founded in the parish church at Appleby, Westmorland, by 1286. Regardless of when the earliest chantry school appeared, their numbers increased rapidly during the late Middle Ages, and by the mid 1540s there were more than 250 of them. Before they were all swept away, Yorkshire prided itself on thirty such schools and Essex on sixteen, while Shropshire and Staffordshire counted sixteen between them.

Although little has yet been discovered about their affairs, the chantry schools seem to have been on a par with those kept by the religious houses, at least in terms of quality. Chantry priests were rarely well paid, seldom receiving more than £6 a year and on occasion as little as £2 or £3 annually. It is true that at Newland, Gloucestershire, where a chantry school functioned from 1445, the priest enjoyed the large yearly stipend of £12 and could collect quarterly fees of 8*d.* from each of his pupils. But that priest was required to pay the expenses of at least one poor student at the school and to distribute a minimum of 5*s.* 4*d.* per year in alms.[34] Thus it seems safe to conclude that most chantry priests were inadequately paid and received far smaller stipends than the average rector, vicar, or prebendary. The academic qualifications of most chantry priests therefore tended to be rather weak, and rarely was a man with more than a year of university training willing to serve in such a position for any length of time.

Because the typical chantry school taught only the basic elements of Latin grammar, a few prayers, the ten commandments, and various other "useful precepts," it is tempting to dismiss these schools as a negligible force in English educational history, as institutions that made a minor contribution to learning and none at all to scholarship. However, some proportion of the chantry schools must have provided able if not commendable instruction, at least during the last years before they were suppressed. At Deddington, Oxfordshire, where a chantry school had functioned since 1445, the last priest, William Burton, was described by royal officials as "'a good school master . . . [who] bringeth up youth very well in learning.'" Similarly, the last priest to preside over the chantry school at Wakefield, Yorkshire, Edward Wood, who was evidently the man of that name who had received an Oxford A.B. in 1522, was declared in 1548 to be "well-learned." Finally, there is the case of Peter Wilegh, a capable scholar who headed the chantry school at Chelmsford, Essex, from 1532 until it ceased to exist in 1548. Like both Burton and Wood, Wilegh received high praise from the royal commissioners who had the sad task of dissolving all the chantries and their affiliated schools. That Wilegh had been an effective teacher is also supported by the subsequent career of his most capable pupil, the great scientist John Dee (1527-1608). Dee, whose father Rowland held a minor office in Surrey, was sent at the age of nine to study with Wilegh, from whom he received a thorough grounding in Latin and mathematics. When he was fifteen, Dee entered St. John's College, Cambridge, where he won immediate acclaim for his skill in both those subjects; and shortly after taking an A.B. in 1546, he obtained a fellowship at nearby Trinity College, which Henry VIII had just established. Thereafter Dee's academic progress was even swifter, and by the early 1550s he was recognized as England's foremost mathematician and scientist. Whether he would have attained such intellectual eminence so quickly had he not spent six years in Wilegh's chantry school seems doubtful.[35]

If the chantry schools had been as poor as most writers hold, it also seems unlikely that they would have attracted as many pupils as they did. Most of those institutions were considerably larger than the schools operated by monasteries, which averaged 22 to 24 pupils each. In the West Country, the chantry schools tended to be especially large. The one at Chipping Camden had 60 to 80 students enrolled during the 1520s, while those at Taunton and Crewkerne boasted over 120 pupils each.[36]

Besides the 250 or so chantry schools that flourished during the pre-Reformation period, many other schools operated at the time. The 170 to 175 schools kept by the monasteries and nunneries have already been considered; so we can now direct our attention to the nine ancient grammar schools that were supported by the secular cathedrals of the realm. These schools, all founded before 1189, were intended to serve the wider needs of the towns in which they were situated and not just to educate clerks and choristers for the cathedrals themselves. For this reason those schools were not located in cathedral closes or courtyards but at more accessible places in their localities. Normally superintended by the dean and chapter of the sponsoring cathedral, they occasionally became rather large. The school at York, for instance, generally had an enrollment of 60 to 70 students during the fifteenth century. Whether these schools dispensed education of a high order is, unhappily, rather doubtful. The stipends paid to the schoolmasters were relatively small; and as time wore on more and more of the actual instruction was assigned to the organist or songmaster, who seldom had more than minimal training in grammar.[37]

Many of the larger collegiate churches of the realm also maintained schools, at least for a time. In London the important churches of St. Martin-le-Grand and St. Mary-le-Bow operated schools until the mid-fifteenth century, when they became superfluous owing to the foundation of three new schools. In 1442 the famous City of London School was opened by means of a bequest left by John Carpenter, the town clerk between 1417 and 1438. As a result of the Carpenter bequest, the municipal authorities received at least £20 a year from a permanent trust, that sum being reserved to pay the cost of educating poor boys. Within four years of the establishment of the City of London School, similar institutions came into being at the churches of St. Anthony and St. Dunstan-in-the East. All three of these new schools seem to have been excellent institutions, since they attracted students from other sections of the realm.[38]

Many trade guilds also made provision for the education of young children. Of the thirty-three guilds studied by A. F. Leach, all maintained song schools to train youths to perform the musical responses that were now an integral part of the mass, while twenty-eight also provided financial subsidies to existing grammar schools. Several of the song schools established through guild action evolved over time into true grammar schools. Such was the case at Ludlow, where the municipal grammar school had originally been operated by the Palmers' Guild, and also at Stratford-on-Avon, where the grammar school was a cooperative venture involving several guilds. Yet in other cases the local school was supported from the outset by an annual appropriation from the town corporation. A good example of this was at Plymouth, where from about 1500 the town council paid £10 a year to a schoolmaster who was allowed the free use of a chamber above the ancient chapel.[39]

During the years 1475–1510, a number of well-endowed grammar schools, superior to all previous institutions with the exception of Eton and Winchester, were established by donors of various stations and ranks. That so many important schools were founded at that time was owing to two general factors: (1) the growing demand for education on the part of all social groups except the very poor; and (2) the great upsurge of philanthropic activity that reached a climax shortly before the

Reformation and then subsided for almost a century before another peak was reached during the 1620s and 1630s.

Of the endowed grammar schools established between 1475 and 1510, perhaps the most significant was Bishop Waynflete's Magdalen College School of 1479, which served as a "feeder school" for Magdalen College in much the way that Eton and Winchester did for King's College and New College, respectively. Magdalen College School was the first permanently endowed school at Oxford that was free to all boys wishing to enter. It operated under the supervision of the president of Magdalen College, who appointed both the master and the usher. Almost as soon as it opened, it acquired a reputation for excellence, owing largely to the capable direction provided by its first master, John Ankwyll (d. 1487). An excellent teacher who received £10 annually and a free house, Ankwyll produced an important Latin textbook for his students to use. Entitled *Compendium Totius Grammaticae*, this work was constructed in the form of questions and answers with prose and verse sections alternating. It was hailed for its usefulness as soon as it appeared and was printed twice at Oxford in 1483, with European editions following at Deventer and Cologne in 1489 and 1493, respectively. On Ankwyll's death, the high standards he set were maintained by his successor, John Holt. Holt had been the school's usher since 1482, and during his term as headmaster he also produced an important Latin grammar which was widely used until the 1540s.[40]

Although Magdalen College School was the most distinguished institution of its kind, many others of considerable excellence were founded during the last years before the Reformation. Of the dozen or so that might be cited, probably the most important were: (1) the grammar school at Westbury-on-Trym, which was established in 1463 by John Carpenter, bishop of Worcester; (2) the College of St. Andrew at Acaster, which was founded during the mid 1470s by Robert Stillington, bishop of Bath and Wells; (3) Jesus College at Rotherham, which Archbishop Rotherham of York endowed in 1483 in order to educate "the many local youths who, though quick to learn, have no desire to attain to the dignity of the priesthood"; and (4) the free grammar school at Macclesfield, which came about through a bequest of Sir John Percivale (d. 1502), who had served as Lord Mayor of London several years before.

Only one other grammar school needs to be considered before we complete this survey of the schools of late medieval England.

This was the great London grammar school for 153 boys that was founded by John Colet, dean of St. Paul's Cathedral from 1505 until his death in 1519. St. Paul's School was, strictly speaking, a refoundation. For several centuries the cathedral had employed a schoolmaster and usher, since St. Paul's was one of the country's nine secular cathedrals, all of which had established schools before 1189. But as was true of the other schools operated by the secular cathedrals, the quality of teaching in the original St. Paul's School left much to be desired, owing to the fact that so much was done by the organist or songmaster. So in 1510 Colet secured letters patent from the crown authorizing him to endow either a new or an existing school. Then he detached the current school from the cathedral chapter and the following September arranged for the Mercers' Company, of which his father had been a prominent member, to oversee it in its reestablished form. After taking all these steps, Colet endowed St. Paul's School with the bulk of the rich inheritance he had acquired on his parents' death several years before. This consisted of some 2,000 acres of lands in Buckinghamshire, Hertfordshire, and Cambridgeshire, which had a collective worth of more than £120 a year at the time.[41]

Why Colet established his school for 153 boys is not entirely clear. Some years ago, C. E. Mallet suggested that he selected that number because of the 153 feast and saints' days that were observed throughout the year as holidays or half-holidays.[42] Yet a more plausible explanation is that Colet was inspired by chapter 21 of the Gospel according to St. John, in which Christ is portrayed after the crucifixion on the shores of the Sea of Tiberias. While conversing with the apostles, Christ instructs St. Peter to pull in his nets and share his catch, which included 153 fish in all.[43] Throughout the Middle Ages it was commonly believed that the world's waterways contained but 153 varieties of fish in all; and just as St. Peter had caught that exact number, Colet intended his school to do its best to "catch" and educate every English boy who was not being trained in another way. Whatever the precise reason Colet chose that particular number, St. Paul's was the largest school of the age, being more than twice the original size of Eton and Winchester and exceeding even the largest chantry schools of the period in numbers.

Like Magdalen College School, which Colet had attended as a boy, St. Paul's soon became known as an outstanding institution, owing to two main factors. First, Colet wisely put the school under the supervision of the Mercers' Company, which had a serious interest in education and discharged its new duties responsibly; and second, Colet made an even sounder decision when he appointed as the school's first headmaster, the noted humanist and grammarian William Lily.

Born about 1468, Lily studied at Magdalen College, Oxford between 1486 and 1488. Then he traveled widely on the continent and even made a pilgrimage to the Holy Land. For a time he lived on the Isle of Rhodes and honed his skills in Greek with native speakers of that language. Subsequently, he worked with such famous Italian scholars as Giovanni Sulpicio and Pomponius Laetus, with the result that he was an outstanding linguist by the time he returned to England in 1492. Between May of that year and November 1495, Lily occupied a Northamptonshire benefice; but after seeing so much of the world, life in a small rural parish had little appeal for him. He therefore resigned the post, moved to London, and became a teacher. Because of great pedagogical gifts, he was soon recognized as the finest teacher of the age; and when Colet refounded St. Paul's School in 1510, he logically turned to Lily to be its first headmaster. Lily retained the position, which paid almost £35 a year and included a free house, until 1522, when he died of an unnecessary medical operation that his friends had warned against.[44]

Lily deserves to be remembered as the first great schoolmaster in English history, the forerunner of Camden, Mulcaster, and Asheton during Elizabethan times. Not only did he preside over St. Paul's School for more than a decade, but he was also one of the first English teachers to instruct his pupils in Greek. Even more important, he produced for his students' use a Latin textbook that was arguably the most successful work of its kind ever published. Completed in 1515, Lily's grammar was in fact something of a collaborative work. Colet wrote the preface, while Erasmus and other scholars made suggestions that were incorporated. Yet the basic format and nearly all the content were of Lily's devising, and the work was always attributed to him alone. Between 1515 and 1540, it was adopted by dozens of schoolmasters, especially in the London area. It was not without competitors, however, including the older textbooks published by John Ankwyll, John Holt, and John Stanbridge, all of which had obvious merits. That there were several competing grammars on the market was disquieting to sixteenth-century minds, which preferred order and uniformity in all important things. Accordingly, Henry VIII issued an edict in 1543 requiring all schoolmasters "as ye intend to avoid our displeasure and have our favour," to make exclusive use of Lily's textbook. The work was then reissued with the title *An Introduction to the Eight Parts of Speech, and the Construction of the Same, compiled and set forth by the commandment of our most gracious Sovereign Lord the King.* From 1543 it enjoyed a virtual monopoly in England's grammar schools; and although it was revised in 1758, it was not finally superseded until 1867, some 324 years later.[45]

In view of the excellence of such schools as St. Paul's and the slightly older Magdalen College School, both of which were models for the future, it appears that the chief problems of late medieval education were being overcome by the early years of Henry VIII. The greatest need was not for a substantial number of new schools, as the various studies of W. K. Jordan seem to suggest.[46] Almost every town of any size had a school of some type by that juncture; and if one considers such diverse institutions as monastic, nunnery, chantry, guild, cathedral, scrivener, and the permanently endowed grammar schools, the average English county—if such an entity actually existed—probably had a dozen or more. Indeed, the largest English county, Yorkshire, with thirty or more chantry schools, seems to have had close to fifty schools in all. Thus the greatest need was not for additional schools but for considerably better ones. And with the establishment of a number of excellent grammar schools between 1460 and 1510, and the simultaneous publication of several outstanding textbooks, England took a long step in that direction.

Moreover, as noted in chapter I, the educational standards of the parish clergy improved steadily during the last century before the Reformation. And since almost all the teaching in the schools was still done by men of the cloth, the general level of instruction was now on a higher plane than it had been during previous eras. In fact, so much progress occurred during the decades after 1460 that it became possible for the universities to banish Latin grammar from the curriculum in 1549. By that year most entering students know their Latin so well that a mastery of its complexities had come to be seen as a prerequisite for admission. This in itself is convincing proof of the degree to which England's pre-Reformation schools had become institutions of considerable excellence.

4

Women and Education

❧ Among the new grammar schools established during the last years before the Reformation were several founded by women. It is surprising that women were as generous in their support of education as they were. Their financial resources were infinitely smaller than men's, since widows alone controlled funds of any magnitude, and females had restricted access to the educational institutions of the time. Girls might receive basic instruction in the chantry, monastic, nunnery, and cathedral schools of the era, but the scrivener and endowed grammar schools, the equivalent of modern secondary institutions, almost never admitted them. For a girl to have aspired to study at a university or one of the Inns of Court would have been unthinkable. Moreover, one seldom hears about women teachers during the late Middle Ages. In 1404 a Matilda Maresflete headed the ancient school at Boston, while four years later a London grocer bequeathed 20s. to one "E. Scolemaysteresse." A female teacher in Taunton received a similar legacy of 3s. 3d. in 1494; whereas the school at Amersham was directed in 1511 by one Alice Harding.[1] Aside from these few examples, there is little evidence that women did any teaching outside the nunneries or the family household. All in all, it seems fair to say that the system of secondary and higher education made no provision for women of any kind; and it would not have been remarkable had they withheld all support from the grammar schools and colleges of the age. Yet most women believed that education was essential for the further spread of Christianity, and during the Yorkist and early Tudor periods they were exceptionally generous with the limited money they had at their disposal.

During the brief reign of Richard III, Elena Burgh, widow of a rich alderman of Hull, left four houses to the local school that Bishop Alcock had established four years earlier.[2] A more important benefactress of the era was Lady Thomasine Percivale, whose third and last husband died in 1503. Within three years, Lady Thomasine established a grammar school in the Cornish village of Week St. Mary, her birthplace, to which she conveyed the manor of Simpson and a 270-acre tract in Devonshire. In her statutes for the school, she specified that it should be administered by a group of lay trustees and that the schoolmaster should always be a priest with an academic degree in either grammar or the arts.[3]

Early in the reign of Henry VIII, two other widows were instrumental in founding schools. In 1512 Mrs. Agnes Morley of Lewes, Sussex, left a generous bequest with which her executors endowed a local grammar school. The following year a Nottingham woman, Agnes Mellers, whose husband had been lord mayor as well as a prosperous bell founder, bestowed "lands and houses of great value" on a school that had been operated for several decades by the wardens of St. Mary's Church. Further, on 22 November 1513, Mrs. Mellers secured a licence from the crown to proceed with the establishment of a free grammar school that would be permanently endowed; and soon afterwards she appointed a Yorkshire priest to be its first headmaster. Thereafter all the school's affairs were handled by the mayor and aldermen of Nottingham, who agreed to administer the institution.[4]

Even before women began to assist the country's grammar schools, they became patrons of existing colleges at the universities. Almost inevitably the society that received the largest measure of female support was the Cambridge foundation that, after several name changes, became known as Queens' College. The founder of that institution was Andrew Dokett, a secular priest who long headed St. Bernard's Hostel, an unendowed hall in Trumpington Street. From 1444 Dokett was also rector of the nearby church of St. Botolph's. In 1446 he devised a plan for a new college, and after securing pledges of support from his parishoners, he applied for a licence to proceed. On 3 December 1446 Henry VI issued a charter authorizing the establishment of a "College of St. Bernard," which would consist of a president, four fellows, and an indeterminate number of under-graduates. The office of president was occupied by Dokett himself until his death in 1484.

In 1447 Henry VI's wife, Margaret of Anjou, developed a fleeting interest in the college and asked to be its official patron. Although Margaret desired to change its name, Dokett voiced no objection in the hope of receiving generous support from her. Thereupon the college charter was returned to the king, to be revoked and reissued in amended form. On 30 March 1448, letters patent under the great seal conveyed to Margaret all the lands and possessions of Dokett's society as well as authorization to reestablish it under a different name. Less than a month later Margaret's charter of foundation was issued. The society was to be the same size as before but now became known as "The Queen's College of St. Margaret and St. Bernard." The bishop of Lichfield and Coventry, William Booth, was enlisted to devise statutes for the society, which was empowered to hold lands worth up to £200 a year. On the same day the queen's charter was issued, her chamberlain, Sir John Wenlock, laid the cornerstone of the original building, which was ready for occupancy by 1454.[5]

After this flurry of interest in the college, Margaret lost all sight of its affairs, doubtless because of the escalating tensions that soon led to the outbreak of the Wars of the Roses. Certainly Margaret never gave the society more than a fraction of the help Dokett had anticipated, since there is no evidence of a direct benefaction by her at all. However, if substantial monetary help failed to materialize, the college still profited from its association with her, as a result of her influential connections. On 4 March 1449, Henry VI himself donated £200 towards the completion of the college buildings, which had been designed by Reginald Ely, the same master mason who had been responsible for the majestic chapel of nearby King's College. The next year Dokett received a similar contribution from the bishop of Carlisle, Marmaduke Lumley, who was seeking promotion to the much richer see of Lincoln. During the 1450s several members of the queen's entourage gave smaller amounts to assist the work of Dokett and his associates, which was an easy way to curry favor with Margaret. Furthermore, in 1464 one of the queen's former attendants, Elizabeth Woodville, became the consort of Henry VI's supplanter, Edward IV (1461-83); and thereafter the college enjoyed increased prosperity. Although

Edward IV made hostile moves towards Eton and King's College, owing to their strong Lancastrian ties, he expressed no animosity towards Dokett's little society and did nothing to thwart its continued growth. Elizabeth Woodville probably rendered no more direct aid to the college than Margaret had done; but many of her friends and relations became benefactors, with the result that eight additional fellowships were established by 1475. When in that year official statutes were finally issued at her suggestion, the foundation changed its name in grateful appreciation to "The Queens' College."[6]

One of the college's most important benefactors during these years was Lady Margery Roos, also a former attendant of Margaret of Anjou and the widow of John, Lord Roos of Hamlake. In 1469 Lady Margery gave substantial funds to the society, enabling it to buy four manors in Huntingdonshire and several lesser tracts. In addition to that generous gift, Lady Margery presented an extensive collection of vestments, service-books, and plate for use in the college chapel, where she herself was buried in 1478. Three other women of the period who assisted the college were: (1) Dame Alice Wyche, who made a monetary donation of £320 in 1473; (2) Lady Joan Burgh, who conveyed a valuable manor on the Isle of Thanet in 1474; and (3) Lady Joan Ingoldesthorpe, who established a new fellowship and procured for the college the advowson of St. Andrew's Church, Canterbury, just before she died in 1494. Thereafter many comparable gifts were made by male and female donors alike, and the society's financial situation improved steadily. By 1534 it was the third richest college at Cambridge, with yearly revenues of £230.[7]

Another Cambridge society that women periodically helped was St. Catharine's, which was established in 1471 by Robert Woodlark, provost of King's from 1452 until his death in 1479. St. Catharine's was the only college at either university that was founded by the warden or principal of another. Being a man of limited means, Woodlark was unable to complete the buildings he began to erect in the 1470s for his little society of a master and three fellows. Probably because of Woodlark's desperate plight, Lady Joan Barnardiston, who belonged to a wealthy Suffolk family that periodically assisted the college over a long period, made an attractive offer. She would donate 100 marks on condition that a fellow of the college prayed daily for the well-being of her soul and any other individuals designated by her. Woodlark quickly agreed to Lady Joan's proposal and thereby acquired the funds needed to complete the original quadrangle. As a consequence, the college was able to accept its first students in November 1473. Six years later Woodlark's own sister Isabella donated her house in Trumpington Street, next to the Bull Inn; while several female donors of the early sixteenth century supported the college in equally significant ways. In 1509 Katherine Miles gave it "considerable property"; in 1514 Lady Elizabeth Barnardiston donated 100 marks; and in 1515 Mrs. Joan Mylbourn helped to establish an additional fellowship. Despite all these benefactions, St. Catharine's remained miserably poor. During the mid 1530s it had total revenues of only £39 3s., whereas the next poorest society, Trinity Hall, had a yearly income of more than £72.[8]

Several other Cambridge colleges, including Corpus Christi and Gonville Hall, received substantial aid from women during the last years before the Reformation. In contrast the generally richer societies at Oxford attracted far less female support at that time. However, the first important gift made to Brasenose College after its establishment by a bishop and a lawyer in 1509 was a valuable contribution from a widow. In 1515 Mrs. Elizabeth Morley granted Brasenose the rich manor of Pinchpoll in Faringdon parish, Essex. The only condition attached to Mrs. Morley's grant was that the college take responsibility for the performance of certain services at St. Margaret's Church, Westminster.[9]

The individual who surpassed all other donors of the era in supporting higher education was Lady Margaret Beaufort, the mother of Henry VII. Lady Margaret functioned almost as the crown's minister for cultural and educational affairs between 1485 and 1509. A person of great gifts, she was extremely learned by the standards of the time. Although she often deprecated her own knowledge of foreign languages, she rendered a Latin tract by Dionysius Carthusianus into the vernacular as *The Mirrour of Goulde for the sinfull soule;* and in 1503 she completed an English version of Thomas à Kempis's *Imitatio Christi,* which William Atkinson had left unfinished. Lady Margaret was also a fluent reader and speaker of French and owned many books in that language which she treasured. Despite this she was a proponent of vernacular literature and especially loved *The Canterbury Tales* and other works by Chaucer. Additionally, she commissioned several romances and devotional works into English.[10] Because of her many interests as well as her genuine piety, Lady Margaret inspired deep affection on the part of all who knew her. Bishop John Alcock, who founded Jesus College, Cambridge, in 1496, was a devoted follower and enjoined the members of that society to remember her faithfully in their prayers. An Italian humanist who arrived in England in 1501, Polydore Vergil of Urbino, shared Bishop Alcock's opinion and characterized her "as a most worthy woman whom no one can extoll too much for her sound sense and holiness of life."[11]

Lady Margaret was one of the most important educational patrons in English history. Her contributions compare favorably with those of William of Wykeham, Henry VI, and her grandson Henry VIII. Professor W. K. Jordan once calculated the capital value of all her educational benefactions at £18,000, an enormous sum for the period.[12]

Lady Margaret had no particular interest in educational matters before 1485. Although the daughter of a duke and the wife of an earl by the age of fourteen, she had received no more training than other well-born girls, whose education normally consisted of religious and moral instruction as well as sewing, music, and needlework. Moreover, she was not even allowed to supervise the early training of her only child, Henry Tudor, from whom she was separated within a few months of his birth in 1457. However, after she helped elevate him to the throne in 1485, he granted her custody of the seven-year-old Edward Stafford, son and heir of the second duke of Buckingham, who had met his death in 1483 at the hands of Richard III. For her young ward, who remained in her household for thirteen years, Lady Margaret established a school of sorts and employed capable men as his tutors. The new duke was, after all, a leading peer of the realm, with estates worth over £5000 a year and a distant claim to the throne. To supervise his early education, the countess* relied mainly on a French priest, Bernard André, "the blind poet of Toulouse." André lived in England from the winter of 1485-86 until June 1501; and he dedicated so many works to his patron that he soon became known as "the King's mother's poet." For a time Lady Margaret also made use of John Skelton, who was also a priest and an accomplished poet, although

---

*Lady Margaret was always known by the title of her first husband, Edmund Tudor, earl of Richmond, who had died of the plague in November 1456, two months before the birth of their son the following January.

his irreverent verses eventually caused her to dismiss him. Because of the care Lady Margaret gave to Buckingham's early training, he grew up to be a learned and cultivated individual with a great love of books, which he bought in numbers. A patron of poets and scholars in his own right, he "was clearly along the first English noblemen to whom the term 'renaissance aristocrat' can properly be applied."[13]

As Lady Margaret came into increasing contact with scholarly individuals while supervising her ward's education, she met the cleric who was to be her friend and adviser for the remainder of her life. This was the saintly and ascetic John Fisher, son of a well-to-do mercer of Beverley, Yorkshire. Fisher, who had been born about 1459 and eventually became a bishop, had been educated at Cambridge, first at Godshouse and then at Michaelhouse, where he obtained his M. A. in 1491. The countess first made his acquaintance in 1494, when she hosted a dinner at Greenwich to which he, as senior proctor of the university, had been invited. She was immediately impressed by his simple and direct manner, his penetrating comments, and his disregard for all material things except books. In 1495 she selected him to be her chaplain, and within a short time she appointed him her confessor as well.[14]

Probably Fisher was not involved in Lady Margaret's first educational project, the establishment of a chantry and attached school at Wimborne Minster, Dorset, where her parents had been buried some years earlier. However, he clearly influenced her decision to appoint divinity lecturers, or professors, at the universities. From the beginning of that enterprise, the countess and her chaplain seem to have envisaged the establishment of permanent, endowed professorships; for in December 1496 Henry VII granted them permission to found such a position at Cambridge, and three months later he authorized a similar lectureship at Oxford. Each was to be supported by lands worth as much as £20 a year. Unaccountably, it took six years to complete all the legal details of the two endowments, but that did not delay the appointment of special lecturers for two-year terms. The name of the first Lady Margaret professor at Cambridge has not been discovered. But at Oxford a theologian from Oriel College, Edward Wylford, was named to the position, probably on Cardinal Morton's recommendation.[15]

By the early months of 1503, the terms of the Lady Margaret professorships had been finalized. Fisher, who had completed his doctorate in divinity in 1501, was named to the position at

Cambridge, while John Roper received the post at Oxford. Both men were to enjoy yearly stipends of twenty marks, payable out of the rents of estates conveyed to Westminster Abbey, and both were to deliver daily talks during term on such matters as the chancellor or the vice-chancellor selected. They were also to lecture during the long summer vacation, although with permission they might have time off during Lent in order to concentrate on preaching.[16]

With the establishment of these professorships, Lady Margaret founded the first such permanently endowed positions at either university. They soon led to improved theological instruction, and in subsequent years they inspired a host of imitators in such fields as medicine, philosophy, rhetoric, logic, Greek, and Hebrew. However, if they were a pointer towards the future in that regard, they represented an attempt to turn the hands of the clock back to an earlier era in another respect. Before the onset of the Black Death, nearly all the teaching at Oxford and Cambridge had been at the university level by young scholars who had received their M.A.s during the two previous years and were officially known as "regent masters." But during the fifteenth century the colleges had grown in numbers and importance. They had admitted more and more students; and as noted in chapter 1, an early form of the tutorial system had begun to spread, with the colleges taking responsibility for most of the actual teaching. As a consequence university-wide lectures were languishing and drawing virtually no auditors. This was openly acknowledged at Oxford in 1518, when those who had just received their M.A.s were excused from the obligation to serve as regent masters "because nobody attends those lecturing."[17] The Lady Margaret professorships, and the many lectureships they inspired, were an attempt, whether conscious or unconscious, to reverse that trend of events. Although they soon led to better teaching in several fields, they were hardly sufficient to halt the further rise of the colleges and the continuing spread of the tutorial system, which Lady Margaret would not have wanted in any event and to which her subsequent contributions gave powerful reinforcement.

Lady Margaret began her greatest educational undertaking in 1505, less than a year after the death of her third and last husband, Thomas, earl of Derby. Once she came into her widow's portion of 800 marks a year, she had such a large income that she was able to finance projects on a grand scale. At first she contemplated making a substantial gift to Westminster Abbey, for which she had a deep love. But she soon chose a different course and went to the aid of the little society known as Godshouse, where Bishop Fisher had briefly studied on his first arrival at Cambridge.

Godshouse had been founded in 1439 by William Byngham, rector of the London church of St. John Zachary. Intended to train men who would become schoolmasters, Godshouse was in fact England's first teacher-training institute, and in 1448 it received substantial assistance from Henry VI, who granted it several estates as well as the advowson of a Lincolnshire church. Yet it always remained a small society and never approached the complement of twenty-four members its founder had envisaged. At the beginning of the sixteenth century, the proctor of Godshouse was John Sycling, a friend of Bishop Fisher's, through whom Lady Margaret's concern for the college was aroused. Ultimately the countess agreed to become its patron, on the grounds of her devotion to the memory of Henry VI and all his "godly intentions." After obtaining a royal license on 1 May 1505, she substantially enlarged Godshouse, which was renamed Christ's College in the process.

Except for nearby King's College, Christ's was larger than any existing Cambridge society, since it consisted of a master, twelve fellows, and forty-seven undergraduate scholars. Except in unusual circumstances, the fellows were all to have A.B. degrees at the time of election and were to take priest's orders by the end of their second year. Sycling, the last proctor of the old society, was appointed to the mastership of the new one, while four of the last six fellows of Godshouse were named senior fellows of Christ's. Building operations commenced almost at once, since the enlarged society would obviously need more spacious quarters, and to that end four attached buildings forming a large trapezoidal court, the longest side of which measured 128 feet in length, were designed. All in all, the countess is said to have spent more than £5,000 on the buildings of Christ's College, which were not completed until 1511.[18]

For the support of her college, Lady Margaret created an unusually generous endowment, which included the advowsons of four parish churches and tracts of land that totaled more than 3,750 acres. The lands she conveyed included three different manors in Cambridgeshire and one each in Leicestershire and Essex. When in July 1507, Henry VII gave his mother the properties of the decayed abbey of St. Mary de Pratis in

Norfolk, which he had suppressed after its last abbot's death, he authorized her to assign them to the college should she wish; and after soliciting the approval of Pope Julius II, she did just that. Although definite proof is lacking, tradition has long held that she persuaded her old ward, Buckingham, to confer several of his estates on the society "for the good of his soul."[19]

In the will she drew up in 1508, Lady Margaret remembered the college handsomely. Not only did she grant it additional lands worth £320, but she also bequeathed her valuable library, some fifty-eight books in all. Of even greater value were the ornaments and clerical vestments she made available to the college chapel. The ornaments included several great processional crosses and two pairs of tall gilt candlesticks, all of which were assessed at £397 4s. 10d., while the vestments were worth even more, being rated for tax purposes at £566 8s. 8d.[20]

Statutes for Christ's College were issued in 1506. Long and detailed, they were compiled by Lady Margaret herself, although they showed the clear imprint of Fisher's thinking. The college master was always to be a theologian, preferably a bachelor or doctor of divinity, at the very least the holder of an M.A. who was an active candidate for an advanced degree in that subject. He was to receive the small yearly stipend of ten marks, although he would have an additional 12d. a week for commons and 20s. a year for livery. The college's twelve fellows were each to receive payments of 13s. 4d. or 16s. 4d. per year, in accordance with their academic attainments. In addition they would have 12d. weekly for commons and 13s. 4d. annually for livery. In all elections to fellowships and scholarships, poorer candidates were to be preferred, and none with personal incomes of more than £10 annually would be permitted to hold a fellowship. In respect for the original purpose of Godshouse, scholars with a talent for grammar would be encouraged to consider careers as schoolmasters. Other students were to concentrate on theology and the arts. Formal lectures on philosophy, dialectic, and the main writings of ancient Rome would be delivered in the hall each day; and recreational activities were prohibited throughout the year except during the Christmas holidays.[21]

Despite her justifiable pride in Queen's College, Bishop Fisher soon persuaded the countess to found a completely new Cambridge society. Given the way her son had tripled the royal revenues since his accession, she had no cause to worry about the financial needs of her descendants, and God's purposes would be well served by the establishment of yet another college for the training of future priests. This could be accomplished by converting the decayed hospital of St. John, a twelfth-century institution, into an academic society comparable to Christ's College. Lady Margaret agreed, and she and her adviser then decided that the new society should be known as the College of St. John the Evangelist.

As early as 1505, the current master of St. John's Hospital, William Tomlyn, was persuaded to resign his post so the work of transformation could begin. Yet before much was accomplished, Tomlyn repented his decision, doubtless because no provision was to be made for him comparable to what was being done for Sycling at Christ's College. Since his resignation had not been cast in legal form, Tomlyn withdrew it and created serious problems thereby. As a consequence little was done before Lady Margaret's death in June 1509. However, in a codicil to her will, she referred explicitly to her "intended college of St. John's." Additionally she stipulated that all her possessions "at the time of her decease and not otherwise bequeathed, should be divided between her colleges of Christ's and St. John's by the discretion of her [nine] executors."[22]

Bishop Fisher had many difficulties to overcome before St. John's became a reality. Although the countess had intended most of her remaining estates to pass to the new society, her will was soon contested by lawyers for the young Henry VIII, and a protracted legal battle in the Court of Chancery resulted. The matter was finally resolved in 1512, when the monarch agreed to pay £2,800 for the lands in question, although he in fact released only £1,200 to his grandmother's executors.[23] An even greater embarrassment occurred because of Tomlyn's persistent refusal to surrender his office. This caused Fisher to turn in desperation to the king, the bishop of Ely, and even the pope, as a way of resolving the matter. Eventually all three ruled in favor of the projected college and against Tomlyn, making it possible for Fisher at last to proceed. On 12 March 1511, the last inhabitants of the old hospital departed for Ely, where new quarters had been readied for them. Four weeks later Fisher and seven of the other eight executors issued a foundation charter for the new society and appointed Robert Shorton its first master. At the same time three fellows named by Bishop Stanley, Lady Margaret's stepson, were officially installed.[24]

Once all these steps had been taken, building operations commenced, an order for 800,000 bricks being placed with a

Greenwich wholesaler about this time. By 1513 the hall, chapel, and master's lodge were almost finished, and even though all the buildings were not completed until 1520, enough were ready for use by July 1516 that the college, now a society of 31 fellows, felt the time had come to admit its first undergraduates. Later that year Bishop Fisher issued statutes for the institution, which he revised in 1524 and again in 1530. The first statutes were almost identical to those drawn up a decade earlier for Christ's College and stipulated the same low payments for the master and fellows. Probably the main difference between the statutes of the two colleges was the provision for regular instruction in Hebrew at the newer society. Presumably Fisher intended for St. John's to stress the three biblical languages. He was therefore pleased when a young English student, Robert Wakefield, returned from the continent in 1523 with skill not only in Hebrew but also in Arabic and Chaldean. Wakefield had taken an A.B. at Cambridge in 1514 and accepted a fellowship at St. John's five years later. Then, undoubtedly with Fisher's blessing, he departed for the European mainland in order to study oriental languages. After lecturing on Hebrew at Louvain and Tubingen, he returned to England and became an active member of the college, giving periodic Hebrew courses until he left the eastern university for Oxford in 1530.[25]

By the mid 1520s, St. John's was recognized as one of Cambridge's leading colleges. This was largely owing to the skillful leadership provided by its third master, Nicholas Metcalfe, who served from 1518 until 1537. One of Fisher's chaplains, Metcalfe was an astute financial manager who shepherded the college's resources carefully. Certainly the endowment grew steadily while he was at the helm, since the yearly revenues increased from £224 in 1518 to £507 in 1535, making the college second only to King's as the university's richest society. Within a few more years it also emerged as one of the largest colleges of the era. In 1545 St. John's had 152 members, while by 1573 it had expanded to 271, according to a reliable contemporary estimate.[26]

Just as significant as Metcalfe's financial ability was his skill in recognizing and promoting capable young scholars. He was an early patron not only of Robert Wakefield but also of Richard Croke, England's foremost Greek scholar during that era. After receiving an A.B. from King's College in 1510, Croke secured financial aid from Archbishop Warham and traveled to Paris in order to study with the great Girolamo Aleandro. Subsequently

Croke taught at several German universities, where his lectures drew enthusiastic audiences. While at Leipzig in 1516 he published a translation of Theodore of Gaza's highly acclaimed Greek grammar of a century before. He also published a small Greek textbook of his own, the first such work by an Englishman. The next year Croke returned to Cambridge and enjoyed immediate academic success. After incorporating for an M.A. degree, he was named to the Greek professorship Fisher had recently established.[27]

Croke was not the first scholar to teach Greek at the younger university. Between 1511 and 1514, Erasmus had offered instruction in that language while serving as Lady Margaret professor of divinity and living in rented chambers at Queens' College. However, after Erasmus's departure from Cambridge, the teaching of Greek languished until Croke's reappearance three years later, and thereafter it never ceased. This was the case because Croke was both an outstanding scholar and something of an academic showman: in 1522 he was elected university orator for life. Because of his extensive knowledge and exuberant teaching, Croke was able to arouse the interest of Cambridge undergraduates in Greek studies, which soon began to flourish.

Croke made his greatest academic contribution while holding a St. John's fellowship between 1524 and 1529. During those years he pioneered the tradition of outstanding Greek teaching, for which the college was long to be famous. For the next three decades a majority of England's leading Greek scholars, including Robert Pember, John Cheke, Roger Ascham, and William Grindal, were all Johnians, as the society's members soon became known. By the last decade of Henry VIII's reign, Greek studies were so firmly established at the college that Ascham wrote exultantly to a friend in 1542:

> Sophocles and Euripides are here better known than Plautus used to be when you were up. Herodotus, Thucydides, Xenophon, are more on the lips and in the hands of all now than Livy was then. What you used to hear about Cicero you now hear about Demosthenes. There are more copies of Isocrates in the hands of young men than there were of Terence then.[28]

Had Lady Margaret Beaufort lived to witness the exceptional progress made by her second collegiate society, she would doubtless have been much pleased.

In view of the many contributions made by women, it would have been ironic and indeed quite unjust had their sex not made some educational gains during those years. Although the grammar schools and universities remained closed to them, a growing perception of the need for more rigorous female training was evident by the second decade of the sixteenth century. To be sure, most male writers of the time—and there were virtually no contemporary women authors—desired only to perpetuate existing arrangements and believed that female education should be limited to reading, spinning, weaving, and music. But a few advanced thinkers, such as Ascham and especially Richard Hyrde, a protégé of Sir Thomas More, expressed the novel view that rigorous intellectual training was unlikely to harm females since it was so beneficial for boys and men. A few writers of the age even maintained that, aside from the extent of her dowry, a woman's education was the most important factor to consider when selecting a mate.

Slightly later, during the mid 1550s, Thomas Becon expressed the most radical opinions of all and advocated a separate but well-endowed system of schools for girls. He justified such a novel proposal by posing a number of important rhetorical questions.

> If it be thought convenient, as it is most convenient, that schools should be erected and set up for the right education and bringing up of the youth of the male kind, why should it not be thought convenient that schools be built for the godly institution and virtuous bringing up of the youth of the female kind? Is not the woman the creature of God as well as the man, and as dear unto God as the man? Is not the woman a necessary member of the commonweal? Have we not all our beginning of a woman? Do not the children for the most part prove even such as the mothers from which they come? Can the mothers bring up their children virtuously, when they themselves be void of all virtue?[29]

Although a few men shared Becon's views, the great majority rejected them out of hand. Even Bishop Fisher, who had such admiration and affection for Lady Margaret, praised her wisdom and abilities chiefly because they "exceeded the common rule of women." Moreover, the man who kept the finest household school of the age for the training of his children, Sir

Thomas More, considered it axiomatic that women's intellectual abilities were inferior to those of men.

Despite his many fine qualities, Sir Thomas More was always
willing to mock women for their alleged foolishness. In fact, he
seldom praised a female except "in contrast to a man whose
vices and ignorance were notorious. Then, by bringing a woman
forward as a virtuous example . . . he made the man's wickedness
all the more striking."[30] Like most of his male contemporaries,
More believed that female virtue consisted mainly of being
properly deferential to their husbands and fathers, and he was
accordingly a harsh taskmaster to every woman in his family
circle. Yet if he never questioned the premise of female inferiority,
he truly believed that "education betters them, so they should
study and learn." Only through education and industry could
the sin of sloth, which More detested above all others, be
conquered and the inherent flaw in women's nature be corrected.

Because he held such views, More was a strong advocate of
the need for more rigorous female instruction. In a letter of
1518 or 1519 to William Gonell, whom he had recently engaged to
teach his children, More maintained that women's minds are
altogether suited "for the knowledge of learning by which reason
is cultivated, and, like plowed land, germinate a crop when the
seeds of good precepts have been sown." His belief in this
regard, he declared, was not original with his own age, for it
had been espoused by "both the wisest and most saintly" of the
ancients.[31] Not only did More preach such views, but he also
attempted to enforce them in the household school he maintained
for his son John, his three daughters, a stepdaughter, and an
adopted daughter. All six children received the same basic
instruction, and in a single classroom they studied the classics
of Greek and Latin literature, the writings of the early Fathers
of the Church, logic, philosophy, and music. In addition, they
learned some astronomy and mathematics from Nicholas Kratzer,
who had earlier lectured on those subjects at Oxford. Because
More himself was interested in science, he tried to ensure that
his children and their classmates had a basic knowledge of such
matters. The most characteristic feature of the school, however,
was the daily routine of translating English compositions into
Latin and the resulting Latin back into English. This was the
so-called "dual system of translation" that such writers as Roger
Ascham strongly advocated and was already becoming a fixture
in the better grammar schools of the realm.[32]

More's household school was a great success by any objective standard. Even the brilliant humanist, Erasmus of Rotterdam, who supported the growing demand for more rigorous female training, was impressed by its excellence. In a letter to a friend, Erasmus described the school in glowing terms.

> You would say that in that place was Plato's Academy. I should rather call it a school or university of Christian religion. For there is none therein who does not study the branches of liberal education. Their special care is piety and virtue.[33]

As the fame of More's household school spread, there was an inevitable tendency for it to become larger. Frances Staverton, one of More's nieces, joined it, and so also did Margaret Barrow, who eventually married Sir Thomas Elyot, a leading educational writer of the 1530s. Even Cardinal Wolsey took notice of the school and placed a royal ward, Anne Cresacre, there. The only child of a Yorkshire landowner who died in 1519, Anne Cresacre was a girl of twelve or thirteen whose hand in marriage was being vigorously sought by both Ralph Rokeby and Sir Robert Constable. To keep Anne from being abducted by either of her suitors, Wolsey enrolled her in More's household school in 1524 or 1525. There she found a safe haven, received an excellent education, and even met her future husband: in 1529 she married More's son John.

Sir Thomas More was a prominent member of the Tudor middle class. Although he became a leading figure of the age and counted dukes and earls as his friends, he was the grandson of a London baker and the son of a municipal judge who lived contentedly in Cheapside. In addition, More's second wife was the widow of a mercer who had traded with European lands through the staple of Calais. Thus it would be wrong to portray More as an aristocrat, although he would doubtless have received a peerage had he supported the king's divorce from Catherine of Aragon. At any rate, More was one—but only one—of the Tudor middle class who acknowledged the need for more rigorous female education. To be sure, vocational instruction and the various domestic skills continued to be stressed for most middle-class girls, but there were scores of bourgeois women besides More's daughters and their classmates who received sound classical training during the period. Another young woman who profited from such an education was Elizabeth Withypoll, daughter of a London merchant and the first wife of a leading member of the Merchant Taylors' Company. Elizabeth Withypoll probably learned most of what she knew from her brother Edmund, who had been a pupil of Thomas Lupset, who in turn had been one of Erasmus's Cambridge disciples. On her death in 1537 at the age of only twenty-seven, Elizabeth was honored by her husband, Emmanuel Lucar, who had a brass plaque proclaiming her accomplishments erected on a wall of the London church where she was buried. According to that plaque, Elizabeth had been fluent in Latin, Spanish, and Italian, and had been noted for her beautiful writing "in three manner hands."[34]

Another middle-class woman who received a thorough education was Margaret Harlestone, who eventually became the wife of Matthew Parker, archbishop of Canterbury from 1559 until 1575. Margaret Parker found her knowledge of ancient languages a valuable aid long before her husband became Primate of all England during the reign of Queen Elizabeth. Between 1544 and 1553, while he was master of Corpus Christi College, Cambridge, she made good use of her classical background as she entertained a succession of learned friends as well as an occasional dignitary from the continent.[35] A much younger woman than Margaret Parker was Rachel Hooper, daughter of the English Protestant divine John Hooper and his European wife, Anna de Tseleras. Born about 1547, Rachel Hooper was a goddaughter of the great Zurich theologian Heinrich Bullinger. She was taught to speak Latin while still in her crib, and in March 1550 Hooper informed Bullinger of young Rachel's progress. "She grows in both stature and talent, and holds out the best promise of a most happy memory. She understands no language as well as she does Latin."[36]

Higher up the social ladder among the gentry, there was also a growing emphasis on the education of women. The greatest exponent of the cause among landed families was Sir Anthony Cooke, the noted educator and politician of the mid-Tudor period. After helping to tutor the young Edward VI, Cooke fled abroad shortly after Mary's accession to the throne. Once he learned of her death five years later, he returned to England and became a radical spokesman in the first parliament of Queen Elizabeth. Cooke was the father of four unusually gifted daughters, on whose education he lavished exceptional care. Their accomplishments became legendary and received rapturous praise as early as 1559 in William Bercher's *Nobility of Women*.

The eldest of Cooke's daughters, Mildred, became the wife of the great Elizabethan statesman Sir William Cecil, Lord Burghley, and was particularly noted for her mastery of Greek. Mildred made a translation of the works of St. John Chrysostom but refused to publish it because an Oxford scholar had recently completed the same task. In 1565 the youngest of the four sisters, Catherine, married Sir Henry Killigrew. Although she too published nothing, Catherine was admired by her contemporaries for both her poetic abilities and her proficiency in the three biblical languages. Yet the most scholarly of Cooke's daughters was probably Anne, the second, who was described in her own lifetime as "exquisitely skilled in the Greek and Latin tongues." The wife of Sir Nicholas Bacon for many years, Anne was a genuinely religious person who published two different editions of Italian sermons by Bernardino Ochino. She also translated a Latin tract justifying the independent status of the Elizabethan church, which had been written by John Jewel, bishop of Salisbury. Bishop Jewel was deeply impressed by Anne's translation; and it was published with his blessing in 1564 as *An Apology or Answer in Defense of the Church of England*.[37]

Perhaps the most interesting—and certainly the most outspoken—of the four Cooke sisters was Elizabeth, the third. Termed an English Sappho by Thomas Lodge, Elizabeth was married first to Sir Thomas Hoby, the translator of Baldassare Castiglione's famous *Book of the Courtier*, which appeared in 1561, and then to John, Lord Russell, son of the earl of Bedford. For both her husbands Elizabeth composed Greek and Latin epitaphs that she had inscribed on their funeral markers. Elizabeth was as interested in science as she was in languages and corresponded with a number of learned men about matters of mutual concern. However, as she grew older she inclined increasingly towards religion, and in 1605 she published an English version of a Latin devotional work as *A Way of Reconciliation . . . Touching the True Nature and Substance of the Body and Blood of Christ*.[38]

It would be a mistake to assume that every prominent woman of the age was as well trained and academically inclined as the four Cooke sisters. Doubtless Honor Grenville, the daughter of a western gentleman during the reign of Henry VIII, was far more typical of the educational attainments of the average female of that class. First married to Sir John Basset, by whom she had seven children, Honor eventually became the wife of Arthur

Plantagenet, Viscount Lisle, an illegitimate son of Edward IV and thus an uncle of Henry VIII. A clever person, Honor was fluent in French but probably knew no Latin. She owned several books of devotions and in 1539 instructed a family agent in Paris to procure an English Bible for her. Clearly able to write as well as to read, she nevertheless handled a pen with difficulty and probably dictated most of her letters, as the Paston women of the previous century had done. She and her second husband, Lord Lisle, who was governor of Calais from 1533 until 1540, were always chronically in debt. Whenever pressed by their creditors for payments, he happily assigned the negotiations to Honor, an especially sharp bargainer, and pledged to abide by whatever she arranged. Moreover, he allowed her to handle important transactions with bailiffs and stewards on their estates in England. She therefore made many decisions of a financial nature, most of which required more than a minimal degree of literacy.[39]

As other females of her class would have done, Honor supervised the instruction of the seven children she had borne her first husband. Not surprisingly, the three boys spelled and wrote far better than the four girls and were more carefully educated in every respect. But the intellectual training of the girls was not neglected. In fact, once Lord and Lady Lisle established themselves at Calais in 1533, they sent the two youngest girls, Anne and Mary, off to live with respectable French families so they could master that language and "be finished." As a result of their stay in France, Anne and Mary enjoyed a relatively lenient period of adolescence and escaped the harsh discipline that was meted out by most English parents.[40]

As has long been known, the average girl of the early Tudor era had to endure a degree of physical abuse that seems almost barbaric today. For example, the admirable Lady Jane Grey (1537–54) had to contend with the frequent "punches, nipps, and bobbs" of her odious and demanding parents. Lady Jane was probably the best-educated but also the most mistreated girl of the age. The eldest daughter of the marquess of Dorset and his wife Lady Frances Brandon, a niece of Henry VIII, Lady Jane was only four years old when a recent Cambridge graduate, John Aylmer, was appointed the family chaplain and tutor. Under his patient direction, which was altogether different from her parents' harsh methods, Lady Jane became an excellent scholar and linguist. By the age of thirteen she could read Plato's dialogues in the original Greek, which caused Roger

Ascham to inform a friend that her mastery of that language was "almost incredible." She was equally adept, it appears, in both Latin and Italian, and in a letter of July 1551 she herself requested advice on a technical point from Heinrich Bullinger at Zurich, "as I am now beginning to learn Hebrew."[41]

There were many other aristocratic girls who received educations along the lines of Lady Jane's. During the mid-sixteenth century the cause of improved female training registered its sharpest gains among the highest social ranks. Probably the first peer to embrace the cause was Henry Howard, earl of Surrey (d. 1547), a gifted poet and one of the first writers of English sonnets. For his three daughters and his lone son Thomas, Surrey employed professional tutors, who included a famous humanist from the continent, Hadrianus Junius. Because of explicit directions from Surrey, Junius instructed all four children in the same subjects and had them study Greek and Latin together. When in 1559 William Bercher published his book praising women's abilities and accomplishments, he gave particular attention to Surrey's daughter Jane, whom he termed "a worthy daughter of a most worthy father." Born in 1537, Jane was known for her own poetry and for her mastery of both Greek and Latin.[42]

Just as the earl of Surrey provided excellent instruction for his daughters, so too did Edward Seymour, duke of Somerset (d. 1552). By sheer coincidence Somerset was also the father of three gifted daughters, on whose behalf he engaged a French poet, Nicholas Denisot, to teach them Greek and Latin. In 1549 the eldest of the three, Anne, exchanged long Latin letters with John Calvin at Geneva, while her sister Jane conducted a similar correspondence with several other notable protestant leaders on the continent. Yet all three girls are especially remembered for the 400 Latin couplets they wrote to honor the memory of Marguerite d'Angoulême and her campaign for religious reform. Soon translated into French and Italian, those couplets were published with some of their other works in a volume that appeared in Paris in 1550 and included an ode praising their achievements by Pierre Ronsard, the leading French poet of the period.[43]

Although Protestant-minded peers were in the vanguard of the campaign for improved female instruction, at least one Catholic nobleman of the age, Henry Fitzalan, fourteenth earl of Arundel, provided excellent educations for his two children, Mary and Anne. Appointed Lord Steward in August 1553, the earl of Arundel was a dedicated bibliophile with a private library of at least 400 volumes, which he used in the education of his daughters. The older, Mary, became famous for her achievements, which were considerably greater than those of her eventual husband, Thomas Howard, fourth duke of Norfolk (d. 1572). The latter had no concern for academic matters, despite the excellent tutors engaged on his behalf by his father, the poet earl of Surrey. But Mary was a capable and diligent student, and during their brief marriage of 1555–57, she read deeply in ancient literature and transcribed passages of Greek and Latin that particularly appealed to her. When she died in July 1557 after giving birth to a son, she left four volumes of such linguistic exercises, which are now among the Royal Manuscripts in the British Library. As for Mary's sister Jane, who eventually became the wife of John, Lord Lumley, the keeper of Nonsuch Palace, she too had a great love of the classics. On her death in 1577 she left a copy in her own hand of an entire play by Euripides, which she had translated into English. Among her personal effects was also a collection of Isocrates' orations that she had rendered from the original Greek into Latin.[44]

Although England could boast a number of female prodigies by the mid-sixteenth century, most girls, even from prominent families, were still rather poorly trained. The accomplishments of the four Cooke sisters, or of the daughters of the duke of Somerset and the earl of Arundel, were far from typical, since the average girl possessed but a fraction of their learning. Yet standards were clearly rising, and most young women were probably somewhat more literate than their late medieval predecessors had been. A variety of religious and cultural factors encouraged the steady improvement of female education, and until the Civil War of the 1640s every generation of Englishwomen was slightly more learned than the previous one, to the obvious advantage of the whole society.

5

Printing, Books, and the Bible

As the sixteenth century progressed, all but the very poor made steady gains in regard to education and literacy. That they did was partly owing to the continuing fall in the price of books. As noted in chapter 2, new cursive scripts had been developed during the thirteenth and four-teenth centuries, with the result that copyists could work more quickly and without the need for the drastic abbreviations that had typified most handwritten works. As early as 1400 books were both more common and far cheaper than they had been before the Black Death. For example, the stocks of two London grocers during the 1390s included a primer priced at 16*d.* and six other books worth an estimated 12*d.* in all. In 1395 the earl of Derby, who would soon ascend the throne as Henry IV, bought seven grammar texts at a total cost of 4*s.* for his eldest son; whereas a mid-fifteenth-century scholar, Simon Berynton, owned fifteen books that were together valued at a mere 6*d.*

It would be wrong to assume that all late medieval books were quite so inexpensive. Many sold for considerably more and were thus beyond the reach of all but the wealthy. In 1374 the earl of March bought a Bible for fifty marks, and about the same time Edward III paid the enormous sum of £44 1*s.* 4*d.* for an illuminated book that he kept safely at his bedside. In 1422 Oriel College, Oxford, acquired a copy of the massive *Golden*

Legend of Jacobus de Voraigne for 100*s*., whereas in 1448 a citizen of Hull bequeathed £5 for the purchase of an antiphoner for Holy Trinity Church. Because carpenters and stone masons made only 6*d*. a day, and plumbers even less, books remained too expensive for the workingman to purchase in numbers, even if he was capable of reading them. Moreover, priests and schoolmasters seldom received over £6 a year, so they too were unable to afford more than a few books. However, once a mechanized form of printing was established in England, books became considerably cheaper and a larger percentage of the population was able to acquire them.

Just how far book prices fell after the introduction of mechanized printing has long been a matter of speculation. Scholarly estimates usually fall within a range of 50 to 90 percent. Probably we shall never know for sure because the evidence is inconclusive and too much hinges on the quality and condition of the relatively small number of pre-1500 books for which definite prices can be established. Yet the comments of a knowledgable Italian observer shed considerable light on the matter. In 1468 Giovanni, Cardinal de Bussi, the Secretary of the new Vatican Library, maintained that the price of books had declined by 80 percent since the advent of the new process. He additionally declared that " '[i]n our time . . . God gave Christendom a gift which enables even the pauper to acquire books.' "[1] This evidence from Italy is corroborated by E. W. Ives's analysis of the library of Thomas Kebell, an English lawyer who died in 1500. At the time of Kebell's death, his collection consisted of eighteen printed books and an equal number of manuscripts, and the price differential between the two categories is striking. As Mr. Ives has written:

> One-half of Kebell's manuscripts are valued at twenty shillings or more, and one in four at two pounds ten shillings or above. By contrast, none of the printed books cost more than ten shillings, two out of every three cost four shillings or less, and one in three, two shillings or less. . . . a [single] shilling provided Sir John Mandeville's *Travels* [printed in 1499] and one shilling and four pence, Caxton's 1481 Cicero or his 1478 Boethius.[2]

Because of the sharp decline in the price of books as well as their greater availability—books were now being offered in markets where they had never been sold before—many individuals considered it extraordinarily important to be able to read the works, particularly those of a religious nature, that now lay within their reach. The new situation was well understood by the anonymous author of *The Pilgrimage of Perfection* of 1526. That writer declared that it is " 'very profitable for all christen people to rede: and in especiall to all relygious persons moche necessary.' "3

The founder of the English printing industry was William Caxton, a Kentishman who was born in 1421. During the late 1430s Caxton was apprenticed to a prominent wool merchant in the capital, and within several more years he was an accredited agent of the Merchant Adventurers' Company at Bruges, the operational centre of England's wool trade with the Low Countries. He remained abroad for many years, although he made occasional visits to London for personal and financial reasons. In 1462 or 1463 he was elected "Governor of the English Nation beyond the Seas," or chairman of the association of English merchants residing in western Europe, a post he retained until about 1470.

During the mid 1460s, Caxton handled tasks of a diplomatic and financial nature for Edward IV. Doubtless his main contribution lay in assisting the king's two special envoys, Lords Scales and Hastings, who arrived from England in 1467 to negotiate a marriage treaty between Edward's sister Margaret and the new duke of Burgundy, Charles the Bold. Once this marriage occurred at Bruges in June 1468, Margaret developed a high regard for Caxton, whose deep knowledge of contemporary literature she admired. They had long discussions about poetry and the problems of language, and within a short time he became her secretary as well as keeper of the ducal library at Ghent. Moreover, he agreed to search for additional works and to secure their translation into English for her. As early as 1469, he himself had begun to translate a French account of the Trojan Wars, which had been written some years earlier by Raoul Léfèvre, the secretary and chaplain of the previous duke of Burgundy, Philip the Good (d. 1467). Because they mistakenly believed themselves to be descendants of the ancient Trojans, fifteenth-century Englishmen had an abiding interest in the Trojan Wars.

Caxton had completed his translation of Léfèvre's book by mid-September 1471. He was obviously pleased with the result, since he hoped to offer it to a wide circle of readers. However, the sheer size of the manuscript (it was eventually published as a folio of 778 pages) required him to find a method to reproduce it mechanically. Since the mid 1450s, German artisans of the Rhineland had been able to print books rapidly and cheaply by means of interchangeable metal letters. From northwestern Germany printing had spread into other parts of Europe, particularly after the devastating sack of Mainz in 1462, where Gutenberg had had his printshop. In 1464 the first printing house in Switzerland was founded at Basle, and within another year the first Italian press was established at Subiaco, a short distance from Rome. By 1470 presses were functioning not only in Rome itself but also at Venice and Paris, while by 1474 print shops had appeared in such additional places as Lyons, Valencia, Utrecht, and Louvain.

During those same years, Caxton resolved to learn the new techniques of mass production, and to that end he set out for Cologne, an early printing center, where he arrived in July 1471. By the time he left Cologne in December 1472, he had mastered the craft with the assistance of Johann Veldener, a Bavarian who subsequently helped to establish it in the Low Countries. Before returning to Bruges, Caxton purchased a press and supply of type and hired a young journeyman printer from Alsace, Wynkyn de Worde, who was to be his foreman for nearly twenty years.

Back in Bruges no later than January 1473, Caxton soon published the first English-language book to be mechanically reproduced. This was of course his own translation of Léfèvre's work, which he entitled *Recuyell of the historyes of Troye*. For several years thereafter Caxton remained in Bruges, where he also issued a popular manual, *The Game and Play of the Chesse*, and various other books. These he exported to merchants in his native land, where he perceived there would be a ready market for them. Yet by the winter of 1475-76 he had decided it was unnecessarily expensive to print books on the continent that were intended for the sole use of English readers. So he recrossed the Channel for the first time in some years and opened the earliest English print shop within a short distance of Westminster Abbey.

For decades Caxton had admired the works of Chaucer, whom he regarded as the greatest of all English writers. Almost at once he prepared an edition of *The Canterbury Tales*, which he intended to be the first book mechanically reproduced in his native land. Caxton lavished exceptional care on this large folio, which was printed by two presses operating concurrently. It has long been considered the most beautiful volume he ever produced, and because of its popularity he published a slightly altered version of it in 1483.[4]

For his printshop to succeed, Caxton felt he needed to attract aristocratic or even royal patronage. Late in 1477 he therefore printed a short quarto, an extract from the earlier *Recuyell of the historyes of Troye,* which he dedicated to the seven-year-old son of Edward IV, "to the intent that he may begin to learn to read English." This extract was entitled *A Boke of the Hoole Lyfe of Jason,* and it prompted the appreciative monarch to become the official patron of Caxton's publishing venture, the success of which was now assured. In 1479 Edward IV author-ized a payment of £20 to him for some service, and two years later the printer dedicated *The Book of Tulle of Old Age* to the king himself.[5]

Meanwhile Caxton had received two commissions from Lord Scales, now second Earl Rivers, whom he had helped to con-clude the Anglo-Burgundian marriage treaty of 1467. Anthony Woodville, second Earl Rivers (d. 1483) was the most cultivated nobleman in the country as well as a royal brother-in-law, since his sister Elizabeth was Edward IV's wife and consort. Most of the Woodville clan loved books—the queen is known to have spent £10 for a single volume on at least one occasion—and Lord Rivers himself had serious intellectual interests. He had prepared a collection of adages from earlier times that he wished to have published, and Caxton was happy to oblige. In November 1477 the earl's brief quarto, *The Dictes and Sayengs of the Philosophers,* appeared, and the demand for it was so great that he reprinted it two years later. Heartened by the enthusiastic response to his work, Lord Rivers soon prepared a second book, *The Moral Proverbs,* which Caxton ran off early in 1478. This small quarto included a selection of Christine de Pisan's moral observations, which the earl himself had translated into English verse.[6]

By the early 1480s, Lord Rivers had persuaded Caxton to undertake the publication of Sir Thomas Malory's celebrated work, the *Morte d'Arthur.* This important book, which had been written during the 1460s, appeared in 1485; and Caxton lavished greater care on its printing than any other work he ever published, except for the first edition of *The Canterbury Tales.* In addition, he demonstrated his outstanding editorial skills by tightening up the long and rambling narrative, compressing accounts of battles, and stressing the central role of King Arthur throughout. In these ways he transformed Malory's book into a genuine work of art and ensured that it would become an important piece of living literature.[7]

It would be tedious to discuss all ninety-six of the books that Caxton published between his return to England in 1476 and his death in 1491. Yet a few general observations will enable the modern reader to understand Caxton's masterly exploitation of the English market, which was the main reason for the success he enjoyed. Since many of his contemporaries had an interest in history, Caxton issued several works of that type. Among the most important of these were: (1) *The Chronicles of England*, which he printed in 1480 and reissued two years later; (2) *The History of Godfrey of Boulogne* (1481), which was based on a French account of the First Crusade; and (3) *Charles the Great* (1485), his own translation of a biography of Charlemagne by a Swiss historian. Yet Caxton's greatest contribution to this genre was his 1482 publication of Ranulf Higden's *Polychronicon*, which has been called "the best general history of the world then available." Translated into English almost a century earlier by John Trevisa, the *Polychronicon* was one of the longest works Caxton ever published since it ran to 430,000 words and nearly 900 pages of print.

Because of the prevailing outlook of the age, Caxton published a number of books that were essentially religious in nature. Indeed, some 45 percent of his total output fits into this important category. Of the religious and devotional works that flowed from his press, probably the most significant were: (1) *The Book of Hours* (1477), a rudimentary prayer book that soon passed through four editions; (2) *The Golden Legend* (1483 and 1487), which included long excerpts from the Old Testament as well as more than a hundred saints' lives, seventy or so written by Caxton himself; and (3) the *Confessio Amantis* of John Gower (1483), a collection of tales that illustrated the consequences of the seven deadly sins. Cast in poetic form by its author, this last book is thought to have been the most widely read, and the most commercially successful, of any that Caxton ever issued.

Because of the obvious success of Caxton's printshop, several other publishers followed his example and set themselves up in business. Probably the first to do so was Theodoric Rood of Cologne, who opened a press in the High Street at Oxford in

1478. An able craftsman, Rood concentrated on the production of academic books and issued critical editions of such works as Leonardo Bruni's *Ethics* and a version of Aristotle's *De Anima* by a thirteenth-century English scholar. In addition, Rood printed John Ankwyll's pioneering Latin grammar, *Compendium Totius Grammaticae,* which had been written for the boys of Magdalen College School. However, Rood published almost nothing of a popular nature, nor did he succeed in attracting royal or aristocratic patronage. After publishing only seventeen books in all, he returned to the continent in 1485 or 1486. Thereafter printing lapsed at Oxford until 1517, when an even briefer venture lasting only three years began under the joint direction of John Seelar and Charles Kyrfeth.

Meanwhile at St. Albans, some twenty miles north of London, another press operated for a short time during the 1480s. The name of the St. Albans printer has never been discovered, although Wynkyn de Worde once referred to him as "the scole mayster of saynt Albons." Apparently this printer was aided to some degree by the abbot of the local monastery, one of the wealthiest abbeys of the period. Eight books in all are known to have issued from this press between 1479 and 1486, when it evidently ceased to operate. The earliest press in northern England functioned from 1509 until 1516, when its printer, Hugo Goes of Antwerp, moved the enterprise to Beverley and thence, after a few years, to London. At Cambridge there was also a brief experiment with printing during the first quarter of the sixteenth century. Between 1520 and 1523 John Siberch ran a press there and published scholarly works by Erasmus, Linacre, and Richard Croke.

Only in London was there a continuous tradition of printing between the 1470s and the 1580s, when permanent presses at last began to function at the two universities. Yet even in the capital only a few printers were able to maintain their operations over an extended period, not because the demand for books was too small but because the European artisans who dominated the industry until the 1520s had little understanding of the tastes of English readers. After Caxton's print shop at Westminster, the earliest venture in the London area was the firm that John Lettou established in 1480. Probably born in eastern Europe, Lettou had learned his craft in Italy. Within a short time of settling in London, he formed a partnership with William Machlinia, a Fleming who had recently arrived on the scene and with whom he co-published a number of legal works and similar tracts designed to appeal to the country's lawyers. Yet within a few years of 1482, Lettou dropped out of sight, leaving Machlinia to carry on alone. By 1491 Machlinia himself had died or returned to the continent, probably after disposing of the business to Richard Pynson, an artisan of Norman birth.

Exceptionally capable and enterprising, Pynson proved to be the most successful publisher of English books since Caxton. His print shop near Temple-bar, which he later moved to Fleet Street, was a thriving place that issued more than 500 works before his death in 1530. Because of his superior technical standards, he won the favor of Henry VII, who in 1508 appointed him to succeed William Facques as official printer to the crown. Thereafter Pynson was responsible for the publication of all edicts and proclamations, and in 1515 Henry VIII doubled his yearly stipend to 80s. Like William Machlinia earlier, Pynson concentrated on supplying the lawyers' needs and printed important treatises by Bracton, Fortescue, Littleton, and others. Yet he also published a variety of literary and historical works, including Sebastian Brandt's *Ship of Fools* and the chronicles of Fabyan and Froissart. Like other successful printers of the era, Pynson printed dozens of religious books, the most important of which were a missal that appeared in 1500 and *The Kalendar of Shepherds,* an especially interesting book that consisted of various prayers, the Ten Commandments, and an open appeal for a new vernacular Bible.[8]

An even more successful printer than Pynson was Wynkyn de Worde, Caxton's longtime foreman, who took charge of the Westminster operation on his master's death in 1491. Between that date and his own death in 1534, de Worde published more than 800 books in all, making him easily the most prolific publisher of the age. In essence, de Worde printed books in three broad categories. Approximately half his output consisted of works of a religious nature; 40 percent were textbooks for use in the schools of the period; while the remaining 10 percent were works of a miscellaneous nature, such as ballads, romances, chapbooks, and informational tracts. All in all, the average book issued by de Worde was 460 pages in length, which was twice as long as the average book issued by Pynson. Yet towards the end of his career, de Worde published smaller and smaller books, including many quartos of only 24 to 32 pages. Most of these he sold for only a penny or two, and in this way he successfully appealed to the growing mass market of the period.[9]

Like de Worde and Pynson, most of the printers of the 1530s and 1540s published many books of a religious nature. Indeed, Thomas Berthelet, who succeeded Pynson as official printer to the crown in 1529, issued more than 125 books of that type, and they accounted for nearly 50 percent of his total production. Other printers of the second quarter of the sixteenth century devoted even more energy to meeting the steady demand for such works. Of the forty-two known books published by Thomas Petyt, at least twenty-five were devotional or inspirational in some way, whereas all but four of the thirty-four books printed by Thomas Reynalde merit such a characterization.[10]

A type of religious work that enjoyed especially brisk sales during these years was the psalter. The first Tudor book in this category, *The Seven Penytencyall Psalms of David,* was compiled by Bishop Fisher in 1508 at Lady Margaret Beaufort's urging. Within a few years of its appearance, an enlarged version of the psalms, in an English translation by George Joye, was printed at Antwerp, probably by Martin Emperor. Yet the most important contributor to this genre was Thomas Sternhold, a Hampshire gentleman who studied for several terms at Oxford and later became groom of the robes to Henry VIII. In 1548 Sternhold published a small book entitled *Certain Psalms,* which consisted of nineteen psalms cast in poetic form by use of the simple ballad stanza. His work won the enthusiastic approval of a Suffolk clergyman, John Hopkins, who soon arranged to become his collaborator. After Sternhold's death in 1549, Hopkins published an enlarged collection of forty-four psalms, with thirty-seven by Sternhold and the remainder by himself. In subsequent years the collection continued to grow, at last becoming complete in 1562, when *The Whole Book of Psalmes* appeared. Popularly known as *The Sternhold-Hopkins Psalter,* this devotional work was in such great demand that it passed through forty editions by 1586 and another 110 by 1621. It continued to appear until 1828, by which year it had been reprinted more than 600 times.[11]

Just as popular as the psalters of the period were the numerous editions of the Bible that appeared from the autumn of 1535. There was in fact such an insistent demand for vernacular Bibles that thirty different editions were issued by 1557 and an additional 170 by 1600. Within another century the English Bible would be reprinted 480 times more! The main figure associated with the publication of a revised vernacular Bible, one that was a great advance on the Lollard Bibles of the fourteenth century, was William Tyndale, probably the most important religious leader of the early Tudor period.

Born in Gloucestershire about 1490, William Tyndale came from a family of prosperous yeoman farmers. After studies at Magdalen College, Oxford, where he completed his M.A. in 1515, he migrated to Cambridge, probably in order to study Greek with Richard Croke, who, as we have seen, had returned from the continent in 1517. Perhaps Tyndale began to learn Greek before leaving Oxford, but it was at the eastern university that he developed his mastery of that language, which was a prerequisite for serious biblical scholarship. During his three or four years at Cambridge, Tyndale may have come into contact with Lutheran ideas, which were then gaining a following in eastern England. Indeed, so many young scholars enthused by Luther's writings met for discussion purposes at the White Horse Inn in Cambridge during the early 1520s that the hostelry became known as "Little Germany." Yet there is no real proof that Tyndale was among those who frequented the Inn, for his name was never mentioned in that context.[12]

In 1521 Tyndale returned to his native Gloucestershire as chaplain to the family of Sir John Walsh, who lived at Little Sodbury, near Bristol. Sir John and his wife, Lady Anne, treated the young priest kindly and encouraged him to read a little tract by Erasmus, *The Handbook of the Christian Knight,* which had appeared two decades earlier. In that work Erasmus insisted that religion was less a matter of formal rites and ceremonies than of personal piety and a detailed knowledge of Christ's life and teachings, the latter being attainable through careful biblical study. Erasmus also held that an improved version of the scriptures, free of all error, was badly needed, so that theologians could provide an accurate summary of Christine doctrine for the laity. These views came as a revelation to Tyndale, who thereupon decided that biblical translation should be the main purpose of his life.

Because of the Constitutions of Arundel, which had been in effect since 1408, no one could undertake a new translation of the Bible without securing authorization from a bishop or archbishop. Accordingly Tyndale soon left Little Sodbury for the capital, where he hoped to secure the necessary permission from Cuthbert Tunstall, the new bishop of London. Tunstall had more progressive inclinations than the average member of the episcopal bench, being the author of a pioneering work on arithmetic and an important collector of Greek manuscripts; and he had recently been praised by Erasmus for his kindness and his sympathy for the New Learning. Tyndale was therefore hopeful that Tunstall would become his patron, and for almost a year he solicited an appointment in the bishop's household. But Tunstall shared the conservative outlook of Sir Thomas More, who believed enough English-language Bibles were available at the time. In 1528 More actually declared that he himself had seen

> . . . and can shew you, Bibles fair and old and written in English, which have been . . . seen by the bishop of the diocese, and left in laymen's hands, and women's, to such as he [the bishop] knew for good and Catholic folk. But of truth such as are found in the hands of heretics, they used to take away.[13]

Because much of central Europe was currently in revolt against the papacy, owing to Luther's strident attacks on clerical abuses, it is easy to see why Tunstall had little interest in lending his name to a new effort to render the scriptures into the vernacular.

Once he realized Tunstall would never become his patron, Tyndale decided to leave England for the continent, where he might begin the undertaking without fear of reprisal. Because there had never been a continental prohibition comparable to the Constitutions of Arundel, the scriptures had been published in a number of European languages by the early 1520s. Among the earliest printed Bibles now owned by the British Library are eleven German versions, all published between 1455 and 1518; three Czech editions dating from the years 1488–1506, a Dutch version of the New Testament that had appeared in 1477, and a complete French Bible of 1510. All in all, more than 400 vernacular editions of the scriptures, or of long excerpts from them, had been printed since the mid-fifteenth century.[14] In view of the way most European readers now had easy access to vernacular Bibles, in addition to the fact that recent advances in Greek and Hebrew scholarship had made the earlier Lollard Bible obsolete, it should come as no surprise that a scholar like Tyndale would desire to produce an acceptable translation for use by his countrymen.

After deciding to go abroad, Tyndale received generous support from Humphrey Monmouth, a wool merchant who had heard Tyndale preach from time to time at St. Dunstan's in the West. (Tyndale had been a priest since 1515.) Monmouth had commercial ties with merchant groups throughout northwestern Europe who might be willing to assist an expatriate English scholar with Protestant leanings. Monmouth himself gave Tyndale £10 and arranged for several other individuals to contribute another £10; and by May 1524 the priest had set sail for Hamburg, whence he traveled inland to Wittenberg. Probably Tyndale was drawn to that university town by Luther's continued presence there, although the two men apparently never met. During his stay of fourteen or fifteen months in Wittenberg, Tyndale did become friendly with William Roy, and English friar of Jewish antecedents. Later the two men fell out and became bitter enemies, but at this early stage Roy was instrumental in helping Tyndale to learn Hebrew, for which language the latter soon demonstrated a definite aptitude.[15]

Meanwhile Tyndale had completed his first version of the New Testament, which he may have begun before leaving England. Whatever the case, Tyndale set out during the summer of 1525 for the important publishing centre of Cologne, where an able printer, Peter Quentel, agreed to run it off. However, after only eight pages had been completed, Tyndale learned he was about to be arrested by suspicious local officials; so he packed his bags and the quires already printed and fled. He journeyed first to Hamburg, where he sought help from merchants in contact with Monmouth's London firm; but later he traveled to Worms, where the large Jewish community might assist him in attaining a total mastery of Hebrew. At Worms in the first months of 1526, the work of printing his New Testament was completed by Peter Schoeffer. Altogether 6,000 copies of this exceptionally important book were published, about half as quartos and the other half as octavos.[16]

Tyndale's New Testament of 1526 was an impressive piece of scholarship that inspired other English translators for decades. It can be compared with the important Graeco-Latin edition published by Erasmus in 1516 and the German edition completed by Luther in 1522. In fact, Tyndale's knowledge of Greek equaled that of his two better-known contemporaries, and he actually remained closer to the original Greek than Luther had done. Moreover, he was surprisingly successful in conveying the literal meaning of the gospels and the various other books of the New Testament, which was his primary objective. In no way pedantic, he took a liberal approach to the problems of translation, refused to worry about minor errors and anachronisms, and produced a work of living literature. Moreover, he promised in an introductory "Letter to the Reader" that he would publish a revised and updated version at some later time.

Despite the merits of Tyndale's New Testament, it was violently criticized in England, where Monmouth evidently handled its distribution from the summer of 1526. During October of that year Bishop Tunstall directed all the archdeacons of his diocese to surrender whatever copies of the offending book they could acquire, and he himself purchased scores of copies that he destroyed. In a sermon delivered during the autumn of 1526, Tunstall claimed to have found 3,000 errors in the work. In February 1527 Bishop Fisher made equally serious criticisms of Tyndale's translation; while in 1528 the government initiated legal proceedings against a Cambridge stationer, Sygar Nicholson, and several other men who had directed its sale in eastern England. Later that same year Cardinal Wolsey sought to arrange the arrest and extradition of both Tyndale and Roy from the Rhineland, so they could be tried for heresy in England.[17]

Because of the harsh reaction to his work and his fear of being apprehended, Tyndale moved about almost continuously between 1527 and 1530. At one time or another he is known to have been in Antwerp, Hamburg, and the old university town of Marburg. Despite the hardships he faced, he was now at work on the most difficult of all his undertakings—a translation of the Old Testament, which he probably began at Antwerp sometime in 1527. Once he completed a preliminary version of Genesis and the other four books of the Pentateuch, he decided to leave Antwerp for the greater safety of Hamburg. But on the voyage his ship capsized in a storm and his precious manuscript was lost. His spirits remained undaunted, however, and on reaching his destination he began the work anew. He was now assisted by Miles Coverdale, an Augustinian friar from Yorkshire, who was destined to be his chief disciple and the inheritor of his mantle. By December 1529 Tyndale's rewritten Pentateuch was ready for the press, and during the next month it was finally run off, apparently by George Richolff. Like his earlier New Testament, Tyndale's Pentateuch of 1530 was a work of outstanding scholarship. Yet his stylistic faults are more obvious in the latter work, since his mastery of Hebrew was not as great as his skill in Greek and Latin. In particular, he paid too little attention to verb forms, which led to minor errors in regard to tense. His love of diversity caused him to make excessive use of synonyms, and he was often guilty of paraphrasing and using indirect discourse. Despite such faults, his translation of the first five books of the Old Testament was an unusually successful pioneering effort by one of England's first great Hebrew scholars.[18]

During the early 1530s Tyndale concentrated on the later books of the Old Testament, in an effort to complete an English-language version of the whole Bible. In 1531 he produced a translation of the book of Jonah, which was immediately assailed by Sir Thomas More in a coarse broadside. (Not one to take criticism lightly, Tyndale responded to More's taunts in kind, which caused him to become known as a quarrelsome and unaccommodating man of violent temperament.) In 1534 Tyndale finished his version of all the Old Testament historical books from Joshua to Second Chronicles, which did not appear during his lifetime, however. Shortly afterwards Tyndale completed what has long been recognized as his masterpiece—an outstanding translation of the book of Job. From the time it was published, Tyndale's translation of Job was hailed for its "arresting phrases, flowing cadences and austere dignity." According to a modern biblical scholar, "All subsequent English translations [of both Job and the whole Bible] bear the imprint of this tragic genius, to whom the English-speaking world owes a debt it can never repay."[19]

While continuing his Old Testament labors, Tyndale became convinced that a revision of his 1526 Old Testament was urgently required. As noted earlier, he had promised in his "Letter to the Reader" to make a second and more accurate version of that part of the Bible one day. Moreover, because of the steady demand throughout England for the work, a number of pirated versions had appeared during recent years. Between 1527 and 1530 at least 6,500 copies had been published without his approval by several different firms in the Low Countries. Inevitably numerous errors crept into the later printings of his translation, since he played no part in seeing them through the press. The matter came to a head in 1534, when two more pirated editions, totaling 4,000 copies and marred by hundreds of "strange renderings," appeared. How long Tyndale spent on producing an improved version of his original New Testament is unclear. But in the words of one authority, "It is not a superficial revision; the whole work has been gone over in scrupulous detail, and nearly always the changes are for the better, reflecting mature judgment and feeling."[20]

Tyndale's second version of the New Testament was his last important work. In May 1535 he was betrayed by Henry Phillips, an English student in desperate need of funds, to agents of Charles V, who six years earlier had banned the circulation of heretical books within the Empire. Once he was arrested at the entrance to the Merchant Adventurers' House in Antwerp, Tyndale was taken to the state prison at Vilvorde, where he was held without trial for over a year. A clamor for his release began, and both the association of English merchants in Antwerp and Thomas Cromwell, England's principal statesman at the time, demanded that he be set free. However, Charles V was still smarting from the harsh way Henry VIII had treated his favorite aunt, Catherine of Aragon, so he refused to intervene on Tyndale's behalf. Ultimately, after a long and grueling interrogation, the English priest was convicted of heresy by theologians from Louvain University. On 6 October 1536, he was strangled before a crowd of jeering onlookers, after which his body was consumed in a bonfire.[21]

Although Tyndale did not live to achieve his life's goal, a complete English Bible was published a short time before his death by Miles Coverdale. A less gifted linguist than his mentor, Coverdale knew little if any Hebrew. Yet he patched together an entire Old Testament by using the various sections Tyndale had finished by 1534 as well as long passages taken from the German Bible Luther had published that same year. He also relied on a Latin version of the Old Testament that an Italian scholar, Santes Paginus, had based on Hebrew manuscripts in 1528. For the New Testament, Coverdale resorted to both the Lutheran Bible and the Zwinglian version that had been printed at Zurich in 1531, but his greatest debt was clearly to Tyndale's New Testament of 1534, long passages of which he incorporated without modification.[22]

Despite his heavy debt to Tyndale, Coverdale wisely eliminated the older scholar's controversial glosses. Almost all of Tyndale's translations had been marred by marginal notes that gave the most Protestant interpretation a disputed passage could be made to bear. These glosses provoked the ire of orthodox Catholics, whose opposition was likely to continue as long as they were retained. Coverdale sensed this, and being a man of gentler temperament than Tyndale, he removed the offending glosses in his edition of the Bible, which had been run off by July 1535. Although the evidence is inconclusive, this new English Bible, the first complete one to appear since the 1390s, was probably printed by the Cologne firm of Soter and Cervicorn.[23]

Because Coverdale wished his Bible to be sold and read without fear of reprisal, the next problem was how to arrange for its legal distribution in England. To this end he sent several copies of the work to Jacob von Meteren, an Antwerp merchant who had long encouraged his efforts. Von Meteren in turn contacted James Nicholson, a printer in Southwark since 1526. Apparently Nicholson was offered exclusive rights to the sale and distribution of the Coverdale Bible, provided he could secure royal permission to allow it. At the time it was unclear whether Henry VIII would grant his approval. Unflinchingly conservative by nature, the king had recently allowed his Lord Chancellor to throw fifteen copies of Tyndale's New Testament onto a public bonfire. However, several influential persons had begun to press the monarch for a vernacular Bible by this juncture. Anne Boleyn and her ladies-in-waiting were in favor of one, and so too was Archbishop Cranmer, under whose leadership the convocation of Canterbury had called for a commission of "certain learned and upright men" to prepare a vernacular Bible. Yet the leading figure who was now an open supporter of the cause was Thomas Cromwell. At the height of his power by the mid 1530s, Cromwell was a committed Protestant of evangelical leanings; and for the past few years he had been aware of Tyndale and Coverdale and the work they had undertaken.[24]

By August 1535, Nicholson had contacted Cromwell and presented him with a copy of Coverdale's Bible, which he urged the chief minister to deliver to Henry. Cromwell agreed to do as he was asked, and with genuine interest Henry examined the book, a small folio with two parallel columns on each page. But before he would authorize it, Henry solicited the views of several conservative bishops, including Stokesley of London and Gardiner of Winchester, who were instructed to comb the work for errors. Because Tyndale's marginal glosses had been removed and the bishops consulted were mediocre biblical scholars, Henry was not apprised of specific passages that had been incorrectly translated. He therefore agreed to licence the book, although he would not allow the title page to state that it had been published with royal authorization, as Nicholson desired. Partly because of the reasonable price of Coverdale's Bible—it evidently sold for 5s. a copy—the supply was soon exhausted. Nicholson therefore reprinted it in 1537, in both a folio and a quarto edition.[25]

Meanwhile two other scholars were about to publish somewhat different versions of the Bible. John Rogers, an able student of both Greek and Hebrew, had been a chaplain to the Merchant Adventurers of Antwerp during the year preceding Tyndale's arrest in May 1535. Rogers obviously admired the older man, whom he probably helped in the last stages of his work, and the Bible he had printed at Paris in 1538 was really a posthumous edition of the work Tyndale had envisaged. Indeed, it included all the translations the latter had finished prior to his arrest, including the Old Testament historical books, which now appeared in print for the first time. In his editorial work Rogers also drew from Coverdale's Bible of 1535 and from two French Bibles that had appeared somewhat earlier. Known as "Matthew's Bible" from the pesudonym Rogers adopted, this work was in some respects an improvement on Coverdale's edition, since Rogers was a better linguist. Yet it sold at the excessively high price of 26s. and reintroduced many of Tyndale's controversial glosses. Moreover, Rogers added more than 2,100 notes of his own in which he attacked the doctrine of purgatory and such practices as pilgrimages, mandatory fasting, and clerical celibacy. Consequently there was little chance that Matthew's Bible would gain popular acceptance.[26]

Almost as soon as Matthew's Bible appeared, its least attractive features were altered by Richard Taverner, a protégé of Cromwell, who had arranged for him to become a clerk of the Privy Seal in 1536. Yet it was not the chief minister but Thomas Berthelet, the royal printer, who persuaded Taverner to revise Matthew's Bible in order to increase its popular appeal. Published in 1539, this newest English Bible was an unequal production since, despite Taverner's mastery of Greek, he knew no Hebrew. His version of the Old Testament was therefore of little significance, but his New Testament marked a worthwhile advance, since it was unusually successful in capturing the nuances of ancient Greek. Most important of all, Taverner eliminated almost all of Tyndale's controversal glosses and Rogers's 2,100 notes.[27]

Even before the publication of Taverner's Bible, work began on yet another version that Cromwell hoped would be a definitive one. The fact that several distinct and competing editions of the Bible had appeared since 1535 was worrisome to a generation that stressed authority in all matters. The king's chief minister was also concerned because much of the recent work seemed only loosely based on the original Greek and

Hebrew manuscripts. He therefore maintained that a single, authoritative text of the scriptures must be established. After securing a five-year monopoly over Bible publishing in England, Cromwell chose Miles Coverdale for this supremely important editorial task.

In his work of producing an improved Old Testament, Coverdale depended on Matthew's Bible as his main guide, but he also relied on a 1535 Latin version with a parallel Hebrew text by Sebastian Münster, an outstanding German Hebraist. For the New Testament Coverdale resorted to four different versions: Tyndale's revised translation of 1534, the Vulgate of St. Jerome, Erasmus's third Latin translation of 1522, and the important Spanish edition of that same year which was known as the Complutensian Polyglot. Although Coverdale hoped to include marginal glosses in the revision, Henry VIII would not permit them; so it was published without any accompanying apparatus, which was clearly for the best.[28]

Although Coverdale had completed his editorial tasks by September 1538, the first copies of the new version did not become available until the following April. This edition, which soon became known as the Great Bible, was destined to have no rival until the appearance of the ultra-Protestant Geneva Bible of 1560. Berthelet, the royal printer, suggested that the Great Bible be sold at the same high price as Matthew's Bible, but Cromwell had invested over £400 of his own money in the venture and refused to agree. The Great Bible was therefore offered at 12s. per copy in hardcover and at 10s. a volume in softcover. Although this was still a relatively high price—a month's wages for an artisan—the Great Bible was an immediate success and passed through seven different editions by the end of 1541. Each of these differed somewhat in typography and phrasing, although the basic text was of course the same.[29]

Altogether nearly 30,000 copies of the English Bible were printed in the four distinct versions of 1535-41. Most of these found ready buyers, but Cromwell nevertheless took steps to promote Bible-reading by the laity. As early as the summer of 1536, the chief minister decided to require every parish church in the kingdom to obtain at least one copy of the Bible, which should be available at all times to the laity. An injunction to that effect was printed but withheld at the last minute because of conservative opposition. However, in September 1538 the injunction of 1536 was revived and at last circulated in the king's name.

Meanwhile the government had instructed local officials not to prosecute anyone for reading or owning a vernacular Bible without explicit authorization. In addition, the justices of the peace of all the counties were commanded to see "that the clergy preached the word of God sincerely and truly, and that they suffered the people to have the English Bible."[30]

These government actions supplemented steps already taken by several prelates on their own initiative. Hugh Latimer of Worcester and Nicholas Shaxton of Salisbury both established precise dates by which their diocesan clergy must acquire individual copies of the Bible, of which they were to study a chapter or more each day. Bishop Shaxton also directed every parish church within his see to chain an English Bible at some convenient point in the nave, so that "literate parishoners might read, and illiterate ones hear 'wholesome doctrine and comfort to their souls.'" After a sharp rebuke from Cromwell for dragging his feet, Bishop Rowland Lee of Lichfield and Coventry took similar steps in June 1538. At that time Bishop Lee directed all the clerics of his diocese to spend more time in Bible study and to exhort their congregations to do the same.[31]

To the authorities' chagrin, the growth of Bible-reading among the laity led to disorders in several sections of the realm. Because the ceremonies of the church remained in Latin and were still conducted in the traditional way, those of advanced opinions developed contemptuous attitudes towards the regular order of worship. In dozens of parishes a dissatisfied minority persisted in reading aloud from the scriptures even after the main Sunday service began. This rude practice disturbed the proceedings and produced so much dissension in some congregations that the government became alarmed. Just as a new parliament opened in April 1539, Henry VIII issued a proclamation intended to promote uniformity and to "silence dispute and keep dissension in hand." Among other things, the king's proclamation ordered a halt to Bible-reading by the laity once a scheduled service began and especially during the celebration of mass. All subjects were commanded to "'use that time in reading or praying with peace and silence as good Christian men ought to do.'"[32]

The first sign of an impending reaction that sought to limit Bible-reading to a small minority, this proclamation did not succeed in maintaining decorum. Periodic disturbances continued, and an unseemly incident occurred at Gloucester in April 1541 when Humphrey Grynshill, a burly weaver, persisted in declaiming from the Bible during a Sunday mass. Moreover,

Grynshill angered others in the congregation by insisting that prayers for the dead were worthless, since there was no scriptural justification for them. The situation was much the same in other places. During the spring of 1541, according to William Malden of Chelmsford, Essex, "divers poor men . . . brought the New Testament of Jesus Christ, and on Sundays did sit reading it in [the] lower end of the Church, and many would flock about them to hear the reading."[33]

The difficulty of maintaining order caused Henry to fear that England was about to be convulsed by Anabaptist uprisings like those which had wracked the Low Countries during the previous decade. In desperation the government adopted a carefully devised dual policy in 1543. On the one hand it decreed that additional Bible-readings in English should be included in more of the daily services, such as matins and vespers. But on the other hand Henry persuaded parliament to pass a special act "for the advancement of true religion and the abolishment of the contrarie." This measure prohibited the use of any but the Great Bible of 1539-41 and specifically forbade all "crafty, false, and untrue translations" that were marred by glosses or annotations of any kind. In addition, it sought to keep unlicensed persons from reading or expounding the Bible to others, either during church services or at other public gatherings. The 1543 statute even sought to limit Bible-reading in private. Men and women of the lower classes were forbidden to read the scriptures in English under any circumstances. Women of higher birth might read the Bible to themselves but to no one else, not even their own children. Only nobles and gentlemen, merchants and lawyers, were permitted to read the scriptures aloud in the hearing of others, and then only to their families and household servants.[34]

The act of 1543 was no more successful than earlier measures in promoting the desired goal. Although driven underground, Bible-reading by the lower classes continued as widely as before; in a tearful speech to his last parliament in 1545, Henry VIII informed the members of his sorrow "to know and hear how irreverently that precious jewel [the Bible] is disputed, rhymed, sung, and jangled in every alehouse and tavern." On 8 July 1546 the king tried once again to recover control of the situation by issuing yet another proclamation. According to this new edict, all copies of the New Testament with glosses by Tyndale, Rogers, or any other writer were to be surrendered to the bishops or other responsible authorities by 31 August. In addition all other books by certain designated writers were to be handed over for public burning no later than 1 October. In the diocese of London and evidently most other sees, this proclamation was vigorously enforced. Although Bishop Bonner had recently taken steps to promote greater Bible study by his clergy, he gathered a large store of books together by the last week of September. On the 26th of that month they were destroyed in a great conflagration at Paul's Cross.[35]

The new situation was deplored by many, and especially by a humble shepherd of Gloucestershire named Robert Williams. On the title page of Langley's *Abridgement of Polydore Vergil,* which he had recently acquired, Williams wrote that, "I bout thys boke when the Testament was obberagatyde, that shepeyerdys myght not rede hit. I prey God amend that blyndness." Because of the restrictions now in force, the business of printing the Bible, which had been so profitable until 1541, came to a grinding halt. During the last years of Henry VIII's reign, only one edition of any part of the scriptures was published in England. This was the New Testament that was taken almost verbatim from the Great Bible and issued in 1546 by Edward Whitchurch.[36]

Once Henry VIII died in January 1547 and Edward VI became king, dedicated reformers gained control of both church and state. Led by Archbishop Cranmer and the duke of Somerset, the new regime revoked the ban on clerical marriage and called for a translation of all the ceremonies of the church, which soon led to the Prayer Books of 1549 and 1552. Moreover, it ended the repressive measures of the previous six years and took steps to promote Bible-reading by all social groups. The changed attitude became apparent as early as 20 February 1547, when a vernacular Bible was carried on a cushion just ahead of the new monarch during the coronation procession to Westminster Abbey. Further, royal injunctions issued on 31 July 1547 directed all the cathedrals of the realm to acquire four copies of the Great Bible for chaining in the choir and the nave, so that the scriptures would be readily available to anyone who wished to read them. These same injunctions ordered every parish church within the kingdom to procure an English Bible within three months and an English translation of Erasmus's paraphrases of the gospels within another nine months.[37]

Because of such clear Protestant policies, men and women who had gone into exile during previous years came back to England. The most important person who now returned from abroad was Miles Coverdale, who since 1542 had resided with his brother-in-law, John Macalpine, a divinity professor at Copenhagen. In March 1548 Coverdale reappeared at Westminster and was received with great favor, being named a royal chaplain soon afterward. In addition he was appointed to succeed the conservative bishop of Exeter, John Veysey, whose ouster was justified on the grounds of advanced age. These were clear signals that the publication of English-language Bibles could be resumed in safety. Between January 1547 and the king's death in July 1553, the whole Bible was reprinted fourteen times, while the New Testament alone appeared in thirty-five separate editions. Despite all these new printings, there was little effort to produce an updated version of the scriptures. A leading Greek scholar of the period, John Cheke of Cambridge, undertook a new translation of the gospels of Matthew and Mark, but his work remained in manuscript until the nineteenth century. Even the two Bibles Edmund Becke has printed in 1551 were nothing but composites of earlier versions that had been available for at least a decade.[38]

If Becke's two Bibles were unimportant for the development of biblical scholarship, the dedications they carried to Edward VI included words of undoubted significance. Becke maintained that if only his readers would spend an hour or more each day with the Bible, they would acquire the strength to conquer their greatest sins, including "pride, prodigality, riot, licentiousness and all kinds of dissolute living."[39] Clearly Becke's words did not fall on deaf ears, since many of the English people were inclined to make Bible-reading one of their principal daily activities. As early as 1531, Sir Thomas Elyot had emphasized the need for regular scriptural study, maintaining in his famous *Boke named the Governour* that:

> The proverbs of Salomon with the bokes of Ecclesiastes and Ecclesiasticus be very good lessons. All the historiall partes of the bible be righte necessarye for to be radde of a noble man, after that he is mature in yeres. And the residue (with the new testament) is to be reverently touched, as a celestiall jewel or relike. . . . [40]

During these years, John Hooper, who was simultaneously bishop of Worcester and Gloucester, evidently believed that the congregations to which he preached throughout the West Country were knowledgable about the scriptures. His sermons often contained precise biblical references that he expected his listeners to read and ponder at a later time.[41] The rapid spread of Bible-reading during Edward VI's reign helps to explain why Queen Mary, a zealous Catholic of the old school, was unable to root out the practice during the course of her reign.

Within sixteen months of her accession in 1553, Mary reestablished the ties with Rome that her father had severed during the 1530s and reinstated the ban on clerical marriage that had been revoked while her half-brother was on the throne. But Mary was powerless to bring a halt to Bible-reading by a majority of her subjects. To be sure, no new editions of the scriptures appeared in England while she was at the helm.* In addition, excerpts from the Bible were no longer read in the vernacular during Sunday worship services, and all English Bibles that had been acquired by cathedrals and parish churches were summarily destroyed. In 1554 Mary even prohibited the painting of scriptural quotations on church walls.

The queen's efforts to prevent Bible-reading by the laity were warmly applauded by Cardinal Pole, who arrived in England from the papal curia in November 1554. In his first speech to the people of London, Pole warned his listeners about the dangers of seeking to interpret the scriptures for themselves and admonished them " . . . not [to try to] be your own masters."[42] Yet an important synod that opened under the cardinal's leadership in December 1555 acknowledged that Bible-reading was so deeply entrenched in most places that it could not be rooted out altogether. Since that was the case, the synod could only attempt to weaken the effect of the earlier English Bibles, which had all been produced by committed Protestants. It therefore called for an authorized Catholic translation of the New Testament, although it expressed no sense of urgency about the matter. By the time a Catholic Bible finally appeared in 1583, most of the English people had decided irrevocably in favor of the Protestant form of Christianity. Because of this it seems obvious that the translation and publication of the scriptures by radical reformers during the 1520s and 1530s was one of the primary reasons for the ultimate triumph of Protestantism in England.

While helping to promote the eventual Protestant victory, the publication of the English Bible also led to greater awareness of

*An important New Testament was published at Geneva in 1557 by a group of religious exiles who were beyond the reach of Mary's government.

the need for more widespread education and literacy. Protestant leaders throughout Europe considered education an effective way to combat superstition and error, and in almost all Protestant households, especially those of England, this was actively encouraged through daily Bible-readings. An Elizabethan woman, Lady Grace Mildmay, reflected the common belief about the need for regular scriptural study when she advised her daughter Mary to read chapters of both Testaments " 'with all diligence and humility every day.' "[43] Largely because of this, a leading historian of the period has observed that, "Christianity is a religion of the book, namely the Scriptures, and once this book ceased to be a closely guarded secret fit only to be read by priests, it generated pressures for the creation of a literate society."[44] Whether Tyndale, Coverdale, and the many others sensed this to be the case seems doubtful, but such was nonetheless an extraordinarily important consequence of their determined labors.

6

Three Steps Forward, Two Steps Backward, 1529-1547

The decades that witnessed the production of England's first Protestant Bibles were a period of almost feverish educational activity. New grammar schools were founded at a steady rate, and important changes at the universities occurred as a consequence of Henry VIII's break from Rome. Large numbers of new scholarships and fellowships came into being, but the decline of the academic halls at Oxford and Cambridge, which was already well advanced by the 1520s, came to an irreversible conclusion. In addition, almost all the schools maintained by religious houses, as well as a few attached to chantries, were swept away. Worst of all, the monastic and nunnery libraries were widely dispersed and many valuable manuscripts lost; while the educational standards of the parish clergy, which had shown steady improvement for over a century, were seriously affected, owing to the frequent appointment of former monks to vacant benefices. All in all, the years 1529-47 should be seen as a period of mixed achievement, although the positive contributions outweighed the work of destruction.

Clerical donors gave almost as much assistance to new or existing institutions as their late medieval predecessors had done. During the last years of his life, William Warham, archbishop of Canterbury from 1503 until 1532, contributed large sums to the endowment of Winchester College. He additionally provided more than £2,000 to complete the construction of both the Oxford Divinity School and nearby St. Mary's Church. On his death in August 1532, Warham divided his valuable library between Winchester, New College, and All Souls. Two other educational benefactors among the prelates of the time were Charles Boothe of Hereford and Richard Nykke of Norwich. In 1532 Bishop Boothe bequeathed three houses in the capital to Pembroke Hall, Cambridge, while four years later Bishop Nykke left £400 to nearby Trinity Hall, to which he had earlier given a tract of 502 acres.

Although the lesser clergy did not become important educational patrons until slightly later, several rectors and archdeacons during the second half of Henry VIII's reign made contributions of undoubted significance. Probably the most outstanding of these was Roger Lupton (d. 1540), who held four different rectories and was simultaneously a canon of Windsor. By 1528 Lupton had established a grammar school at his birthplace of Sedbergh, Yorkshire, which he linked to St. John's College, Cambridge in two ways. First, he authorized the master of St. John's to appoint the schoolmaster at Sedbergh; second, he gave £600 towards the establishment of six scholarships at St. John's for the aid of promising graduates of the Sedbergh school. A few years later, probably in 1537, Lupton donated £400 more to St. John's for the establishment of two additional scholarships and two fellowships. During these same years Lupton was an equally generous benefactor of Eton, where he served as provost from 1504 until 1535. Because he expanded that school's facilities by erecting several new buildings at his own expense, it seems entirely fitting that his name is commemorated at Eton by Lupton's Chantry and Lupton's Tower.[1]

During the 1530s and 1540s, rich merchants were probably the most active founders of new grammar schools. Only the most important can be mentioned here. In his will of June 1532, William Ratcliffe, a London alderman and well-to-do merchant of the staple, left funds for the establishment of a grammar school at Stamford, Lincolnshire, which was probably his birthplace. Four years later a grocer of the capital, Nicholas Gibson, founded a free grammar school in his native village of Stepney, several miles east of London. Gibson paid for the construction of a schoolhouse and a residence of the master, and until his death in 1540, he underwrote all the expenses of the school, which soon had sixty boys enrolled. His widow Avice continued his support of the school and in 1552 settled lands worth £333 on it in perpetuity. In June 1542 another rich grocer, Thomas Chipsey of Northampton, granted several tracts of land for the town corporation to use in maintaining a free grammar school. During the next five years similar institutions were founded at such places as Findon, Walthamstow, Newcastle-upon-Tyne, and Tavistock, where in each case local merchants took the lead and provided most of the funds.

Nobles and gentlemen played a surprisingly small part in the expansion of educational institutions during this period. Aside from the earl of Bedford, who assisted the work of the two founders of the Tavistock school,[2] the only rich landowner who founded or otherwise aided a grammar school during Henry VIII's reign was the earl of Derby. As noted in chapter 3, Lord Derby endowed an existing school at Blackburn, Cheshire, in 1514.

That so few aristocrats assisted the schools of the early Tudor period is especially curious in view of the high regard now felt for education at court. During the course of his twenty-four-year-reign, Henry VII had generally turned to scholarly bishops and lawyers to staff the central government, while during the decades after 1509, Henry VIII relied almost as heavily on capable young men with formal training in the New Learning. One of those young men, Richard Pace, rose to become Henry VIII's private secretary, and in a letter of 1517 Pace declared that learned men of humble status now had better chances for advancement than ignorant individuals of noble background.[3]

A few unredeemed aristocrats resented the growing stress on education as a prerequisite for high office. During the course of an entertainment in 1515, an irate gentleman garbed in hunting clothes made a violent retort to those who had just expressed unqualified praise for higher education. Indeed, this confirmed rustic declared that university studies would lead only to poverty in the end, after which he angrily maintained, "By the body of God, I would sooner see my son hanged than a bookworm. It is a gentleman's calling to be able to blow the horn, [and] to hunt and hawk. He should leave learning to clodhoppers."[4] Such views were typical of a dwindling minority, however, and within another generation almost all aristocrats came to see that formal education was no longer an optional matter, as it had been during earlier centuries. Because of Henry VIII's practice of employing qualified men in high office without regard to social background, the upper classes bowed to the unhappy realization that their sons must prepare themselves for important government posts by attending a university, an Inn of Court, or both.

It would be wrong to suggest that Henry VIII was a social egalitarian who rejected the concepts of hierarchy and degree that his age held dear. Nevertheless he had an abiding interest in all his subjects, regardless of class, and he saw no reason to deprive himself of the services of able men who happened to be humbly born. As a consequence his government enjoyed a broader social base than that of any other English regime before the 1650s. Ministers like Thomas Wolsey, a butcher's son, and Thomas Cromwell, whose father had worked as both a tanner and a blacksmith, were typical of those who rose to high office and considerable wealth because of extraordinary abilities. Others who might be compared with them include Sir John Mason, Sir Thomas Audley, Sir Thomas Pope, and Sir Nicholas Bacon, whose fathers had all supported themselves as yeoman farmers or even as humble sheepreeves and cowherds. Henry VIII's practice of employing well-educated men without consideration of social background was especially evident during the 1530s, while Cromwell was his chief minister. Indeed, during Cromwell's term of office, "the principle of ignoring rank . . . became known policy," and poor scholars regarded him as a special friend whom they often solicited for government appointments.[5] The regime's willingness to employ humble but learned men drove home the point that England's bluebloods were now expected to acquire advanced education as a way of equipping themselves for service to the state. Not even the greatest aristocrats had an inherent right to high office. In this way a conscious government policy added momentum to the educational advances that had begun well over a century earlier.

Although Henry VIII's indirect encouragement of education was apparent from the time of Richard Pace's 1517 declaration, he did not give direct help to the educational advances of the period until the 1530s. Admittedly, he supported a few students at Oxford and Cambridge during earlier years, and he also assisted several scholars, including John Mason and Reginald Pole, who matriculated at continental universities between 1518 and 1525.[6] But it was not until he went to the aid of Wolsey's great academic society, Cardinal College, that he emerged as a leading educational patron.

During the early 1520s, Henry's chief minister for nearly a decade, Thomas, Cardinal Wolsey, had conceived a bold and grandiose plan. The great cardinal, who was also Lord Chancellor, an archbishop, and a papal legate for life, decided to establish an Oxford college that would eclipse every other foundation at either university as well as a network of fifteen feeder schools throughout the countryside, which would send their best graduates on to the new Oxford society for advanced work. This visionary scheme led to the establishment of Cardinal College in 1525 for the support of whose 176 members Wolsey suppressed the large Oxfordshire priory of St. Frideswide's along with twenty smaller abbeys around the kingdom. Altogether these 21 religious houses had collective revenues of nearly £1,830 a year, or considerably more than what any existing college enjoyed at the time.[7] When Wolsey attempted to establish the first of his projected feeder schools, he encountered stiff opposition. The people of Tonbridge Wells, Kent, objected strenuously to the suppression of the local priory, even though a new school became possible thereby. Obviously annoyed by this unexpected criticism of his actions, Wolsey gave up his plan to found a permanently endowed school in that small town. However, in 1528 he did succeed in establishing a grammar school in his birthplace of Ipswich. The statutes of that institution called for seventy members to belong to the foundation. For their maintenance the cardinal intended to settle revenues of £600 a year on the school.[8]

After Wolsey's fall from power in 1529 and his subsequent trial in the King's Bench, his two educational institutions came into jeopardy since he had failed to take all the necessary steps to convey the intended endowments to the societies themselves. Thus their revenues still legally belonged to Wolsey and, like all his other wealth, were subject to royal confiscation. Because of impassioned pleas from several quarters, Henry was at first inclined to spare the Oxford foundation. But within a short time his mercenary instincts prevailed, and in 1530 he suppressed it along with the Ipswich school and began to parcel out the lands reserved for the two institutions. Those intended for the Ipswich school, which included six manors in Norfolk, were granted to the master and fellows of Christ's College, Cambridge, as a way of making amends for estates withheld from that institution two decades earlier.[9] As for Cardinal College, its intended endowment was distributed more widely. In 1531 Lady Lucy Clifford received the manor of Sandewell, while the advowson of Ellesborough Church was assigned to the Charterhouse at Sheen. Another segment of the property was used to increase the revenues of St. George's Chapel, Windsor.

Ultimately the king doubted the wisdom of allowing such a potentially useful college to vanish. Moreover, he was probably encouraged to reconsider his actions by Stephen Gardiner, who had been his private secretary since 1528 and would be appointed bishop of Winchester in 1531. Another strong advocate of Cardinal College was Thomas Cromwell, who had been Wolsey's main assistant during the 1520s and was sworn of the council during the winter of 1530–31. Cromwell was particularly concerned to improve the quality of the civil service and believed that a reestablished Cardinal College might serve as a nursery for royal officials.

At any rate, Henry soon decided to reserve all that remained of Wolsey's foundation for the support of a society that would look to him for patronage, and he named Cromwell to handle all the legal details, including the settlement of conflicting claims, the transfer of property, and the preparation of a new charter. On 18 July 1532, letters patent for the new society were issued. It was now to be known as King Henry VIII's College in the University of Oxford and consisted of twelve canons, eight priests, and a variety of choristers and students. John Higden, the sole dean of Wolsey's society, was appointed to lead the new foundation, but since he died within a few months, Dr. Richard Oliver succeeded to the post. Among the original canons of the new college were such distinguished scholars as Richard Croke and Robert Wakefield, who had previously had brilliant careers at St. John's College, Cambridge. Another early member of the society was John Leland, probably England's greatest antiquary before the time of John Stow.

Despite its relatively small size, the new society had insufficient revenues since Henry settled lands worth less than £670 a year on it. As a consequence the dean and canons sent periodic appeals to the king and his minister for assistance. On 24 January they addressed the following plea to Cromwell:

> Last year we supplicated the King to pity our destitution, but were not a little discouraged because you were absent. However, the King granted us to be of his yearly exhibition, until he could provide better for us. It is now half a

year ago, and we are therefore compelled to sue for it. The sum is £28 7s. 2d.[10]

Less than a month later the dean and canons called their plight to Cromwell's attention again: "We have not received our stipends. We beg you to mediate with the King . . . and to have us in remembrance for the establishment of his college."[11]

Before Cromwell could solve the college's financial problems, his attention was diverted by other matters. The year 1534 was in many ways the most important of that critical decade. A revolt in Ireland, triggered by false reports of the earl of Kildare's execution in London, prompted fears that enormous military expenditures were about to be required. Moreover, because of the king's lavish building projects at Hampton Court, Whitehall, and St. James's Palace, additional sources of revenue had to be found. Within a short time the decision was taken to survey all the lands of the church, which might be divested of much of its wealth as a way of raising the necessary funds. This decision led to the gigantic enquiry known as the *Valor Ecclesiasticus,* which was the prelude to the dissolution of the smaller religious houses and a series of unequal land transfers between the crown on the one hand and the bishops and archbishops on the other. Also in 1534, the break between England and Rome, which had begun with several tentative measures passed earlier, was finalized by a series of legislative enactments drafted almost exclusively by Cromwell. These included the Act of Succession, the Definitive Act against Annates, and the Act of Supremacy, by which parliament recognized the king as Supreme Head of the Church of England.

The creation of an independent state church without ties of any sort to Rome led to significant changes at both universities. Cromwell, who had become a convert to evangelical views by this juncture, did not want remnants of papalism to survive in any guise at Oxford or Cambridge. This was likely to happen if the study of canon law, for which the universities had long been famous, continued unabated. In 1535 he therefore persuaded Henry to issue injunctions forbidding the further teaching of that subject, in which no more degrees should be awarded. With this action the profession of canon lawyer was abolished, along with an important field of higher study.[12]

The 1535 ban on the study of canon law not only extinguished a profession and a traditional academic field, but put a final stamp on the decline of the unendowed halls, many of which had stressed legist studies. Yet it is wrong to hold, as a distinguished historian does,[13] that the prohibition was directly responsible for the disappearance of the halls, which had actually began to decay much earlier. During the mid-fifteenth century, there had been approximately fifty halls at Oxford; by 1501 there were only about thirty. Additional halls vanished during the next few years, so that by 1514 only a dozen or so remained at the older university. The same process occurred at Cambridge during those decades, with the seventeen or so halls of the 1450s all disappearing by the eve of the Reformation, their properties passing to nearby colleges that wished to expand. Thus the 1535 prohibition against the further study of canon law cannot be blamed for the decline of the halls, which faced an uncertain future as soon as the permanently endowed colleges began to admit large numbers of undergraduates.

Just as Cromwell hoped to weaken papalism by forbidding the study of canon law, he sought to achieve that goal by another injunction sent in October 1535 to Cambridge, of which he had recently become chancellor. According to this new injunction, all divinity lecturers were henceforth to limit themselves to the Bible itself, giving no attention to "the frivolous questions and obscure glosses of [John Duns] Scotus." In addition, no scholar was to study or discuss the various commentaries on Peter Lombard's works, while all undergraduates were now free to read the Bible in the privacy of their own rooms.[14] In order to ensure compliance with this injunction, Cromwell sent commissioners to both universities in 1535 with directions to destroy as many works of scholastic theology as possible. In a famous letter addressed to the chief minister before the end of the year, one of the commissioners wrote jubilantly:

> We have sett Dunce [*i.e.,* Duns Scotus] in Bocardo [an ancient jail], and have utterly banissheded hym Oxforde for ever, with all his blinde glosses ... And the second tyme we came to New Colege affter we had declarede your injunctions, we fownde all the great quadrant court full of the leiffes of Dunce, the wynde blowing them into everie corner.[15]

The destruction of books and manuscripts was not as great as this letter suggests, however. College libraries of that era usually possessed two categories of works: rare and valuable tracts that were kept in the non-circulating collections, like costly reference works in a modern library, and cheap copies for student use, which were usually lent out each November. It was books in the second category that were destroyed in record numbers during the autumn of 1535. As a consequence many Oxford and Cambridge colleges still possess many of their original scholastic tracts.[16]

In 1535 Cromwell took additional steps to regulate academic conditions at the universities. He decreed that each college should sponsor daily lectures in both Greek and Latin, while in another injunction he stipulated that all university graduates must formally renounce the authority of the bishop of Rome. In yet another directive, he instructed the richer clerics of the realm to support a poor undergraduate or a grammar-school student for each £100 of yearly income.[17] A parliamentary act of 1536 that shows Cromwell's influence decreed that all holders of benefices who had reached their fortieth year and were still in residence at either university must depart immediately in order to discharge their parochial duties. Younger men who remained were to be regular in their attendance at the new daily lectures and were to participate frequently in disputations and other scholarly exercises. They were definitely not to spend their time in idle amusements, as many were alleged to have done in the past.[18]

While helping to regulate the universities' affairs, Cromwell was overseeing the suppression of the religious houses, more than 835 in all. The smaller houses were dissolved under the terms of a parliamentary act of 1536, which called for the suppression of all abbeys and priories with fewer than twelve inmates or revenues of less than £200 a year, whereas the larger convents survived only until the passage of a similar measure in 1539. Just how much additional wealth accrued to the crown as a result of the Dissolution is impossible to determine. According to a government report of 1539, the religious houses had gross revenues of more than £152,500 a year.[19] However, some scholars believe that figure to be much too low. Professor David Knowles, who studied the Dissolution in detail, maintained that all the religious houses together had gross revenues of approximately £200,000 during the early 1530s.[20] In addition to the seizure of vast amounts of landed wealth, perhaps four times as valuable as the entire royal demesne, the crown enjoyed an immense windfall in the form of gold and silver crucifixes, candlesticks, vestments, and the like. For example, more than 9,500 ounces of gold and silver items were surrendered by the abbey of Bury St. Edmunds alone. The actual worth of all those valuables is beyond calculation, although Christopher Hill once declared that goods with a market value of between £1.0 and £1.5 million were obtained from the religious houses.[21]

While an immense boon for the crown, the suppression of the religious houses was a staggering blow to education for obvious reasons. As late as the mid-1530s, approximately 175 monasteries and nunneries were still engaged in some kind of educational work, and nearly all their schools disappeared at a stroke with the dissolution. Indeed, *all* the nunnery schools collapsed except for the one associated with Polesworth Abbey, Warwickshire. That school was kept in being by the prominent Goodere family from 1539 until they bestowed a permanent landed endowment on it in 1573.[22] As a consequence, the education of young women suffered a devastating blow from which it took generations to recover, this being the single most harmful effect of the Dissolution.

As for the schools previously kept by monasteries, most of them also disappeared, although many alternative institutions for male education remained. In addition more than a few monastic schools were soon reestablished in altered form, albeit almost invariably for boys alone. On the suppression of Bedford Abbey, for instance, its ancient school for boys was handed over to the mayor and burgesses of the nearby town. Thus its operations were not disrupted, although it did not receive a permanent landed endowment until 1552. At Sherborne the inhabitants banded together in less than a year and arranged to buy the former monastic school at their own expense; while shortly after the suppression of Evesham Abbey, the king himself took steps to reestablish the former school and allocated £10 a year "for a master to instruct the children of the Town in *Latin*." At such additional places as Bruton, Reading, Chichester, and St. Albans, the former monastic schools also sprang back to life within a brief time.

Not only did numerous monastic schools quickly reappear, but in most cases they were stronger institutions in their reestablished form. At Abingdon, for instance, a somewhat longer period elapsed between the suppression of the local abbey and the reappearance of its ancient school. Not until 1563 did a local man, John Roysse, who had prospered as a mercer in the capital, resurrect the school in a building 63 feet long, for 63 boys, during the course of his 63rd year. Roysse not only erected the school building at his own expense, but also contributed valuable lands to its endowment. A. J. Fletcher therefore contends that the reestablished school at Abingdon "was vastly superior to the school connected with the monastery that it replaced."[23] Thus it is probably true that the Dissolution was a blessing in disguise for the education of boys. Local energies were unleashed by the sudden realization that schools long taken for granted might disappear altogether, and in most instances barely adequate institutions gave way to better-funded and directed ones. However, if the Dissolution was much less harmful to male education than it might have been, it dealt a serious blow to the cause of female instruction.

Just as male and female education were affected unequally by the Dissolution, so were the fortunes of the universities. At Cambridge the number of student monks and friars had always been comparatively small. Indeed, the surrender instruments that accompanied the suppression of the Dominican and Franciscan friaries in 1538 bore only four signatures in all. Moreover, there seem to have been but four Augustinians and two Carmelites in residence at the eastern university during the years 1535–39.[24] How many Benedictine monks were enrolled at Buckingham College is a thorny question for which there is no documentary evidence, although there were probably less than thirty. At Gonville Hall and the various other secular colleges that provided lodging for members of the regular clergy, perhaps a dozen or so monks were in residence. All in all, there were probably not more than 70 or 80 students of that sort at Cambridge on the eve of the Dissolution, so their sudden disappearance from the scene was not particularly harmful to the university's size or prosperity.

At late medieval Oxford, the monkish element had always between more than twice as large, and as the Dissolution entered its final phase in 1539, the university authorities complained to Cromwell that student numbers had declined by 50 percent.[25] This was clearly an exaggeration, but the four friaries operated by mendicant orders all vanished from the Oxford scene by the end of that year. In addition, the sole Cistercian college, St. Bernard's, collapsed, as did one of the three societies established and supported by the Benedictines—Gloucester College. The other two Benedictine establishments, Canterbury Hall and Durham College, did not formally surrender to the crown until 1545, although they evidently ceased to operate during the winter of 1539-40. As a result of the sudden disappearance of perhaps 200 monks and friars in all, considerable turmoil developed at the older university that was destined to last until the mid 1550s.

In the long run, however, the disappearance of the regular clergy proved an unexpected fillip for the universities. Many wealthy families had long been hesitant to send their eldest sons to study there, lest they be persuaded to take holy orders or induced to join a monastic or mendicant order. With the new state of affairs, that traditional apprehension weakened, and in subsequent years boys from landed families with such concerns arrived at Oxford and Cambridge in a growing stream. During the late 1540s, a leading Cambridge scholar, Roger Ascham, complained about the presence "of wealthy undergraduates in excessive numbers." In a sermon preached at court in April 1549, Hugh Latimer made a similar point, declaring that " 'There be none now but great men's sons in colleges and their fathers look not to have them preachers.' "[26] If more and more wealthy boys arrived to study for a time, some families retained the old fear that their offspring might choose to take holy orders and insisted that they go elsewhere to attain the training that was now considered essential. This helps to explain the remarkable growth experienced by the Inns of Court during the Elizabethan period.

The disappearance of the student monks and friars also aided the universities by enabling new or existing societies to adapt for their own ends medieval buildings that had recently fallen vacant. For example, during the early 1540s Lord Chancellor Audley, whose income had soared as a result of the estates he acquired from suppressed religious houses, decided to found a new college at Cambridge, which he had briefly attended as a young man. Known as the College of St. Mary Magdalene, this college was formally established in 1542 and received lands worth only £43 7s. 5d. a year from its founder. This was an unusually small endowment for a new society, and consequently its early existence was precarious. But Lord Audley did persuade Henry VIII to aid the foundation by granting it the site and buildings of Buckingham College, which had collapsed when its parent body, Croyland Abbey, surrendered to the crown.[27] In a similar way, the vacant Dominican and Franciscan friaries at Cambridge were eventually acquired by secular colleges established during Queen Elizabeth's reign, while at Oxford the facilities of the three Benedictine societies and also of the single Cistercian institution, St. Bernard's College, were used for similar purposes, and in earlier years, as we shall soon see.

A number of existing university societies also benefited from the Dissolution in a somewhat less direct way. More than half the religious houses had controlled one or more presentations to church livings, and once the Dissolution ended, those rights of advowson passed to the new owners of monastic estates. In some instances individual Oxford and Cambridge colleges purchased advowsons directly from the crown for nominal sums. In 1541 or 1542, Clare Hall, Cambridge, elected to do so when it bought the rectory of Everton for £144.[28] Occasionally Henry VIII granted advowsons free of charge to specially favored colleges. During the early 1540s, he gave two such rights of presentation to The King's Hall, Cambridge, which he wished to help. When in 1546 he founded Trinity College, Cambridge, he conferred *forty* such appointments on it, almost all of which the crown had acquired from dissolved religious houses.[29] In most instances rich laymen who obtained valuable patronage over the church preferred to keep it securely for themselves. But in a few cases new owners were motivated by religious or other considerations to bestow advowsons on new or existing colleges. One prominent individual who chose that course was Henry Hastings, third earl of Huntingdon. In 1586 Earl Henry made "a generous grant of livings" to Emmanuel College, Cambridge, which had been established two years earlier by his friend Sir Walter Mildmay in buildings once owned and occupied by the Dominican friars.[30]

Although the Dissolution was not a complete disaster for education, it was virtually that for the books and manuscripts that had existed in many abbey libraries. On the eve of the Dissolution, Henry VIII had foreseen how the monastic collections might suffer irreparable damage and had deputized John Leland to survey their holdings, with an eye to transferring the rarer and more valuable items to the royal libraries at Greenwich, Westminster, and Hampton Court. Leland, an outstanding antiquary as well as a canon of Henry's Oxford college, did his work thoroughly, and once the Dissolution began, the three royal libraries enjoyed a steady stream of acquisitions. Within a few years they increased from several hundred volumes to almost 1,000, while by the end of the reign they grew to approximately 1,450. In addition, the king arranged for tracts from the Carmelite friary in London to be delivered to Richard Morison, an able diplomat and publicist in the crown's service.[31]

Although Henry salvaged well over 1000 books and manuscripts from the monastic shipwreck, incomparably more vanished without a trace. Among the most important collections that disappeared were those at Robertsbridge Priory in Kent, where only one book among several hundred is known to have survived, and at the Augustinian friary in York, from which only 6 items out of nearly 650 have been traced. All the chapters of Trinitarian friars suffered heavy losses, as did most of the monasteries of the Cluniac, Gilbertine, and Premonstratensian orders. At Malmesbury Abbey the destruction was so great that the loose pages of discarded books are said to have "fluttered like butterflies through the streets of the town." According to John Bale, an ex-Carmelite friar of Norwich who deplored this development, the new owners of monastic estates used whatever books and manuscripts they found in deserted libraries "to scour their candlesticks, and . . . to rub their boots." Others who suddenly acquired large numbers of unappreciated items disposed of them as profitably as they could, selling them to tradesmen for wrapping paper or sending them overseas to foreign buyers. The irate Bale even held that the callous treatment of so many important collections had caused the English to become known throughout western Europe as "despisers of learning."[32]

Although a major tragedy obviously occurred, some historians have begun to question whether the destruction was quite as great as generally believed. Mr. Neil Ker, for instance, writes that, "We have about five hundred manuscripts from Durham . . . [and] about three hundred [each] from Christ Church, Canterbury and St. Augustine's." In addition some 130 identifiable manuscripts survive from the cathedral priory at Rochester, approximately 100 each from eight other monastic collections, and 10 to 70 from each of fifty lesser libraries.[33] The traditional view holds that at least 95 percent of all books and manuscripts disappeared at the time of the Dissolution. But because Mr. Ker has traced nearly 4500 such works, it now appears that the destruction was closer to 80 or 85 percent.

That a considerable number of items survived was owing to the efforts of several dedicated individuals who undertook the work of salvage. Archbishop Cranmer acquired at least 49 volumes, while two of his successors on the throne of St. Augustine, Matthew Parker (1559-75) and John Whitgift (1583-1604), obtained even more. Parker's outstanding holdings passed mainly to Corpus Christi College, Cambridge, whereas Whitgift reserved his books for a new library at Lambeth Palace.[34]

If several prelates were active in this regard, a number of laymen made an equally significant contribution. One such layman was Sir John Prise, a lawyer who assisted in the suppression of the religious houses. Married to one of Cromwell's nieces, Prise had serious antiquarian interests and preserved a number of chronicles, charters, and similar works that had belonged to Cirencester Abbey, St. Guthlac's Priory, and the monastery of Bury St. Edmunds. On Prise's death in 1555, his holdings passed to the library of Hereford Cathedral, from which many of his books were later conveyed to Jesus College, Oxford.[35] A more important collector than Prise was Henry, Lord Stafford (1501–63), who lived in the west midlands but had close ties with London booksellers. By 1556 Lord Stafford had a diverse collection of approximately 300 books, most of which came from the religious houses.[36] Probably the most discriminating collector of the period was Thomas Allen, who became principal of Gloucester Hall, Oxford, in 1577. Although Allen donated twenty choice manuscripts to the new Bodleian Library in 1598, he still owned more than 250 when he died in 1632. Of those 250, almost a third have been traced to monastic houses, including Witham, Tavistock, Canterbury, and Battle. Allen is known to have purchased a substantial number of manuscripts from Gerbrand Harkes, an Oxford stationer who traded in such items over a long period.[37]

That Henry VIII left so much to private initiative and did comparatively little to use the abbeys' resources for social and educational betterment has long been accounted a major tragedy of English history. Various suggestions were naturally made from the time the Dissolution was perceived as eminent. Leland, and John Dee during the 1550s, dreamed of a national repository where many of the works that ultimately disappeared might have been preserved, whereas Thomas Starkey, a scholar and publicist with close ties to Cromwell, hoped to see St. Albans or some other large monastery converted into a boarding school for aristocratic boys. In 1538 the bishop of Worcester, Hugh Latimer, petitioned unsuccessfully for the lands of a large western friary, which he desired to use to endow a school at Worcester. Archbishop Cranmer's plan to convert one of the Canterbury monasteries into a college was also disappointed.

The Cambridge authorities were especially anxious to profit

from the Dissolution and in 1538 beseeched the king to "give the University one of the dissolved monasteries, and found a college as an eternal monument of his fame." When this plea was ignored, the Cambridge officials wrote again to Henry on 12 October 1538. After recalling his many past favors, they declared their fervent desire "that the monasteries formerly given over to superstititon . . . may henceforth be made colleges to promote good letters and the true doctrine of Christ." Largely because of this second letter, which was soon followed by an appeal from Queens' College, the monarch allowed the possessions of the Carmelite friary at Cambridge to be added to the endowment of Queens'.[38]

Henry ignored nearly all such pleas because he was in no position to divert resources from the naval and military programs he had initiated in 1538. During that year, England's international position suddenly became precarious when the pope issued a bull of deposition and urged the English people to rise up and overthrow their king. In addition, the pope helped negotiate the Truce of Nice, by which the king of France and the Holy Roman Emperor accepted a cease-fire in Italy and agreed to support a joint campaign against heresy everywhere, including England. To make matters worse, James V of Scotland concluded a dynastic pact with France in 1538 and took as his second wife Mary of Guise. Thus the Franco-Scottish alliance of past centuries became stronger than ever, and it briefly looked as if Henry might be attacked by three hostile powers encouraged to such action by the papacy.

Given the dangerous situation that had materialized, Henry had little choice but to use much of the new monastic wealth to enlarge the navy, which grew from twenty-four to fifty-one ships within a short time. In addition, he felt the need to upgrade England's coastal defenses, and to that end he employed a number of German artisans and engineers along the Channel coast. Because of such expensive undertakings, many of the ex-monastic lands had to be sold quickly, at less than their real value, and a never-to-reoccur opportunity for educational and cultural projects failed to be exploited as effectively as it should have been.

Nevertheless, Henry accomplished several worthwhile goals during his final years, and none more important than the establishment of six new bishoprics. During the late Middle Ages England had only seventeen episcopal sees, whereas the little Mediterranean island of Sardinia had eighteen and the Italian mainland

266! The number of English bishoprics was thus absurdly small, and many prelates were responsible for dioceses too large to be administered effectively. Complaints about non-residence were often heard, since the bishoprics' great size promoted absentee-ism on the part of their incumbents. Clearly, then, additional sees were badly needed, and before his fall in 1529 Cardinal Wolsey had proposed the establishment of thirteen new ones. Once the Dissolution occurred and the crown obtained vast new estates, Henry hoped to create eighteen additional dioceses, and in 1539 he obtained parliamentary approval for such an undertaking. Altogether he intended to earmark lands worth £18,000 for the support of the new bishops and their cathedral chapters. But this project proved too ambitious in practice, and it was implemented only partially. By the mid 1540s Henry had established six of the planned sees—at Bristol, Gloucester, Chester, Oxford, Westminster, and Peterborough. Even if Henry's full goal was not achieved, its partial realization still marked a worthwhile advance for the religious life of many of his subjects.

At the same time he founded his six new bishoprics, Henry made several other religious arrangements of consequence. He converted a number of dissolved abbeys, including Beverley, Manchester, and Ripon, into collegiate churches, and at the seven former monastic cathedrals,* he replaced the previous monastic chapters with colleges of secular canons. Linked with those of the six new bishoprics as "cathedrals of the new foundation," all the former monastic cathedrals benefited from the establishment or reestablishment of an associated grammar school.[39] For example, at Durham Cathedral Priory before the Dissolution there had been a monastic school consisting of a master, an usher, and eighteen scholarship students, all main-tained by the priory. When Henry created a college of secular canons at Durham in 1541, he resurrected the school that had disappeared along with the priory, although he did not issue statues for the school until a few years later.[40] Perhaps the most important school Henry reestablished in this way was the one attached to Canterbury Cathedral, which accepted its first stu-dents in 1542. It soon became known as "The King's School" and consisted of a master, an usher, and over fifty students.[41]

As for the six new bishoprics, Henry attached schools to all their cathedrals with the exception of the one at Oxford, where

*Durham, Norwich, Ely, Carlisle, Canterbury, Rochester, and Coventry.

there was no need for another grammar school. Issued in 1544, the statutes for the school established in conjunction with Chester Cathedral are typical of the arrangements that prevailed in many schools that date from this period. The Chester statutes stipulated that the master should receive a yearly stipend of £16 13s. 4d. and the usher, £8 annually. The two men were to teach Latin grammar to twenty-four "poor and friendless boys" between the ages of nine and fifteen, who would receive individual payments of £3 6s. 8d. per year. In addition the master and usher were to provide instruction in Greek, although a suitable Greek textbook did not become available until 1575. Eighteen choristers of the cathedral would be permitted to attend classes at the school, their musical training being left to another master, however. The teachers and pupils were all to be nominated by the dean and chapter of the cathedral; and at midday they would dine together in the refectory, a special allowance for that purpose being provided.[42]

Henry also contributed to the establishment of numerous other schools, nearly two dozen in all. In 1539 he reendowed the old abbey school at Carlisle, and two years later he authorized the bishop of St. David's to convert a portion of the endowment of Abergwili College into a source of support for a new grammar school at Brecon. In 1542 the king established a school in Lincolnshire to replace the institution that had vanished at the same time as Thornton Priory. In July 1543 he issued letters patent for a free grammar school at Abergavenny, Monmouthshire, to which he granted the tithes of six rectories that had once belonged to two different monasteries. Two years later he sold lands in Coventry at a bargain price to John Hales, a local merchant, who pledged to use the properties in question to endow a free grammar school that would be known as "King Henry VIII's School."

During these years Henry was just as concerned about the universities, where conditions were so confused that teaching and learning suffered serious hardships and the number of degrees awarded each year declined precipitately. In addition, proposals for further and more drastic reform emanated from several quarters, causing even greater apprehension for the future. In January 1537 John Parkyns suggested to Cromwell that all the colleges at the universities should be radically reorganized, with their affairs entrusted to laymen and not to men of the cloth. Parkyns also contended that the number of civil and canon lawyers in each of the colleges, but especially at New College, Oxford, should be substantially reduced.[43]

Partly to allay the alarm generated by such proposals, Henry decided in 1540 to establish ten praelectorships, or professorships, at the universities. Equally divided between Oxford and Cambridge, these new positions were also founded in part because, for the last five years, the universities had been obligated to support a number of public lecturers, and the universities, in sharp contrast to their component colleges, had almost no means to pay the stipends of those highly visible academicians. New professorships with stipends supplied from a different source would relieve the universities of that heavy burden. It is also possible, as Professor Kearney contends, that Henry established the praelectorships as a way of controlling appointments "in sensitive academic areas."[44]

Thus Henry probably hoped to realize several goals at a stroke when he founded endowed professorships in Greek, Hebrew, and the three traditional fields of higher study—divinity, law, and medicine. The holders of these prestigious appointments soon became known as Regius professors, and they received large stipends of £40 each, which were to be paid out of the recurring revenues of the bishopric of Westminster. At Oxford, scholars of no particular distinction were named to the new professorships. For example, the first holder of the divinity chair was Richard Smith of St. Alban's Hall, an old-fashioned theologian who in 1546 published *A Defence of the Sacrifice of the Mass*. At Cambridge the story was somewhat different. To be sure, two of the original Cambridge professors, Eudo Wigan and John Blythe, were men of few accomplishments. But the other three were outstanding young scholars who made notable contributions in their respective fields. The chair of Hebrew went to Thomas Wakefield, one of the first Englishmen to develop a real mastery of that subject, while the chair of Greek was conferred on the equally capable John Cheke of St. John's College. As the first Regius professor of civil law, the king appointed the brilliant Thomas Smith, who might as easily have been named to the Greek chair. Because his legal knowledge was not what he felt it ought to be, Smith prepared himself for his teaching duties by traveling abroad and attending lectures at Paris, Orléans, and Padua for over a year. Then he returned to Cambridge and lectured enthusiastically about the work of contemporary law reformers on the continent.[45]

Shortly after the establishment of the Regius professorships, the cathedral chapter at Westminster petitioned to be relieved of the responsibility of providing the yearly stipends of the new professors. The king agreed but insisted that the cathedral chapter surrender lands worth £400 annually to the crown in return. Once this financial transaction occurred, Henry had to make new arrangements for the support of the ten positions, which he soon decided to link to permanent foundations at either university. This in turn caused him to embark on the most ambitious of all his educational undertakings — the refoundation of his 1532 Oxford society on a much grander scale and the establishment of an equally impressive college at Cambridge.[46]

As noted early in this chapter, King Henry VIII's College in the University of Oxford had been poorly endowed by the crown, and as a consequence it never played a meaningful part in the life of the university. By 1545 Henry had concluded not only that the college ought to be strengthened and made the permanent home of the Oxford Regius professors, but that it should also be united with the new bishopric of Oxford, which was currently operating out of buildings once owned by Oseney Abbey. On 20 May 1545, an important dual event occurred when the dean of the college, Richard Oliver, surrendered all its estates to the crown and the bishop, Robert King, did likewise in regard to the properties of the see. A short while later the dean of Canterbury, Nicholas Wotton, renounced whatever claims his chapter still had on the lands and buildings of the long-vacant Canterbury Hall, which Henry intended to use for the new society. Once these three surrenders occurred, the king proceeded to reconstitute the college, which was simultaneously merged with the bishopric. This unique hybrid body, created by letters patent of 4 November 1546, was centered on the former monastery of St. Frideswide's and was officially named The College and Cathedral of Christ Church.[47]

Henry died in January 1547, before issuing statutes to regulate the affairs of Christ Church. But in December 1546 he made detailed arrangements for the foundation and created an extensive endowment for its support. In all he conveyed lands worth £2,200 annually to the society, including all that remained of Canterbury Hall and St. Bernard's College, a portion of the grove of Durham College, and the sites and buildings of the three abbeys of Oseney, Rewley, and St. Frideswide's. Even if £1000 of those revenues had to go each year for the bishopric's needs, the new society was still richer than any existing foundation at either university. King's College, Cambridge had yearly revenues of just over £1,000 at that time, but no Oxford society enjoyed a comparable income. In fact, only five Oxford colleges received more than £200 annually from their lands, while such societies as Balliol, University, and Exeter drew less than £100 a year from their estates. Thus the exceptionally generous arrangements Henry made for Christ Church fully justify Professor Kearney's description of it as "an academic palace . . . intended to dominate the university without precedent."[48]

In his letters patent of November 1546, Henry appointed Dr. Richard Cox, provost of Eton and chief tutor to Prince Edward, to be the first dean of Christ Church, in both a diocesan and a collegiate capacity. He additionally nominated the college's original eight canons, five of whom had previously been attached either to the cathedral at Oseney or to King Henry VIII's College. Thereafter the foundation expanded rapidly, having ninety students enrolled by January 1548 and more than 130 resident members by 1552, when only Magdalen exceeded it in size at Oxford.[49]

The last of Henry's many educational contributions occurred during the autumn of 1546, when he established an even grander academic society at Cambridge. Probably he intended this last college to be his final monument. Certainly he was determined it should eclipse nearby King's College and its only serious rival, St. John's. To found a society of unprecedented size and grandeur, he began by suppressing two existing foundations, The King's Hall and Michaelhouse, both of which dated from the reign of Edward II. Citing a 1545 act that allowed him to dissolve and take possession of any chantry within the kingdom, Henry sent letters in October 1546 instructing the wardens and fellows of both institutions to surrender all their properties forthwith to the crown. Both surrenders occurred within a week, although they were not officially registered at Westminster until 17 December. Two days later, a formal charter for the new society was issued, which was to be known as Trinity College. To include a master and sixty other paid members, the foundation received a formal deed bestowing the endowment on 24 December.[50]

For the support of Trinity College, Henry granted all the lands obtained from The King's Hall and Michaelhouse, which had a combined worth of £350 per year. In addition he conveyed the vacant buildings of the Cambridge Franciscans, the sites of two ancient unendowed halls, nine complete manors, a number of scattered tracts, and the advowsons of forty parish churches. All these lands and rights together were intended to produce a clear annual revenue of £1,640, although their real value seems to have been several hundred pounds less. Nevertheless, from the time it was established Trinity College was unquestionably the richest academic society at Cambridge and a worthy rival of Christ Church, Oxford.[51]

Although formal statutes for Trinity were not issued until 1552, Henry made detailed arrangements for the college before being paralyzed by the stroke that contributed to his death in January 1547. To head the new society he selected John Redman, a distinguished scholar who, since 1542, had been warden of The King's Hall. Thus it fell to Redman to surrender all the lands and possessions of his institution to the crown during the autumn of 1546. Because he actively helped to bring the new foundation into being, his role can be compared with that of John Sycling, who in 1505 had helped convert Godshouse into Christ's College. As master of Trinity until he died in 1551, Redman was certainly well paid. His yearly stipend was £100, whereas the master of King's received £74 and his counterpart at St. John's £18. The heads of the smaller Cambridge colleges were still paid as little as £6 annually.

Like Christ Church, Trinity grew at a rapid rate during its first years. By 1548 there were 110 members on the foundation in addition to scores of fellow-commoners who paid substantial fees for room and board. In 1564, when the entire university had a resident population of 1,267, Trinity accounted for nearly 25 percent of the total, since it included 306 members in all.[52]

Only one other point about the establishment of Trinity needs to be mentioned here. When Henry created the society in December 1546, he was inspired to some degree by the example of Magdalen, Oxford, which had long kept a grammar school to prepare future undergraduates with weak backgrounds for the rigors of advanced work. In his foundation charter of 19 December, Henry stipulated that there should be a similar grammar school for the youngest students accepted by Trinity. However, by the mid-sixteenth century most of the country's schools had improved to such an extent, and the average first-year student at the university was so well prepared, that basic Latin grammar was now considered too elementary a subject for study at the college level. So in 1549 the grammar school attached to Trinity was allowed to disappear.

If Henry's expectations for his second foundation failed to be realized in that respect, the king would doubtless have been pleased by its progress in all other regards. Indeed, Trinity soon eclipsed King's College and nearby St. John's as the largest and most prestigious society at the university. By the 1560s it dominated the Cambridge scene just as Christ Church loomed over all the other colleges at Oxford. In this way both institutions were unusually successful reflections of the commanding personality of their founder and appropriate monuments to his exuberant will.

7

Developments During
Two Reigns, 1547–1558

The six-year reign of Edward VI was dominated by two great figures in turn: Edward Seymour, duke of Somerset (1547–49) and John Dudley, earl of Warwick (1549–53), who eventually became duke of Northumberland. Although the two men disagreed about social problems and foreign policy, they had a common approach towards education. As a consequence the two sub-periods of the reign will be treated as a unit here, since there was a high degree of continuity between them. Both the Somerset and the Northumberland regimes actively promoted reform at the universities and encouraged education at all levels as a way of achieving a common religious goal—the establishment of a genuine Protestantism in place of the Anglo-Catholicism of Henry VIII's last years.

As noted in chapter 5, the royal injunctions of 1547 required every parish church in the realm to acquire an English Bible within three months and a copy of Erasmus's paraphrases of the gospels within nine more months. Both books were to be chained at a convenient place in the nave so that all parishoners might have easy access to them. At the same time the government announced that Protestants who feared for their lives on the continent would be welcome in England. Within a few months a number of European emigrés arrived and settled in London, Glastonbury, and other places. In a few cases noted

Protestant theologians were granted pensions or posts in the church or at the universities. For example, in 1548 Bernadino Ochino of Siena received an annuity of forty marks out of the Hanaper in Chancery, while Peter Martyr of Florence was appointed Regius professor of divinity at Oxford.

During this same period the government declared that all clerics could marry and directed Archbishop Cranmer to translate the rites of the church into the vernacular, which led in 1549 to the adoption of the first Book of Common Prayer. In addition, it began the removal of men regarded as uncommitted Protestants from college headships at the universities. One of the first individuals ejected was Owen Oglethorpe, president of Magdalen College, Oxford. Oglethorpe was replaced by the far more militant Walter Haddon, whose appointment drew fire because he did not meet all the requirements of the statutes. At nearby New College, Henry Cole, who had been the warden since 1542, was either deprived or persuaded to resign, also for being too tepid a Protestant for the enthusiasts on the Privy Council.[1]

During the first two years of the reign, various proposals to reorganize the colleges at both universities were received and considered. The details of these proposals need not concern us here, since they were never implemented. However, they essentially called for the creation of specialized legal colleges, with All Souls, Oxford, serving as the nucleus for such a society at the older university, and Trinity Hall and Clare Hall being consolidated to form a similar society at Cambridge.[2]

More fruitful than these proposals was the campaign to overhaul the university curriculum. In 1549 royal commissioners carried out full visitations of Oxford and Cambridge; then, on the basis of their recommendations, the Privy Council issued sweeping regulations regarding curricular matters. In this way it was hoped that standards could be raised, the existing program made more relevant to contemporary needs, and a greater knowledge of mathematics and science promoted. To this end the Trivium, which had long governed undergraduate instruction, was altered in several ways. First, the study of basic Latin grammar was abolished, since a mastery of that subject was now considered a prerequisite for admission to either university. Second, the place formerly occupied in the Trivium by Latin grammar was assigned to mathematics; and third, a greater stress was put on rhetoric, although logic and dialectic were not banished altogether. Despite the need for such changes, they were harder to realize in practice than in theory, owing to the dearth of suitable textbooks. For example, because there were almost no modern mathematical tracts, aside from those on arithmetic by Tunstall and Recorde, the statutes of necessity prescribed the writings of such ancient scholars as Euclid, Ptolemy, Pomponius Mela, and Strabo. The same thing was done in regard to the teaching of logic and philosophy, where the works of Plato, Aristotle, Cicero, and Pliny were inevitably required. Thus the basic texts remained much as they had always been, although the writings of most scholastic theologians were specifically forbidden.[3]

Probably the most radical change attempted in 1549 related to instruction in medicine, where students seeking bachelor's degrees now had to study for six years, observe at least two dissections, participate in two or more disputations, and pass a final examination. For the doctor's degree they had to attend two additional dissections, participate in two further disputations, and pass two qualifying examinations. However, because dissections were seldom if ever performed at this time, the effect of these changes was considerably less than the authorities had hoped.[4]

The government's efforts to strengthen the university curriculum were offset in part by a parliamentary act against "superstitious books and images." Once this measure was passed in 1550, royal commissioners returned to the universities and inflicted greater damage on the college libraries than their predecessors of 1535 had done. In a sense the new statute was an extension of the Act of Uniformity of the previous year, which had made the first Prayer Book mandatory throughout the realm. Specifically, the 1550 measure ordered the destruction of all processionals, grails, and other works "heretofore used for the services of the Church" that might compete in any way with the new Prayer Book. Although the statute did not require the destruction of non-religious works, it included no safeguards to prevent overzealous commissioners from discarding books and manuscripts they considered suspect. Consequently many works that had not been earmarked for destruction were removed and lost. At Balliol College, for instance, more than twenty important works owned by that society since 1478 were taken out to the marketplace and burned. These included translations of Plato's dialogues, the letters of Petrarch, and the orations of Poggio Bracciolini and Guarino da Verona.[5]

The libraries of several other Oxford colleges suffered even greater damage. Lincoln and Exeter lost almost all their books, while the holdings of nearby Queen's were ravaged so badly that almost nothing remained when a new inventory was made in 1555. Yet the collections of Merton, Corpus Christi, All Souls, and New College escaped from the crisis almost unscathed. At Cambridge there was also considerable variation regarding the damage inflicted on individual collections. At King's College, St. Catharine's, and Clare Hall, the destruction was almost complete. But at Peterhouse, Pembroke, and Gonville, the commissioners took little if any action.

Despite the way a dozen collections remained intact, the general libraries owned by the universities were almost totally ruined. At Oxford, Duke Humphrey's Library, which had occupied a large chamber above the Divinity School since 1488, was completely dispersed, and only a few books from that once outstanding collection have been discovered in modern libraries. In 1556 the library chamber was so barren and depleted that the authorities ordered the sale of all the desks and book presses in the room, since they were no longer needed. At Cambridge less harm was inflicted on the university collection, doubtless because it had already declined to an insignificant size. Since the 1520s the books had been improperly cared for, and lax security had led to the theft of dozens. By 1547 so much damage had resulted that a proposal of that year suggested the library's conversion into a school for the Regius professor of divinity, for "in its present state it is of no use to anybody." A catalogue of 1557 revealed that approximately two-thirds of the books had vanished and that the collection had shrunk to 175 volumes.[6]

If the governments of Somerset and Northumberland made almost no contribution to higher education, their actions in regard to primary and secondary education were even more controversial, owing to their part in dissolving the chantries and closing the nearly 300 schools kept by them. A. F. Leach, the first scholar to study the disappearance of the chantry schools, was scathing in his denunciation of the two ministers and also of the young Edward VI, whom he labeled the great "spoiler of schools." In addition, Leach held that Edward VI's reputation as the founder of some twenty-four new schools was totally undeserved: a view quickly embraced by R. H. Tawney, who observed rather wittily that, "the grammar schools that Edward VI founded, are the ones that Edward VI did not destroy."[7]

Such an interpretation is not really borne out by the facts, however. Even if the governments of the period had not been so inclined, they would have been compelled by popular opinion to preserve the better chantry schools intact, while in areas where such schools actually disappeared, voluntary action usually led to the swift establishment of new and stronger institutions to take their place. As a result the dissolution of the chantries and their affiliated schools was not the disaster for primary and secondary education that Leach and his disciples believed it to have been.

The vast majority of the 2,500 or so chantries that existed at the end of the Middle Ages were dissolved during the early months of 1548, although the process had actually begun nine years earlier. The 1539 statute that had decreed the suppression of all the remaining monasteries and nunneries had also allowed the monarch to proceed against any chantries, free chapels, hospitals, and colleges whatsoever, as he deemed wise. Almost at once a few chantries were dissolved, including a large and wealthy one at Colchester before the end of that year. Because of the high cost of the wars against France and Scotland after 1542, the crown resorted increasingly to the 1539 act, and by the summer of 1545 Henry VIII had dissolved 54 chantries, colleges, and hospitals in all.[8] When a new parliament met the following November, another parliamentary measure was passed, encouraging the king to continue the process of dissolution but also creating barriers to the private confiscation of chantry endowments. However, the new act seems to have been based on the assumption that some proportion of the chantries would be allowed to continue, since no attack had yet been made on the doctrine of purgatory and the efficacy of masses for the dead. Thus the act of 1545 was a permissive rather than a peremptory measure, and only eight additional institutions are known to have been dissolved before Henry VIII died in 1547 and the act of 1545 expired with him.[9]

Once Edward VI ascended the throne and zealous Protestants took charge, the crown decided to proceed with the dissolution of all the remaining chantries and hospitals except for those that might be deliberately exempted. The necessary legislation was introduced in the House of Commons on 30 November 1547; but because of its radical intent and its open attack on the doctrine of purgatory, it aroused heated controversy, with the burgesses of Coventry and Lynn taking the lead. When the bill was debated in the upper house, even Archbishop Cranmer spoke against it, thereby assuring its defeat. Somerset and his assistants then withdrew and refashioned the bill, to which they added a pledge that all chantry endowments would be converted "to good and goodly uses, as in erecting Grammar Schools . . . [and] the further augmenting of the Universities." Once it was reintroduced, the bill was passed by both chambers on 21 and 22 December, although six bishops voted against it in the Lords. The act of 1547 was peremptory in nature and established Easter 1548 as the final date for the dissolution of all the remaining chantries and hospitals in the kingdom.[10]

As soon as the measure was passed, the government appointed twenty-four sets of commissioners to survey the lands and possessions of the institutions now facing extinction. These commissions, of five to thirteen men each, were responsible for a single county or a pair of adjacent counties, and once they completed their work, they submitted certificates of their findings to the crown. On the basis of these certificates, it has long been held that some 2,374 chantries and free chapels were dissolved, along with more than 100 hospitals. Yet a recent study of the fate of the chantries in four sample counties suggests that that figure is too low and needs to be revised upward.[11]

Regardless of the exact number of chantries dissolved in 1548, the government had pledged to preserve all the schools maintained by them. Accordingly, the Privy Council decided that, while it would confiscate all existing chantry endowments, it would assume responsibility for whatever schools were judged to be doing an acceptable job and would henceforth support those schools out of the recurring revenues of the Court of Augmentations. Once this policy was adopted, the Council appointed two special commissioners, Sir Walter Mildmay and Robert Kelway, to examine all the certificates submitted in order to make the final determination regarding which chantry schools to preserve and which to suppress along with the chantries themselves.[12]

That Mildmay and Kelway honestly sought to rule in favor of the better chantry schools, which would thereby continue at government expense, is obvious from the large number that survived. These included so many chantry schools throughout the realm that it would be tedious to list them. However, in the southwest, a region carefully studied by Nicholas Orme, approximately 80 percent of all the chantry schools were allowed to continue, and of the 20 percent that disappeared, none had had their existence clearly stated in the chantry certificates sent to the capital and subsequently examined by Mildmay and Kelway. Thus the government should not be criticized for failing to provide for them.[13]

In several instances schools that might otherwise have vanished were saved by timely intervention on their behalf. In 1548 Sir William Cecil secured a special parliamentary act by which the school at Stamford, where he had studied as a boy, was preserved and assigned to the management of the town corporation. In a similar way Sir Edward North arranged for the mayor and aldermen of Great Grimsby to purchase the lands of a local chantry in order to reestablish its affiliated school, and in that manner the intentions of the 1547 act were also circumvented. At Stockport the ancient chantry school was saved in similar fashion, while in the capital the famous City of London School, which had been coupled to a chantry throughout its century of existence, was resurrected by the municipal authorities within a short time.[14]

Although several dozen chantry schools continued to operate without interruption, considerably more were suppressed in 1548. Indeed, Foster Watson calculated in 1916 that approximately 260 schools vanished as a result of the various measures passed between 1539 and 1547.[15] Doubtless this number is too high, since neither Watson nor his mentor, A. F. Leach, understood how the government assumed responsibility for the payment of schoolmasters' salaries at the very time it was confiscating chantry endowments. However, even if only 90 to 100 schools disappeared, several counties suffered especially heavy losses. Cornwall saw five of its six schools collapse, while Hertfordshire lost a third of its fifteen schools. Many of the chantry schools in Cambridgeshire and Kent also vanished at this time, as did a large number in Wales.[16]

Thus, even though well over half the chantry schools survived in altered form, enough had disappeared by the end of the 1540s to provoke angry outbursts from Hugh Latimer, Thomas Lever, and other forceful preachers of the era. Several sermons delivered before Edward VI during the winter of 1549-50 assailed the "despoiling of schools" to such an extent that the government adopted a radically different policy in two important respects. First, because the crown itself had aided only a few schools since 1547, it was resolved that the monarch should play a more active role in this regard. Second, the Council also decided in 1550 that its current policy of paying the yearly stipends of most schoolmasters had failed to work satisfactorily:

hence a return to the old system of a separate landed endowment for each school seemed in order.[17]

In 1550 the officers of the Court of Augmentations were therefore instructed to oversee the establishment or reestablishment of schools in all sections of the realm. Almost at once dozens of petitions requesting swift action arrived from the localities, and before Edward VI's death in 1553, at least twenty-six former chantry schools were reestablished, reendowed, or both, at considerable government expense. In addition, some twenty-five other schools reappeared as a result of local initiatives, making a total of fifty-one schools erected on new foundations during the brief period 1550-53.[18]

In almost every case the schools that date from these years were stronger institutions than those of the late Middle Ages. A case in point is the former chantry school at Newark-upon-Trent, which had been founded as recently as 1532. By his will of 1551, a prominent cleric, Thomas Magnus, rector of Sessay as well as archdeacon of the East Riding of Yorkshire, bequeathed £766 to serve as a permanent endowment for the school at Newark. At current rates of return, that bequest should have produced a yearly income of almost £40, which would have been almost four times that of the former chantry school.[19]

Of the more than fifty schools founded during these years, the most important was the Free Grammar School of Edward VI at Shrewsbury. That school, which soon established itself as one of England's best, resulted from two different petitions submitted by leading citizens of the town. The second petition (of 1550) claimed to have wide popular support and hinted that the properties of two nearby colleges that had been dissolved would serve nicely as an endowment for the proposed school. On 10 February 1552, a royal charter for Shrewsbury School was at last issued, and the crown generously allocated £20 per year out of the revenues of the two former colleges. The school was to be directed by a master and an usher appointed by the municipal corporation, which on its part was instructed to confer with the bishop of Lichfield and Coventry about appropriate statutes for the school.[20]

Almost as soon as the school opened, the local bailiffs purchased a building for £20 to serve as the schoolhouse, and a cleric known only as "Sir Morris" was named to serve as master. How long "Sir Morris" held the post is unclear, although he must have been succeeded within a year or two by John Eyton. Evidently the relations between Eyton and the local bailiffs were far from happy, since the school seems to have closed for a time during the late 1550s. However, as almost no records survive from that period, the school's early history is obscure. Finally, in 1561, a schoolmaster of exceptional ability, Thomas Asheton, was appointed, and he remained at the helm for a decade. Asheton managed to establish the school on firm foundations, and by the mid 1560s approximately 360 students were enrolled. During the remainder of the sixteenth century, Shrewsbury was the largest school anywhere in England, and it attracted upper-class boys from all parts of the country.[21]

The upsurge of school foundations that began during Edward VI's last years continued during the reign of his half-sister Mary (1553–58). Additional communities petitioned the monarch for grants of lands, and by 1558 at least seventeen towns had succeeded in the quest. As a result schools were established at such places as Boston, Hampton, Walsall, Clitheroe, Ripon, Bangor, Bromsgrove, York, and Ipswich. Not only did Mary herself give direct assistance to nine schools, but she also granted licenses so that sixteen others could be founded through private action.

Affluent members of the parish clergy emerged during these years as important patrons of education. John Deane, rector of a London church and a prebendary of Ely, established a new grammar school at Wilton, Cheshire, and about the same time a school was founded at Wrangle, Essex through a bequest of the former vicar, Thomas Allenson (d. 1555). In May 1558 a Staffordshire rector, Thomas Allen of Stevenage, left funds for the endowment of three different schools, while contributions of comparable importance were made by William Armistead, rector of Birstall, Yorkshire between 1537 and 1556. As early as 1548 Armistead reestablished the former chantry school at Skipton in Craven, where he had studied as a boy. Eight years later he gave £300 towards the establishment of a new school at Birstall, and in his will of 1558, he left lands worth more than £143 to the trustees of the Leeds Grammar School, which had been founded by another cleric in 1551.

The laity were as active as the clergy in establishing new schools during Mary's reign. In 1553 Sir Andrew Judd, a London skinner who had earlier served as Lord Mayor, founded a school in his native town of Tonbridge Wells and assigned it to the management of the Skinners' Company. The next year another prominent merchant, William Dawkes, left a bequest of £40 for the construction of a school building at Droitwich, on which institution he also bestowed a landed endowment of £10 per year. In 1556 a free grammar school was established at Thaxted, Essex, by the collective action of that town's citizens, while a year later a London brewer of some wealth, Richard Platt, founded a school at Aldenham, Hertfordshire, which he eventually entrusted to the direction of the Brewers' Company.

During these years rich landowners and lawyers finally began to assist the kingdom's schools. In 1554 Anthony Cave of Buckinghamshire established a free grammar school at Lathbury. He additionally founded two Oxford scholarships for promising graduates of that school. Another gentleman who contributed to the educational expansion of this period was Sir John Port of Etwall, Derbyshire. In 1557 Sir John left lands worth nearly £18 a year for the maintenance of a free school at Repton. About the same time a school was founded at Brentwood, Essex by a prominent lawyer, Anthony Brown, and his wife Joan.

Because of more serious concerns as well as the relative poverty of the crown—in 1558 the royal debts stood at approximately £250,000—Mary was unable to make large gifts to the universities. Yet on 2 May 1554, she granted Oxford lands worth more than £131 annually, and she also helped several colleges that had suffered financial hardship during recent years. In February 1555 she authorized the president of Magdalen College to purchase lands worth up to £100 annually as a way of increasing its revenues. A short while later she made a direct gift of lands to New College, which Henry VIII had deprived of a Bedfordshire manor, several Essex tracts, and Peckwater's Inn in Oxford itself. To compensate New College for those losses, Mary granted it the advowson of a Gloucestershire church and several estates that had formerly belonged to Tewkesbury Abbey.[22]

It is often said that Mary was consumed by bitter memories of her father and desired to weaken, if not destroy, all his work. Such a view is not in accord with the facts, since she strengthened the endowment of his great Oxford foundation, Christ Church. Moreover, she rendered especially valuable aid to his other academic institution, Trinity College, Cambridge. In 1556 she began the construction of the Old Library at Trinity and also of a large new chapel, which took nine years to complete. Because of persistent complaints that the lands settled on Trinity in 1546 had failed to produce the intended revenue of £1,640 annually, Mary made a substantial gift to the college in 1554. At that time she granted it four wealthy rectories that had a combined worth of over £376 a year.[23]

Despite Mary's obvious concern for the universities, there was considerable turmoil at Oxford and Cambridge at the beginning of her reign, owing to her staunch Catholicism and her known intention of restoring papal power to England. The Regius professor of divinity at Oxford, Peter Martyr, departed at once for the continent, while the militantly Protestant head of Magdalen College, Walter Haddon, took flight almost as quickly. Probably the most radical changes at the university occurred at New College, where the first married warden, Ralph Skinner, a man of the cloth, was soon induced to resign. In addition, seven fellows of New College were deprived within a few months because of their steadfast refusal to renounce Protestantism.[24]

Similar alterations occurred at Cambridge, where several college heads were summarily ejected for religious reasons. The master of Corpus Christi, Matthew Parker, was ousted, as was the provost of Christ's, Richard Wilkes. At Peterhouse, King's, and Pembroke Hall, all three masters were also removed within a brief time. However, the most dramatic changes at the younger university took place at St. John's College. There Thomas Lever was expelled from the headship after which he and twenty other members went into foreign exile, causing that society to lose its most eminent members.[25]

Despite these changes in personnel, both universities enjoyed steady growth, and thus recovery from the downturn of the previous twenty years, while Mary was on the throne. From the mid 1530s until the mid 1550s, there had been a sharp decline of the student population and in the number of degrees awarded each year by the universities. Whereas an average of 127 degrees had been bestowed at Oxford between 1506 and 1533, only 33 degrees were granted on average during the period 1548–53. At Cambridge a somewhat less precipitate decline seems to have occurred, although the surviving date for the younger university is patchy and, in some respects, contradictory. Regardless of the exact decline that took place at Cambridge after 1535, both universities enjoyed a greater measure of health during Mary's reign. Probably her intensely conservative views led many to conclude that the days of radical upheaval were at last over. In addition, many of the dispossessed monks who had become secular priests after 1536 were now dying off, so that parochial livings were again becoming available and ambitious young men were consequently willing to contemplate clerical careers.* Whatever the specific reason, or reasons, enrollments at Oxford and Cambridge rose steadily after 1553, and there was a corresponding increase in the number of degrees awarded each year, although the peak conditions of 1506–35 were not equaled until the end of Queen Elizabeth's second decade on the throne.[26]

If Mary's reign was important because of the reviving fortunes of the universities, there is another reason why her years at the helm were significant ones in the annals of higher education. At that time two new Oxford colleges—Trinity and St. John's—were founded, while at Cambridge the ancient society known as Gonville Hall was expanded and strengthened, its name being changed in the process to Gonville and Caius College.

Trinity College, Oxford was founded in 1555 by Sir Thomas Pope (1505–59), the son of a yeoman farmer in Oxfordshire. Educated at Banbury and Eton, Pope eventually became a lawyer and, by 1532, held a responsible post in the Court of Chancery. Probably because of his friendly relationship with Sir Thomas Audley, who was Lord Chancellor for more than a decade, Pope was appointed treasurer of the new Court of Augmentations in 1536. Thus he was in an advantageous position to share in the spoils of the religious houses, and within five years he acquired some thirty monastic estates. Knighted by Henry VIII in October 1537, Pope was appointed late in the reign as keeper of all royal woods and forests south of the Trent. On Mary's accession in 1553, he was sworn of the Privy Council and recognized as one of the leading politicians in the kingdom. After the discovery of the Dudley Plot of 1556, he was sent by Queen Mary to reside at Hatfield and stand watch over her half-sister Elizabeth. Although Pope married three times, he had no surviving children and was thus free to use his fortune as he wished. He assisted scores of poor relatives and bequeathed large sums to churches, hospitals, prisons, and other worthy causes. His most

---

*That laymen with rights of advowson often appointed former monks to vacant benefices was understood and generally deplored by contemporaries. In a letter of 1550, Martin Bucer complained from Cambridge to John Calvin at Geneva that, "The nobility . . . have, in many parishes, preferred those who have been in monasteries, who are most unlearned and altogether unfit for the sacred office; and this merely for the sake of getting rid of the payment of their yearly pension." See Hastings Robinson, ed., *Original Letters Relative to the English Reformation*, II (1847), p. 546.

important educational contribution was the foundation of a new Oxford college in 1555.

Pope was probably inspired to establish Trinity College by his earlier efforts on behalf of Magdalene College, Cambridge, which his friend Lord Audley had founded in 1542. For almost a decade Pope was periodically involved with arrangements for that society, since Audley died in 1544 and Pope was one of the principal executors of his will. Once statutes for Magdalene College were issued in February 1554, Pope decided to endow a college as well as a free grammar school of his own creation. On 8 March 1554, he obtained the queen's authorization to establish a society known as Trinity College, which was to consist of a president, twelve fellows, eight scholarship students, and a large number of fellow commoners. In addition, Mary issued a licence for him to found a free grammar school at his birthplace of Deddington or any other Oxfordshire town he selected. Within a short time Pope opened negotiations for the purchase of a site for his Oxford college, and in the early months of 1555 he acquired the lands and vacant buildings of Durham College, which had earlier been purchased from the crown by two private gentlemen. In addition Pope bought a portion of the grove that had once belonged to St. Bernard's College.[27]

On 28 March 1555, Pope issued a foundation charter establishing Trinity College and its endowment. The latter consisted of three manors, the advowsons of four parish churches, and several scattered tracts in Oxfordshire, all worth just over £226 a year. In addition, Pope gave the new society an ample supply of clerical vestments for use in the chapel, along with some "splendid silver" for the hall. To equip a library, he provided twenty-nine manuscripts and seventy printed works, including several large and handsome patristic books. In addition, he appealed to the generosity of the first president of the college, Thomas Slythurst, and to a number of his associates, all of whom donated from their own collections. So the college developed substantial holdings within a short period.[28]

On 1 May 1556, statutes for the college were issued by Pope and his wife Lady Anne. They declared that the main purposes of the college were to encourage "the growth of the orthodox faith and Christian religion, and [to provide for] ... the perpetual maintenance of poor scholars in the University." Perhaps because of the latter objective, the various members of the foundation received smaller stipends than most of their counterparts of the era. The president's salary was only £10 a year, while the twelve graduate fellows were paid a mere £2 13s. 4d. each. The eight undergraduate scholars had to make do with even less, since they were limited to £1 13s. 4d. annually.[29]

On 30 May 1556, the college was officially opened and the president and other original members installed. Six weeks later the founder paid a ceremonial visit in order to inspect his handiwork. He must have been pleased by what he saw, for on his death in 1559 he bequeathed 500 marks to construct a president's house and £100 to complete the building of a long garden wall. In addition, he donated more valuable silver, including thirteen spoons, six goblets, six drinking pots, a large ewer and basin, and a handsome chalice.[30]

At the same time Trinity College was coming into existence, St. John's was being founded by Sir Thomas White (1495–1567). The son of a Hertfordshire clothier, White had spent several years at the Reading Grammar School, after which he was apprenticed to a merchant tailor of the capital, Hugh Acton. When Acton died in 1520, White received a legacy of £100 from him. Three years later White benefited from a similar bequest from his father. This dual inheritance enabled the twenty-eight-year-old entrepreneur to open his own business, and within a decade he was one of the richest men in the capital. He also developed an interest in politics and served as an alderman for many years. During the early 1550s he was a charter member of the corporation that soon became known as the Muscovy Company, and after his election as Lord Mayor in October 1553, he was knighted by Queen Mary. Once his term in London's highest office ended, White bent all his efforts to the establishment of an Oxford society whose officially stated goal was " 'the increase of the orthodox faith in so far as its has been weakened by the damage of time and the malice of men.' "[31]

For the endowment of his college, White spent over £4,000 to purchase six manors, two rectories, and various smaller tracts, all of which were then worth £230 a year. On 1 May 1555, he obtained a royal licence to establish the college, which was to consist of a president and up to thirty paid members, who were to study theology and the arts. During the spring of 1555, White also acquired a site for the intended society by purchasing part of the grove of Durham College and a smaller tract in Walton Field. Shortly afterwards he leased the lands and vacant buildings of St. Bernard's College from their current owner, Christ Church. Late in May 1555, White issued the official foundation deed and named a canon of Christ Church, Alexander Belsire, to be the first president. By that juncture he had begun to renovate the chapel, refectory, and other decayed buildings of St. Bernard's, on which task he spent approximately £1,000 in all.[32]

Issued in 1557, the college statutes were revised in 1562 and again in 1566, when they at last became complete. The president received £20 a year and each of the senior fellows £8. The twenty junior fellows and twenty scholarship students were allotted payments of £5 10s. or £4 10s. a year apiece, respectively. The statutes also specified that there should be weekday lectures in the hall on Greek, logic, and rhetoric, and that once every three years a legist was to serve as vice-president of the college.[33]

When St. John's officially opened its doors on 25 June 1557, it consisted of only twenty members. Within a short time the founder decided to increase its maximum size from thirty to fifty men, although he did not increase the endowment until he died in 1567. As a consequence the college struggled during its first decade and lost many able members to nearby societies. As late as 1568 it consisted of only twenty-four men, and not until the 1580s did it include the full complement of fifty that he had envisaged. In actuality, the society did not surmount all its financial problems until 1593, when White's widow died and her jointure of 400 marks a year became available.[34]

Despite its early financial problems, St. John's had a large library from the outset. White himself donated dozens of works, probably 100 or more in all, which were mainly religious tracts and early editions of the classics he had acquired from the suppressed religious houses. White's brother John presented a number of manuscripts he had obtained on purchasing Southwick Priory, while William Roper provided copies of various printed books written by his late father-in-law, Sir Thomas More. Even before the college admitted its first undergraduates in June 1557, its library included more than 150 works. In succeeding years a stream of such gifts flowed to the college, including 49 valuable books given in 1560 by Henry Cole, whom Queen Elizabeth had recently ousted as dean of St. Paul's Cathedral. Despite the library's rapid growth, it was some years before a special room was reserved for the burgeoning collection. However, a small library chamber existed by 1583, when the most important tracts were chained in the medieval manner, a system that remained in use at the college until the eighteenth century.[35]

The third academic society to be founded during Mary's reign was, as already noted, a refoundation: Dr. John Caius's reestablishment and substantial enlargement of Gonville Hall, which was renamed Gonville and Caius College in the process. In some ways this event in September 1557 was of greater significance than the establishment of either Trinity or St. John's, since Gonville and Caius soon emerged as a major centre of medical and scientific studies in England.

Dr. John Caius, who occupies an honored place in English educational and medical history, was born at Norwich in 1510. He entered Gonville Hall in 1529 and received his A.B. and M.A. degrees in 1533 and 1537, respectively. A graduate fellow of the college from 1533 until 1545, he was originally attracted to the study of theology but gradually inclined towards medicine. In 1539 he went abroad and worked for four years with the great anatomist J. B. Montanus at the university of Padua. In addition he became a close associate of the brilliant Andreas Vesalius, a Belgian who taught at Padua from 1537 until 1544. Vesalius was about to complete his epoch-making tract *De Fabrica Humani Corporis,* which was published at Basle in 1543, and because he and Caius were fellow lodgers at a rooming house known as the *Casa degli Valli* for eight months, it seems probable that the Englishman learned a great deal from his outstanding contemporary, one of the fathers of the Scientific Revolution.[36]

Early in 1541 Caius began to lecture on Aristotle's logic and philosophy at Padua, and on 13 May of that year he received an M.D. degree from the university. Until July 1543 he remained there, teaching and editing various works by Galen and St. John Chrysostom. Then he departed for Florence, where he stayed a short while before moving on to Pisa to study with Matthew Curtius. Ultimately he visited Rome, Ferrara, and Venice before crossing the Alps to Switzerland in 1543 or 1544. While at Basle in 1544, he published his first medical treatise, *De Medendi Methodo* (On the Art of Healing), and formed a lifelong friendship with the great Swiss naturalist Conrad Gesner, for whom he later wrote a pioneering tract on English dogs. Then he traveled down the Rhine to the Low Countries, where he boarded a ship for England. Back in his native land by September 1545, when he resigned his Gonville fellowship, he settled in London and developed a lucrative medical practice, soon becoming the most eminent English doctor of the age. After the accession of Edward VI, he was engaged as a royal physician and served in that capacity during the reigns of Mary and Elizabeth as well.

As a royal physician from 1547, Dr. Caius was probably consulted about the attempted reform of the medical curriculum at Oxford and Cambridge in 1549. By that government measure, mentioned earlier in this chapter, students seeking bachelor's degrees were required to observe at least two dissections, while those working towards doctor's degrees had to witness two additional ones. Recently a leading historian has noted that Dr. John Warner, the Regius professor medicine at Oxford, had long been concerned about medical training and had attempted to use a university committee on standards to which he belonged from 1545 in order to achieve reform.[37] However, it seems unlikely that Dr. Warner would have attempted to sponsor fundamental changes without outside assistance from some quarter. Because Dr. Caius was elected to the Royal College of Physicians in February 1547 and had already embarked on the weekly lectures and demonstrations he delivered in Barber-Surgeons Hall for twenty years, it follows that Dr. Warner or the Privy Council, or perhaps both, may have consulted him about his views. Certainly the reform that emerged, although less effective than intended, embodied principles that he advocated.

During the early 1550s, Dr. Caius published several important books, including a zoological tract on the characteristics of animals and a work on the nature and treatment of the sweating sickness, which has been called "the first clinical description of a disease by an English writer." In addition he became increasingly active in the College of Physicians, of which he served as president in 1555 and on eight subsequent occasions.

During his second or third term as president of the College of Physicians, Dr. Caius was approached by Thomas Bacon, master of Gonville Hall since 1552. Bacon was a pleasant man but a poor administrator, and the society was then nearing bankruptcy. Bacon hoped the wealthy Dr. Caius would come to the aid of his old society, and Dr. Caius tentatively agreed to do just that. He was willing to increase the college's endowment, provided he could appoint the holders of whatever new fellowships and scholarships were to be established. He additionally made it clear that he expected to be consulted about all the college's future affairs. Once Dr. Caius's terms were approved by the society's leadership, Bacon sought royal authorization to proceed. On 4 September 1557, Queen Mary gave her consent and decreed that the college's name should be changed to Gonville and Caius, with Dr. Caius henceforth to be regarded as its co-founder. He was empowered to issue new statutes for the society, so long as they did not countermand the original ones given two centuries earlier. Bacon was thereupon named to the mastership of the expanded college, and the ten current fellows of Gonville Hall were all reappointed, with the stipulation that two or more additional fellows should be nominated by Dr. Caius.[38]

Once the royal charter of 4 September 1557 was issued, Dr. Caius granted the college two manors in Norfolk and one in Hertfordshire, which had a combined worth of more than £120 a year. After increasing the endowment in this way, he established twenty undergraduate scholarships and three graduate fellowships, two of the latter being reserved for medical students and the other for a prospective theologian. On 25 March 1558, an elaborate ceremony attended by Dr. Caius and many high university officials took place at the college. With great pomp the new foundation was officially opened and Bacon installed as its first master. A week later the appreciative university authorities conferred an honorary M.D. degree on Dr. Caius.[39]

Sometime during the next seven months, Dr. Caius issued statutes for the college. They are of no particular interest except in regard to the two medical fellowships he established. He was well aware that medicine was the weakest part of the graduate curriculum of the English universities. Accordingly he stipulated that the recipients of his two fellowships should be allowed generous periods of leave in order to continue their studies abroad, as he himself had done. He specifically mentioned Padua, Bologna, Montpellier, and Paris as places where English students might profitably go for advanced training.[40]

Despite the stress on foreign study in the statutes of 1558, Dr. Caius promoted better medical training at Gonville and Caius itself. In 1564 he secured royal authorization for the society to claim the corpses of two executed criminals each year for purposes of dissection. When in January 1573 he revised the college statutes, he gave careful directions concerning those dissections, and with rare consideration he decreed that:

> . . . every year, during winter, there shall be spent by the students of our College, on anatomy and the worthy burial of the dissected bodies at St. Michael's [Church] 26s. 8d. The president and every one residing in the College to attend the burial of the remains with as much respect and ceremony as if it were the body of some

> more dignified person. . . . And the master shall see that
> the students do not treat the body with any lack of
> humanity.[41]

Despite the sensitivity of those provisions, Dr. Caius was a difficult and demanding person who was often churlish towards others. Only slightly over five feet tall, he had virtually no tact and never tolerated opposition to his ideas. As a consequence, once Bacon died and he became master of the college in 1559, he encountered recurring difficulties with the fellows and scholars. In fairness to his memory, it should be acknowledged that he did not seek the mastership, believing it should properly be held by a theologian. Moreover, the men who opposed him so bitterly were an undistinguished group who accomplished nothing of importance. Yet he did not help the situation by keeping in his chamber a large collection of medieval relics, in the unlikely event Elizabeth were overthrown and Catholicism restored for a second time. Neither was it politic for him to assign a room at the college to his old friend Edmund Cosin, an unwavering Catholic who had resigned the mastership of St. Catharine's College in December 1558. The predominantly Puritan fellows of Gonville and Caius were incensed by such actions and denounced their master as a tyrant, a papist, and even an atheist. He responded by expelling one fellow after another, although the replacements he chose were just as ardent in their opposition. As long as he remained at the helm, Gonville and Caius knew no peace, and shortly before his death in July 1573, he felt compelled to resign the mastership.[42]

Although he failed in leading his own college, Dr. Caius was passionately devoted to its welfare. During his fourteen years as master, he accepted no pay for his work. In fact, he strengthened the endowment even more by conveying two manors he had recently purchased for almost £600. During the mid 1560s he bought a tract adjacent to the original college buildings, now known as the Gonville Court, and began the construction of a second quadrangle, which subsequently became known as the Caius Court. For this ambitious project he obtained stone and other materials from the ruins of Ramsey Abbey, and by the time he died he had spent almost £1,840 to that end. After his death in 1573 his executors released an additional £304 3s. 6d. from his estate to complete the work he had begun.[43]

Although of no real importance as a book collector, Dr. Caius left the college nine volumes of manuscripts, chiefly works by

Galen and Hippocrates that he had acquired during his travels in Italy. Moreover, he encouraged his friends to donate materials to the library. In 1560 Dr. Thomas Wendy, who had held a Gonville fellowship during the 1520s, left the college a valuable collection of books, which included Plato's complete works and the earliest printed edition of Thucydides. Four years later Dr. Henry Walker left a bequest of sixty-eight additional books, while Archbishop Parker stipulated in his will of 1575 that the society should receive twenty-five volumes of theology and medieval documents from his extensive holdings.[44]

Archbishop Parker was probably Dr. Caius's closest friend and briefly served as his literary executor. In January 1572 the archbishop rendered direct assistance to the college by giving over £60 to endow an undergraduate scholarship in medicine. The recipient of this award was to enjoy an annual stipend of slightly more than £3, and he was to have free tuition and lodging provided by the college itself. After spending three years on "subjects useful to medicine," he would be expected to concentrate on medicine itself for three additional years. Without a doubt the most important man ever to hold the Parker Scholarship was William Harvey, a yeoman farmer's son. Famous for his eventual discovery of the circulation of the blood, Harvey enjoyed the award from 1593 until 1599, when he departed for Padua to hone his skills.

By the time Harvey was elected to the Parker scholarship in 1593, various types of medical and scientific studies had become well established not only at Gonville and Caius but also at a number of other academic societies at the two universities. Because that important development occurred during the second half of Queen Elizabeth's reign, it seems best to defer consideration of it until the next chapter.

8

Religion, Science, and Society: The Universities During the Elizabethan Period

When Queen Elizabeth ascended the throne in November 1558, the primary role of the universities was still to train young men for clerical careers, although a secondary function had developed by that time. More and more boys from landed families were enrolling in order to gain a veneer of polish and learning before becoming suitors at court, taking charge of their estates, or begining a period of legal studies at the Inns of Court. These latter boys usually had no intention of seeking degrees or fulfilling the statutory requirements for graduation. With guidance from their tutors they studied whatever subjects were of mutual interest and read somewhat different books from those assigned to candidates for degrees.

If a two-track instructional program existed by the late Tudor period, all students, regardless of their goals, were expected to be active participants in Christian worship. In virtually all the colleges, and especially the three new ones established during Elizabeth's reign, the requirement of regular daily prayers was far from nominal. In 1571, just a few years before his death at an advanced age, Dr. Hugh Price, treasurer of St. David's

Cathedral, founded Jesus College, Oxford. In his statutes for that foundation, Dr. Price decreed that the 5:00 A.M. daily service in the chapel was mandatory for all members of the society except those with advanced degrees in divinity, whose presence was nonetheless required at daily evening prayer at 9:00 P.M. On Sundays and feast days, all members of the college were expected to attend the 8:00 A.M. and 4:00 P.M. services, while all were similarly required to accompany the college principal to the periodic university sermons.[1]

At Emmanuel College, Cambridge, which Sir Walter Mildmay founded in 1584 as a seminary for a pastoral preaching ministry, the requirement of an active Christian life was also far from nominal, although Mildmay gave less detailed instructions than Dr. Price. Attendance at daily evening prayer in the chapel was obligatory for all members of Emmanuel, and in addition all students without graduate degrees were required to attend the prayers of their tutors " 'everie night at eight of the clock, so everie tutor may see him at that time and be answerable for their good behaviour.' "[2] At nearby Sidney Sussex College, which was established in 1596 by the executors of Frances, countess of Sussex (d. 1589), the daily chapel services were taken just as seriously. The Sidney Sussex statutes specified that those who were tardy should be fined ½d., while those who failed to attend at all should be penalized a whole penny for each absence, these exactions being reserved for the support of the Fellows' Table, which ensured that they would be collected.[3]

The statutes of the older colleges prescribed the same kinds of religious observances, although the fines for nonattendance naturally varied from society to society. At Trinity College, Oxford, the fine for each unexcused absence was 2d., but at Trinity College, Cambridge, it was only ½d. for those who were over eighteen, whereas the younger students were to be publicly thrashed in the hall for each absence.[4]

In view of the continued importance of religion at both universities, the national government could hardly follow a lax policy and allow the colleges to espouse whatever doctrinal views they preferred. If the crown was to achieve any measure of religious unity within the realm—and religious unity was felt essential for political stability—it had to inquire into the beliefs of the college heads and insist on their conformity with official policy. This had been apparent to successive regimes since the 1530s, when Cromwell engineered the break from Rome and iniated the era of the Reformation. The dukes of Somerset and North-umberland after 1547 had been equally aware of the need to exert control over the universities' religious affairs, and once Mary ascended the throne, as we have seen, massive changes at Oxford and Cambridge occurred. Yet no ruler of the period was more aware of the need to regulate what was taught and prac-ticed at the universities than Queen Elizabeth.

At her accession in November 1558, Elizabeth was confronted by religious problems of major proportions. Because of her parentage and personal convictions, she was determined to break the ties with Rome once again, although she knew that a large percentage of her subjects were still Catholic at heart. At least a third, and possibly far more, continued to be convinced Romanists. The Spanish ambassador to England in 1558, Count de Feria, believed that as many as two-thirds were still wedded to the Old Faith, while the respected Victorian scholar J. R. Green held that 70 to 75 percent continued to be. In our own century most Catholic historians maintain that at least half the English people still had pronounced Catholic sympathies as late as 1570, when Pius V made a belated attempt to depose the queen by means of the bull *Regnans in Excelsis*.[5] Whatever the exact proportion of the population still inclined towards Rome at the outset of the reign, Queen Elizabeth had to win their acceptance and tacit approval if an independent national church was to have any chance of survival. Moreover, she had to make alterations at the universities, where Mary's appointees, if left in office, would train a new generation of clerics to preach and mobilize support for the Old Religion.

Accordingly, once the new monarch and her advisers took charge, a series of changes at the universities began. These changes were less drastic than they might have been because Elizabeth desperately hoped to avoid the 300 martyrdoms that had turned public opinion violently against her half-sister. As a result she was more concerned about a man's outward behavior and professions of faith than with his inner beliefs, and because of her dislike of religious enthusiasm, she had no intention of trying to force individual consciences. In addition, the need for extreme action was lessened, at least at Cambridge, by several timely deaths among the ranks of the college heads. Just before Mary herself died on 17 November 1558, the conservative provost of King's College, Robert Brassie, expired of natural causes, and during the next six weeks the heads of both Trinity and Jesus College departed this earth also. Thus Elizabeth's ministers faced no obstacles in appointing men to direct those three societies who would support the policy of the new regime. Meanwhile at nearby Magdalene College, the ultra-conservative Richard Carr was ejected to make way for Roger Kelke, while Edmund Cosin of St. Catharine's was replaced with John May. There were similar changes at Queens', Christ's, St. John's, and Pembroke Hall.[6]

At Oxford even more deprivations occurred during the winter of 1558-59. Both the warden and sub-warden of Merton were expelled, while at All Souls Seth Holland was replaced with his predecessor, John Warner, whom Mary had ejected. At nearby Trinity the first president, Thomas Slythurst, was ousted to make way for Arthur Yeldard, a canon of Windsor. William Cheadsey, who had been president of Corpus Christi for less than a year, not only lost that post but also suffered a long captivity because of a chronic inability to hold his tongue. Both the rector of Lincoln College and the dean of Christ Church were deprived, as were the heads of such neighboring societies as Balliol, Magdalen, Queen's, and University. The principal of St. Albans Hall was likewise replaced, and so too was Alexander Belsire, the first man to preside over St. John's College. However, as Belsire was soon named rector of Hanburg and adhered to the order of worship in the Prayer Book of 1559, his removal was prompted less by religious considerations than by a financial dispute with the college founder, Sir Thomas White.[7]

Once these twenty or so changes of college heads were complete, Elizabeth did not lose interest in religious developments at the universities. Indeed, she maintained a careful watch over the course of affairs there, although in 1562 she delegated a general supervisory power to the Court of High Commission. Authorized by the Act of Supremacy of 1559, the High Commission was specifically directed to correct any "enormities, disorders, defects, surplusages, or wants" in the statutes of all schools and colleges established during Mary's reign and to draw up such new regulations "as may best tend to the honour of Almighty God, the increase of virtue and unity in the same places, and the public weal and tranquillity of our realm."[8] Archbishop Parker was the first president of the High Commission, whose membership included the bishops of London and Ely and such prominent laymen as Sir Anthony Cooke and Sir Francis Knollys. The court exercised a powerful influence, although, because of its members' ardent Protestantism, it had to be prodded by the queen into suppressing Puritan agitators at the universities.

Puritanism became a strong force in English life during the 1560s, when a campaign to simplify all religious ritual occurred. Now known as the Vestiarian Controversy because of the Puritans' opposition to elaborate clerical vestments, this agitation became especially intense in the capital, where thirty-seven ministers were suspended for refusing to wear the required robes, and also in several important colleges at the universities. Early in 1566 the new dean of Christ Church, Oxford, Thomas Sampson, who had helped produce the ultra-Protestant Geneva Bible of 1560, lost his post and was even held under house arrest for a time. Not long after Sampson was deprived, Laurence Humphrey of nearby Magdalen was threatened by the High Commission with similar punishment unless he and his fellows conformed, which they grudgingly agreed to do.[9]

Meanwhile, Puritanism had gained scores of adherents at Trinity College, Cambridge, where in December 1565 there was a boycott of the despised vestments, which were denounced as "rags of Rome" and "the livery of Anti-Christ." Within a short time the outburst at Trinity spread to nearby St. John's, where scores of members refused to don the surplice for ceremonies in the chapel. The protest at St. John's was especially worrisome to the university chancellor, Sir William Cecil, a devoted alumnus of that college. Cecil instructed the vice-chancellor and all the college heads at Cambridge to prohibit public preaching for a time and to warn the firebrands to conform or expect expulsion. In addition, he wrote directly to his former society and ordered the members to halt their agitation for "vainglorious innovations," after which he summoned the current master, Richard Longworth, to appear before him at Westminster. Although Longworth had been away from the college when the disturbances began, he had taken no disciplinary action since his return, so he was ousted from the mastership. However, his successor, William Cole, soon proved incapable of suppressing the agitation, and after a brief term of office he gave way to Nicholas Shepherd.[10]

By that juncture a more significant change had occurred at Trinity College, where in 1567 the hapless Robert Beaumont was replaced with John Whitgift, the grim and determined Lady Margaret professor of divinity. At the same time Whitgift received that college headship, he was elevated to the most prestigious academic chair at the university, that of Regius professor of divinity. Curiously, he was succeeded as Lady Margaret professor by Thomas Cartwright, a senior fellow of Trinity but also the ringleader of the earlier Puritan agitation in the college. The appointment of Cartwright to one of the leading chairs at the university proved to be a mistake of major proportions.

During the autumn of 1569 Cartwright gave a series of public lectures on the Acts of the Apostles, in which he made thinly veiled criticisms of the administrative structure of the Elizabethan church. In his view, the Apostolic church had been organized along congregational lines, with individual parishes free to elect their own ministers and adopt whatever ritualistic practices they liked. The obvious conclusion was that the present system of church government, which was hierarchically structured, was altogether wrong and required fundamental change. As a consequence Cartwright's lectures generated considerable excitement, since they were perceived as a clarion call to attack the two basic principles of episcopacy and royal supremacy over the church. Should those two principles be discarded, the Elizabethan church would be completely transformed. Moreover, the Puritans might then secure the changes regarding vestments and ritual that they had failed to win during the Vestiarian Controversey, which had been ended in 1566 by Archbishop Parker's *Book of Advertisements* threatening the agitators with extreme punishment.

From the time Cartwright delivered his 1569 lectures, he was a marked man. In 1570 he was ousted from the Lady Margaret professorship, whereas the next year John Whitgift resorted to a technicality to deprive him of his fellowship at Trinity College. Thereafter the two men were bitter enemies, and between 1572 and 1577 they were the chief figures in a pamphlet war known as the Admonition Controversy. During that acrimonious dispute, Whitgift provided a ringing defense of the principles of episcopacy and royal supremacy over the church, whereas Cartwright produced a blueprint for reform and urged parliament to seize the initiative and establish a more democratically structured church, whether the queen approved or not. Because of his appeal for radical action, Cartwright's chances of recovering his influence at Cambridge collapsed altogether. At the same time Whitgift won the undying gratitude of the queen, who elevated him to the episcopal bench at her first opportunity. In 1583, after Archbishop Grindal's death, Elizabeth even transferred him from the relatively unimportant see of Worcester to the most powerful religious office in the realm.

If the High Commission had to be prodded into action against Puritan agitators, it was tireless in attempting to extinguish the lingering Catholic sympathies of several university colleges. In fact, concerted opposition from the High Commission compelled the master of New College, Oxford, Thomas White, to proceed against that society's most conservative members between 1559 and 1561. During those years five men were deprived of their fellowships, and four others withdrew voluntarily before going into exile on the continent. Then there was a brief respite until the latter part of 1562, by the end of which year the High Commission had forced the ouster of eleven more New College men from their fellowships. Between 1564 and 1568 nine additional members were expelled, and by the early 1570s another five had been deprived. All in all, New College lost thirty-four of its seventy fellows during the first fifteen years of Elizabeth's reign, which was far more than any other college. By the mid 1570s, New College had been transformed from a Catholic into a Protestant society, although at heavy cost. The repeated purgings of the college ranks led to the expulsion or withdrawal of most of the ablest scholars, causing the society to lose the reputation for excellence it had enjoyed for nearly two centuries.[11]

Although Warden White gradually rid New College of its Catholic members before he himself reigned in 1573, the High Commission faced a more formidable task at nearby St. John's. There the new president, William Elye, who had taken office during the summer of 1559, was a more ardent Romanist than his ousted predecessor, Alexander Belsire. During Mary's reign Elye had openly debated theological issues with Archbishop Cranmer just before the latter's execution in 1556. He was thus a poor choice for the headship of an Elizabethan college, and in 1563 he was deprived for continuing to uphold papal authority. Elye's successor as president of St. John's was William Stocke, also a partisan of the Old Religion. After a year in office, Stocke laid down the reins, probably because he too feared deprivation, whereupon he returned to the more tolerant atmosphere of Gloucester Hall. Only with the appointment of yet another president of St. John's, Henry Robinson, did Protestantism make inroads at the college. A fellow of Pembroke Hall, Cambridge, Robinson was a protégé of the forceful John Whitgift, who proposed his name to Elizabeth's chief minister, Sir William Cecil. Robinson held the presidency of St. John's from 1564 until 1572, during which time Protestantism finally became established. It was during his term of office that almost a dozen Catholic fellows, including Gregory Martin and Edmund Campion, departed for the continent, where they took instruction in the tactics of Catholic missionary activity from William Allen at Douai.[12]

By any objective test William Allen was the most important English Catholic to go into exile during Elizabeth's reign. Long associated with Oxford, Allen had taken an A.B. there in 1550 and briefly served as principal of St. Mary's Hall. He first went abroad in 1561 but returned to England after a few months and took refuge with the duke of Norfolk, a well-known Catholic sympathizer. His second and final departure for the continent occurred in 1565. Ordained a priest two years later, he soon secured papal support for a large seminary at Douai, in the Low Countries. He opened that institution in 1568 and thereafter trained young Englishmen in the most effective ways of winning their countrymen back to the Old Religion.

In 1574 the first of Allen's students returned to England to work among the people of the north and west. At first the missionary campaign proceeded so smoothly and made so many converts that Henry Shaw boasted in a letter of 1575 to Allen that even Sir William Cecil was alarmed. As for Allen himself, he informed an associate in 1577 that several young students who had just arrived at Douai had assured him that " 'the numbers of those who daily returned to the Catholic church almost surpassed belief.' "[13]

Although more than 120 missionary priests had reappeared in England by 1580, the optimism of Allen and his supporters proved unfounded. Always on guard, the English government was aware of the campaign being waged against it and took effective countermeasures. Arrests occurred with grim regularity, and as early as 1577 the first of Allen's students to be executed, Cuthbert Mayne, was put to death. By the middle of the next decade, some twenty-three missionary priests, including several Jesuits trained in Rome, had paid the supreme penalty, while seventy others were being held in various English prisons, where they often remained until they died.

Because Allen and many of the missionary priests were former Oxonians, the authorities at the older university were seriously embarrassed and took vigorous measures to eradicate Catholicism there once and for all. In 1580 the earlier Oath of Supremacy was made mandatory for all fellows and scholars, while each student at Oxford was directed to reside in a college or an approved hall (of which there were now only six) so as to be less vulnerable to the missionaries' appeal. In 1581 a new matriculation statute was passed which effectively closed the university to students with Catholic sympathies. That statute decreed that all individuals who were at least sixteen years of age must publicly subscribe not only to the queen's supremacy over the church but also to the Thirty-Nine Articles of 1563, and it additionally required all tutors who wished to continue in that capacity to avoid all suspicion of papal leanings.[14]

At Cambridge after 1558, Catholic sentiment was never as strong as at the older university. So measures comparable to the 1580 and 1581 Oxford enactments were not adopted by the Cambridge authorities until 1606, during the hysteria generated by the Gunpowder Plot of the previous November. Even then the younger university did not close its doors completely to Catholic students, who could still come and study, although to be admitted to a degree they now had to subscribe openly, and without mental reservations of any sort, to the Thirty-Nine Articles of 1563.

Despite the continuing importance of religion at the universities and the violent controversies that often disturbed their peace, mathematical and scientific studies made steady progress at Oxford and Cambridge during the Elizabethan period. Curiously, one of the first centers of such studies was Gonville and Caius, Cambridge, which probably had closer ties to the missionary movement than any other society at the younger university. Between 1574 and 1588, at least five graduates of Gonville and Caius were tried and executed as missionary priests, while seven others became Jesuits and one entered the great Benedictine monastery of Monte Cassino in Italy. Of course the college continued to furnish recruits for the Anglican priesthood during those years. Between 1558 and 1625 approximately 75 percent of the men who took degrees at Gonville and Caius became clerics in the state church.[15] Nevertheless, Gonville and Caius emerged as an important center of scientific activity, which suggests that the dichotomy which sometimes exists between science and religion was more of an illusion than a reality at that time.

Whatever the normal relationship between science and religion, the scientific activity at Gonville during the late Tudor period was largely owing to three men. The first was Thomas Legge, who, like Dr. Caius, had been born at Norwich. From 1568 until 1573, Legge held a fellowship at Jesus College, where he became known as an outstanding tutor of undergraduates. When in the summer of 1573 Dr. Caius resigned the mastership of his own college, he recommended Legge as his successor, and the latter served in that position until he died in 1607. During that thirty-four-year period, Legge maintained an atmosphere conducive to scientific investigation, of which he strongly approved, and thereby made possible the work of two younger men, Richard Swale and John Fletcher. Also a respected tutor of undergraduates, Swale became widely known as a mathematician. He took his M.A. in 1572, and from 1573 until 1578 he held office as the university mathematical lecturer. The youngest of the three men, John Fletcher received his A.B. in 1581 and his M.A. three years later. Nothing is known of his movements between 1584 and 1587, when he was elected to a fellowship that he retained until his death in 1613. Periodically he held such college offices as bursar and salarist, but he too made his principal contribution as a tutor. He was especially interested in mathematics, astronomy, and astrology and is known to have owned an astrolabe made about the year 1490.[16]

Despite the teaching contributions of Legge, Swale, and Fletcher, the most original mathematician produced by the college during these years was Edward Wright (1558-1615). Wright received his M.A. in 1584 and held a Gonville fellowship from 1587 until 1596. He belonged to a learned circle that included not only members of his own college but also such able young scientists as Henry Briggs of St. John's College and Mark Ridley of Clare Hall. In 1589 Wright became a pensioner of George Clifford, third earl of Cumberland, who had taken an M.A. at Cambridge several years before and whom he accompanied on a voyage to the Azores in 1596. During that same year Wright resigned his Gonville fellowship and settled in London. Shortly afterwards he began a collaboration with Emery Molyneux, a well-known maker of globes and other navigational instruments. He also became a close associate of Dr. William Gilbert, the great Cambridge-trained physician who had practiced in the capital since 1573. When Gilbert's pioneering tract on magnetism and geology, *De Magnete*, appeared in 1600, Wright wrote a valuable preface for it. Wright's most important contribution, however, was the book he himself published in 1599. This was his *Certain Errours of Navigation detected,* which was particularly helpful to men piloting ships in the high latitudes of the North Atlantic.[17]

Gonville and Caius was only one of several Cambridge colleges in which mathematical and scientific studies flourished during the Elizabethan period. At Peterhouse such work was encouraged by Dr. Andrew Perne, master of that society from 1554 until 1589. Perne had a sincere interest in mathematics, astronomy, and geography and owned many up-to-date instruments, including astrolabes, quadrants, dials, and globes. On his death in 1589, he bequeathed all those instruments, along with his personal library, reputedly "the worthiest in all England," to the college. In this way Peterhouse acquired important works by Copernicus, Frisius, Mercator, Ortelius, Peurbach, and Digges, which provided a strong foundation for later empirical work at the college.[18]

Like Dr. Perne, William Fulke, who was master of Pembroke Hall from 1578 until 1589, had an abiding interest in scientific subjects. Fulke's main concerns were zoology and mathematics, and while holding a fellowship at St. John's, where he took his M.A. in 1563, he is said to have kept a veritable menagerie in his bedchamber. His most important writings, however, were in the fields of astronomy, astrology, and mathematical games. At nearby Trinity College, important contributions were made by Thomas Hood, the gifted son of a London merchant tailor. Born in 1556, Hood entered Trinity in 1573 and received his A.B. and M.A. degrees in 1578 and 1581, respectively. He held a college fellowship for several years and was university mathematical lecturer in 1582. However, he had left the university by 1588 for London, where he gave public lectures on mathematics, geography, and navigation at the behest of an aristocratic patron, John, Lord Lumley. Although there is no clear proof, Hood probably directed the undergraduate studies of William Bedwell, who received his A.B. in 1585 and was elected to a Trinity fellowship the next year. In 1588 Bedwell proceeded M.A., and he soon developed such an extensive knowledge of astronomy that a contemporary described him as "Our English Tycho." He had an equal mastery of mathematics and has recently been termed "one of the best mathematicians of the last quarter of the sixteenth century." He spent little time at Cambridge during the 1590s, however, being employed as a chaplain by agents of the Levant Company at Aleppo. Perhaps because of his time in the Near East, he eventually became a great Arabic scholar and assisted in the preparation of the King James Bible of 1611.[19]

King's College was also fortunate in having bright young scholars to instruct its undergraduates during the Elizabethan period. Robert Dunning held a fellowship at King's from 1567 until 1577 and received his M.A. there in 1572. A highly esteemed mathematician, he was the university mathematical lecturer in 1574-75. However, he was expelled from his fellowship two years later when he was unable to substantiate charges of misconduct he had brought against the provost, Roger Goad. If Dunning's ouster led to a declining interest in such studies, it cannot have lasted long. In 1582 the equally capable Joseph Jessop (d. 1599) was elected to a fellowship, and in 1588-89 he too served as university mathematical lecturer. It was probably Jessop who directed the undergraduate work of William Oughtred (1575-1660), who took his M.A. degree in 1599 and subsequently became an outstanding mathematician himself, although he spent the last fifty years of his life as a country parson and teacher. Oughtred's brilliant undergraduate essay, "Easy Method of Geometricall Dialling," circulated widely, brought him instant fame, and shows how closely the university remained abreast of contemporary developments in regard to navigation and the allied sciences.[20]

Meanwhile at Oxford, there was also a growing interest in science and mathematics during these years. Paradoxically, the Oxford statutes of 1564-65 put almost no stress on such subjects. Indeed, they emphasized grammar, rhetoric, and dialectic for undergraduates and banished mathematics, science, and philosophy almost totally to the M.A. program. Yet virtually all undergraduate teaching was now in the hands of tutors who normally instructed their pupils as they saw fit, particularly if the latter had no wish to complete the A.B. course, as was increasingly the case. In a few instances the statutes of individual Oxford colleges required some instruction in the more modern subjects. At Trinity College, for example, the founder had decreed in 1558 that there should be a daily "logic lecture" immediately after morning prayers in the chapel. The logic lecturer was required to teach arithmetic and geometry to all members of the college, while during the long vacation he was to address them three times each week on either astronomy or geography. To ensure that these lectures were taken seriously, unjustified absences were punishable by fines of 2*d.* each, while failure to take notes also merited a 2*d.* exaction.[21]

Regardless of the exact statutory requirements of the various Oxford colleges, an interest in mathematics and science was evident throughout the older university and, just as at Cambridge, it was characteristic of more than a few societies. Partly because of its medieval tradition, Merton College was in the vanguard of this important movement. By 1588 a younger member of Merton, Henry Wotton, had such extensive knowledge of medicine and anatomy that he was able to give three lectures on the physiology of the human eye. Yet a more prominent part was taken at Merton from the 1570s by the Savile brothers, Henry and Thomas. Henry Savile (1549–1622) had matriculated at Brasenose in 1561 but was elected four years later to a fellowship at Merton, where he seems to have studied mathematics with the respected scholar John Chambre. In 1570 the elder Savile was deeply impressed by the publication of Sir Henry Billingsley's masterly translation of Euclid's *Elements,* with a brilliant introduction by John Dee. Within a short time he launched a series of lectures on the general topic of Greek geometry, to which he invited the entire academic community. He continued these lectures until 1578, when he resigned his fellowship to free himself for foreign travel. On his return from the continent he was named in 1585 to the wardenship of Merton, which he retained until his death and from which he championed mathematical and scientific teaching throughout the university. The younger Savile brother, Thomas, was a student at Merton during the late 1570s and received his A.B. in the spring of 1580. Admired for his expertise in both mathematics and history, he was soon elected to a college fellowship, which he held until his death in 1593 at the age of about thirty. A man of broad interests, he corresponded with Tycho Brahé, who sent him one of his books in 1590. Had Thomas Savile lived to a riper age, he might well have made a significant contribution.[22]

At Christ Church and All Souls, an enthusiasm for such matters was also becoming evident. The famous mathematician and clergyman Nicholas Torporley (1564–1632) developed a lifelong interest in astronomy while a student at Christ Church during the early 1580s. Torporley took his A.B. in 1584 and his M.A. seven years later. By the latter year he was both an accomplished mathematician and respected astronomer, although he had honed his skills during a stay in France. The two most capable scholars produced at All Souls during this period were Richard Forster and Thomas Heth. Forster was awarded an M.A. in 1567, which was probably the year he received a fellowship at the college. He had a deep interest in mathematics and astronomy, but in later life he supported himself as a medical doctor. He wrote several scholarly tracts; and shortly after his death in 1616, the famous historian William Camden eulogized

him as "medicinae doctor et nobilis Mathematicus." Thomas
Heth, who was a member of the college from the mid 1560s
until the mid 1580s, was also esteemed for his skills in astronomy and "physical affairs." Especially admired by John Dee,
Heth published a brief work in 1583 in which he denounced
the mathematical and astronomical ignorance of the average
astrologer of the period, although he did not attack the cult of
astrology itself.[23]

Like Christ Church and All Souls, Balliol produced several
accomplished scientists during these years. In 1579 Lawrence
Kemyss matriculated at Balliol, where his outstanding mathematical abilities prompted his election to a college fellowship
three years later. He remained at the college until 1589, when
he accepted service with Sir Walter Raleigh, who often engaged
capable young scholars with scientific interests. An exact contemporary of Kemyss, George Abbot, who eventually became a
bishop and, ultimately, primate of all England, enrolled at Balliol
in 1578, took his A.B. in 1582, and received an M.A. three years
later. For more than a decade Abbot held a Balliol fellowship
and tutored large numbers of undergraduates in geography, his
own special interest. Between 1597 and 1610, he was master of
nearby University College, and in 1599 he published the first
real geography textbook, A Briefe Description of the Whole
Worlde.[24]

Like many Oxford scholars of the late Tudor period, Abbot
was deeply influenced by Thomas Allen of Gloucester Hall, who
had a deep knowledge of mathematics, geography, and other
scientific subjects. Born in Staffordshire in 1540, Allen matriculated at Trinity College at age twenty-one, which was considerably later than most entering students. He received his A.B. and
M.A. degrees in 1563 and 1567, respectively, and held a Gloucester
fellowship from 1565 until he became principal of that small
college in 1577. A man of moderate Catholic beliefs that he kept
quietly to himself, Allen had a genuine scientific temperament
and was hailed in his own lifetime as a new Roger Bacon.
According to John Aubrey, he kept "a great many Mathematicall
Instruments and Glasses" in his private chamber at Gloucester
Hall, over which he presided for fifty-five years, until he died
at the age of ninety-two. In 1572 the earl of Leicester took
him to court to explain to Queen Elizabeth the supernova that
had suddenly appeared in the constellation Cassiopeia, and
on several occasions he visited John Dee's laboratories at
Mortlake and witnessed chemical instruments conducted there.

Among the many important figures influenced by Allen's teaching were Richard Hakluyt, Walter Warner, Robert Hues, and Thomas Harriot, all major scientists and geographers of the next generation.[25]

Partly because of the growing stress on scientific subjects, which were taught to their pupils by tutors of obvious learning and enthusiasm, the universities attracted more and more boys from well-to-do families after 1558. Of course there were other reasons as well why aristocratic parents chose to send their sons to Oxford and Cambridge during the second half of the sixteenth century. In the first place, the monks and friars of late medieval times were now absent from the scene, which was bound to be reassuring to men who had been fearful that their sons might be pressed into joining a monastic or mendicant order. Second, considerably higher educational qualifications were now required for government service than before the beginning of the Tudor period. Queen Elizabeth, who had been instructed as a girl in foreign languages, music, and other subjects, had a strong preference for cultivated individuals, and for the first time almost all the men on the Privy Council had profited from university training. Finally, the universities themselves were anxious to attract rich young students and took various steps to make their programs more attractive. For example, an Oxford University decree of 1591 made it possible for the eldest sons of esquires to qualify automatically for their A.B.s after twelve terms of residence, without even nominal compliance to the statutory requirements for graduation.[26] Doubtless this step was taken to entice rich young students to enroll, since they could be assessed substantial fees, not only at the time of entrance but also during each term of residence. Further, whenever such a boy completed his program of studies, he might present a valuable piece of plate to the college as a parting gift. Should such a boy grow up to be rich and influential, he might well remember his old college with donations of land, books, and money, and perhaps even with presentations to valuable church livings. Before founding Emmanuel College, Cambridge, in 1584, Sir Walter Mildmay supported his university alma mater, Christ's College, in just such ways.

At any rate, there were several reasons why wealthy families developed the practice of sending their sons to study at Oxford and Cambridge. One Elizabethan gentleman who provided university educations for all his sons was Sir Edward Montagu

(1532-1602), a Northamptonshire squire who was sheriff of his county a number of times. Montagu chose to enroll his eldest son and namesake at Christ Church, Oxford, where he received his A.B. in 1579. However, Montagu sent his three younger sons—Henry, James, and Sidney—to Christ's College, Cambridge, where their paternal grandfather had preceded them.[27] The distinguished lawyer Sir Thomas Egerton, who became Lord Keeper of the Great Seal in 1596, sent his two sons, Thomas and John, to Brasenose, Oxford, the same college he himself had attended as a young man, while Sir Nicholas Bacon, Lord Keeper from 1559 until his death twenty years later, enrolled his sons Anthony and Francis at Trinity College, Cambridge, whence they later departed for Gray's Inn in order to study the common law. Perhaps a few more examples of this sort will suffice. In 1564 the earl of Shrewsbury placed his two sons at St. John's, Oxford, at which society the three male offspring of the earl of Derby matriculated eight years later. During the late 1570s, John Holles, scion of a rich Nottinghamshire family and the future earl of Clare, became a student at Christ's College, Cambridge, while in 1585 the twelve-year-old Henry Wriothesley, heir to the earldom of Southampton, became a fellow commoner at St. John's, Cambridge. In 1594 the officials of nearby Christ's College were no doubt pleased to admit George Manners, the young earl of Rutland, and his two brothers.

In his classic study of the aristocracy during these years, Lawrence Stone contends that, "University education never became the *sine qua non* of the cultivated nobleman."[28] No serious student of the century 1540-1640 would dispute that assertion. Yet the influx of so many sons of aristocratic families, in addition to boys from the gentry and *haute bourgeoisie* — a Nottingham goldsmith, Walter Travers (d. 1575), provided university educations for his four sons—indicates that the social composition of the universities changed, and changed fairly dramatically, during the period under review.

The social status of entering students began to rise even before Queen Elizabeth's accession to the throne in 1558, however. As early as the 1540s, a few perceptive observers, including Roger Ascham and Hugh Latimer, had complained about the growing number of rich students who had no intention of preparing themselves for clerical careers.* Yet Ascham and Latimer may well have exaggerated the situation. In a 1559

*See above, page 124.

memorandum to parliament, Sir William Cecil held that the nobility ought to be *required* to provide a university education for their sons and that a third of all college scholarships should be reserved for the heirs of landed gentlemen with financial problems. Even as late as 1570, when Sir Humphrey Gilbert proposed a special academy to train the sons of the aristocracy, there were many who felt that the education of upper-class youth was still woefully inadequate. Gilbert himself held that view, and in his plan for an institution to be known as "Queene Elizabethe's Academie," he argued that, "By erecting this Academie, there shall be hereafter, in effecte, no gentlemen within this Realme but good for somewhat [*i.e.,* something], Whereas now the most parte of them are good for nothing."[29]

As it happened, the need for a special institution like the one Gilbert envisaged had already been overtaken by events. By the early 1570s, the influx of upper-class boys into the universities had begun in earnest, and from that decade on, bitter complaints about what was happening were frequently heard. During the mid 1570s the Reverend William Harrison of Colchester noted that the various colleges of the universities had been "erected by their founders . . . only for poor men's sons, whose parents were not able to bring them up into learning; but now they have the least benefit of them, by reason the rich do encroach upon them."[30]

To what degree the Reverend Harrison accurately described the situation is difficult to tell. Insufficient evidence survives for a statistical analysis of the social composition of the two universities, which kept almost no records about entering and graduating students. Although Gonville and Caius College initiated an admissions register as early as 1557, in which it recorded pertinent social facts along with the names of each new entrant, the other colleges followed suit only gradually. St. John's, Cambridge, did not begin such a register until 1630. However, by means of complicated research, Lawrence Stone has analyzed the social origins of all students enrolled at Oxford between the 1570s and the 1630s. As a result of that analysis, Professor Stone argues convincingly that, despite the influx of boys from aristocratic and bourgeois families, students from humble backgrounds managed to keep from being crowded out. Indeed, the sons of "plebeians"—glovers, tailors, dyers, drapers, husbandmen, and the like—still accounted for at least half of all the entrants to the older university during that period. In Professor Stone's words:

Students describing themselves as sons of plebeians were [still] coming to Oxford in very considerable numbers in the late 16th and early 17th centuries. They comprised the largest single element in the university, amounting to over 50 percent in the 1570s and 1630s. . . . Even if allowance is made for the higher level of non-registration by the social élite, the proportion must still have been about the fifty percent mark.[31]

That lower-class boys did not disappear from the universities during those years was owing to several related factors. Foremost among these, no doubt, was the growing recognition on the part of the poor that higher education was an essential qualification for social, economic, and political advancement. For several centuries the more farsighted among the poor had suspected this to be the case, and since the time of Henry VIII, their belief had been strengthened by the growing awareness that even aristocratic youth must equip themselves through advanced study for service to the state. As long ago as 1531, Sir Thomas Elyot had openly proclaimed that message to the gentry in his influential *Boke named the Governour*, which was consulted by readers of all classes. If the social elite now acknowledged the value of university training for their sons, was this not clear proof that the lower-class attitude towards higher education had been correct all along?

The genuine desire of the poor for formal education was often encouraged by the elite during these years. Thomas Cromwell had done as much during the 1530s, but in the period after 1558 the strongest proponent of university training for boys from humble families was probably Sir Nicholas Bacon, himself a sheepreeve's son who became an imminent lawyer and, for two decades, Lord Keeper of the Great Seal. A generous supporter of the grammar schools at St. Albans and Redgrave, Bacon donated substantial sums to establish six scholarships at his Cambridge alma mater, Corpus Christi, for poor graduates of those grammar schools. In the opinion of Bacon's modern biographer, those six scholarships are clear proof of his "recognition that the humbly born might use formal education as a stepping stone to social advancement."[32]

A second factor that contributed to the continued presence of large numbers of poor boys at the universities was the growing feeling that advanced academic studies were necessary for those who wished to preach the reformed religion. To be sure, the social status of the parish priest was improving at the time, this development being as important as the rise of the gentry.[33] However, the value of most clerical livings was still too low to attract many boys from wealthy families, so a majority of parish ministers inevitably came from the ranks of the poor, who comprised the bulk of the population. If the parish ministry was to be a learned one, fully capable of spreading the new precepts, provision had to be made at the universities for the education of poor boys destined for the church. Such considerations led to the establishment of the two new Cambridge colleges of the era, both of which were intended exclusively for poor boys who hoped to become country parsons. Indeed, Sir Walter Mildmay decreed in his original statutes for Emmanuel College, which he founded in 1584, that all entrants were to be "candidates for the ministry, poor and able," and that those elected to graduate fellowships "were to be poor men of pure religion." Should a fellow accept a benefice worth over £10 annually, he was to resign his place immediately, so it could be assigned to another poor student.[34] Issued more than a decade after Emmanuel's, the statutes of Sidney Sussex College stipulated virtually the same things. In fact, the younger society's regulations decreed that any fellow named to a benefice worth over £20 a year would automatically forfeit his place on the foundation. In addition, any member of the society who nominated a rich man's son for a scholarship would be fined half his own yearly stipend.[35]

A third and final factor that contributed to the continued presence of poor boys at the universities might be described as the variety of ways enterprising students without means could secure help with their expenses. The first source of such assistance was from the colleges themselves. Since the appearance of the original colleges during the thirteenth century, work-study students known as "sizars" had been appointed to perform menial duties, like the tasks of stewards and butlers in private households. In more recent times, students generally described as "private" or "proper" sizars had been added to the foundation in order to serve the personal needs of the master, the senior fellows, and rich fellow commoners. Being such a student was not considered degrading since, in almost all respects, they were treated like other undergraduates. Although they often waited on fellow members during meals in the hall, they participated in the usual examinations and scholarly exercises and progressed towards their goals at speeds dictated by their abilities. Between 1558 and 1603 many more sizars appeared on the scene than ever before, since the large number of fellow commoners in attendance led to an increased demand for humbly born servants to perform personal services. In essence, therefore, an able and enterprising boy could "work his way through college" in this fashion, without prejudice to his future prospects. Of the eight men who succeeded Dr. Caius as master of Gonville and Caius College between 1573 and 1700, exactly half began their rise up the academic ladder as sizars.[36]

Another way poor but enterprising boys managed to attend the universities was by securing help from a wealthy patron. Peers, bishops, and important government officials often assisted boys from humble families to secure the advanced training that was now essential to get ahead in the world. Sir Walter Mildmay, Queen Elizabeth's longtime Chancellor of the Exchequer and the worthy founder of Emmanuel College, is known to have rendered such aid to poor boys, and on at least one occasion so did Sir Thomas Smith, who held the important post of principal Secretary of State for a time. In 1566 Smith provided funds so that Gabriel Harvey, the precocious son of a humble farmer and ropemaker of Saffron Walden, Essex, could attend Christ's College, Cambridge, where he compiled a distinguished academic record and was elected in 1570 to a fellowship at Pembroke Hall.[37] In much the same way Mildred Cecil, Lady Burghley, wife of the queen's chief minister, occasionally helped poor boys without means to attend a university. In 1580 she arranged for Richard Neile, the promising son of a tallow chandler whose death had left the family almost destitute, to study at Cambridge at her expense. Neile eventually became a distinguished cleric and, after serving as bishop of Durham for fifteen years, capped his career as archbishop of York.[38]

From time to time a master or fellow of one of the colleges of the age agreed to pay the expenses of an able student without means. This happened between 1578 and 1584, when Paul Gould of Gonville and Caius College stood sponsor to John Fletcher, who has already been mentioned in another context in this chapter. The son of a poor Yorkshire husbandman, Fletcher was what is today known as a "late bloomer." He did not even begin his grammar-school studies until the age of eighteen, when he became a pupil of a Mr. Hargraves of Leeds. Yet in less than three years he mastered everything Mr. Hargraves could teach him and hoped to find a way to enroll at either of the universities. How his plight came to the attention of Paul Gould at Cambridge is unclear; but beginning in February 1578 Gould paid all the expenses of his protégé, whose academic progress was rapid. Fletcher took his M.A. in 1584, and three years later he was elected to a college fellowship. Until his death in 1613, he remained at Gonville and Caius, tutoring scores of undergraduates and pursuing his own scientific interests.[39]

On a number of occasions rich individuals bequeathed funds to assist needy students already enrolled at the universities. During the mid 1570s, Edward, Lord Hastings and Lady Elizabeth Dennis left sums of £40 or more apiece to be disbursed among the poorest undergraduates of all the colleges. Perhaps the largest donation of this sort was made by Dame Alice Smith, who in 1593 bequeathed £200 to "the poore scholers in the 2 Universities." A generous person, evidently, Dame Alice left well over £300 to other charities.[40]

During the Elizabethan period hundreds of recurring scholarships worth between 10s. and £21 a year were established to help poor boys attend the universities. In 1569 Robert Nowell, a distinguished lawyer and the attorney of the Court of Wards and Liveries, left a bequest of £912 for two related purposes: the endowment of a former chantry school at Middleton, Lancashire, where he and his two younger brothers had all studied many years before, and the establishment of seven university scholarships for the most qualified graduates of that school. Nowell's wishes were implemented in 1572 by his brother Alexander, dean of St. Paul's Cathedral and one of Queen Elizabeth's favorite clerics. Not only did Alexander Nowell honor his late brother's intentions, but he himself established six scholarships to help poor boys from Middleton School to attend Brasenose College, Oxford, his own alma mater. Thus by the end of the 1570s there were thirteen scholarships for graduates of this one Lancashire school, which had some 200 students enrolled by 1600.[41]

Women donors were especially active in establishing new scholarships, although any benefits their sex derived from this form of philanthropy were indirect at best. In 1563 Mrs. Joan Trapps of London left funds to establish four scholarships at Lincoln College, Oxford, and four others at Gonville and Caius, Cambridge, each worth £2 13s. 4d. annually. Less than a generation later Mrs. Trapps' daughter, Joyce Frankland, widow of a wealthy Hertfordshire clothier, proved one of the greatest benefactors of the universities during the entire period. In her will of 1587, Mrs. Frankland left £1,200 to be split equally between

Lincoln and Brasenose Colleges, Oxford and Emmanuel College, Cambridge. To her favorite collegiate society, Gonville and Caius, Cambridge, she left the large sum of £1,540 along with a yearly rental of £33 6s. 8d., the latter sum always to be used for the support of twelve poor undergraduates each year.[42]

Many other women of the age made similar, albeit less valuable, contributions. In 1575 Lady Margaret North gave £500 to the Mercers' Company, the interest from which was to be used to assist poor boys in the grammar schools and then, "if they should be found apt for [advanced] learning," at either of the universities. Three years later Lady Burghley established two scholarships at her husband's Cambridge society, St. John's, to which she later presented £20 and a valuable polyglot Bible. In 1585 Queen Elizabeth herself established an annuity of 25 marks out of the revenues of ex-monastic lands for the maintenance of five poor students at Emmanuel College, Cambridge. About the same time she also founded six comparable scholarships for the aid of poor but deserving undergraduates at Brasenose College, Oxford. At her death in 1596, Mrs. John Titley of King's Lynn left £130 to the municipal corporation of that town, on condition that her bequest be coupled with any funds the corporation could raise for the support of two local boys at Emmanuel, Cambridge. In 1603 this benefaction bore fruit in the establishment of two scholarships worth £4 apiece for terms not to exceed seven years. Meanwhile Peterhouse, Cambridge had received a bequest in 1601 from Lady Mary Ramsey, by which it was able to establish four scholarships and two fellowships.[43]

The founding of new scholarships was one of the main ways by which contemporaries demonstrated their approval of the universities' work. There were other ways as well, including the gift of substantial funds and building materials to help with construction projects. Corpus Christ College, Cambridge, received especially generous aid during the late 1570s, when it erected a new chapel at a cost of £650. Sir Nicholas Bacon donated £200, while the earl of Bedford sent 146 tons of stone from his quarry at Thorney Abbey. Queen Elizabeth also contributed to the undertaking, presenting thirty loads of timber from various royal estates.[44] Soon after its establishment in 1584, Emmanuel College profited in much the same way. A former Lord Mayor of London, Sir Wolstan Dixie, gave £650 to help finance the original quadrangle, while the rector of Croxton, Dr. Edward Leeds, contributed 1,000 marks.[45] During the years 1596–98, St. John's College, Oxford, received generous gifts from several donors when it erected a new library at a cost of over £765. Robert Barkley of Marden, Kent contributed £100 to the building fund, and largely because the college founder, Sir Thomas White, had been a respected member, the Merchant Taylors' Company of London gave another £100. In addition, two individual members of that company, William Craven and Robert Dow, donated £50 each, while Dow provided another 25 marks for the purchase of books to be chained in the new library.[46]

Sidney Sussex, Cambridge was one of the most fortunate colleges of the era in attracting benefactions. The £5,000 bequest left in 1589 by Frances, countess of Sussex, for the establishment of a new society was hardly sufficient for the purpose. Lady Sussex feared as much, for in her will she specified that the whole amount should be offered on certain conditions to Clare Hall, should her executors decide a new collegiate body could not be maintained with such limited funding. After several years' reflection, the countess's executors, led by her nephew Sir John Harington and Henry Grey, earl of Kent, decided to proceed with the foundation of a new society, which was officially opened in 1596. Both Harington and Lord Kent waived the legacies of £100 left to them by the countess so the college's meager resources might be augmented. Harington made a number of valuable gifts to the college as well, including money for the building fund, stone to pave the chapel floor, and lands to increase the endowment. All in all, he contributed almost as much money to the project as his aunt and therefore should be remembered as the college's co-founder.[47]

At the turn of the sixteenth century, the imposing second court of St. John's, Cambridge, was built largely at the expense of Mary Cavendish, countess of Shrewsbury, a woman of serious intellectual interests. Designed by the noted architect Ralph Simons, the second court of St. John's was expected to cost £3,400, and the countess pledged to contribute the full amount. However, after four years of construction, the cost had risen to £3,655, while, because of unexpected expenses of her own, Lady Shrewsbury could supply no more than £2,760. The college bore the other £895 out of its own funds but nevertheless felt deeply grateful to the countess, whose coat-of-arms was subsequently erected over the main gateway to the new court.[48]

One last way Elizabethan benefactors aided the institutions of higher education was through gifts of valuable books and manuscripts. During the years 1558-1642, almost all the college libraries grew at a steady rate. For example, Trinity College, Cambridge, owned only 325 books during the early 1560s, but by 1640 its collection had increased to approximately 1,900 volumes. Of course, not all the growth of that period was owing to the generosity of alumni and other donors. From the latter years of Henry VIII, most of the colleges used a portion of their revenues for the purchase of library materials. In 1544 Oriel College, Oxford, even sold silver plate to the value of £30 in order to buy important tracts on theology and other subjects, while in 1572 nearby Magdalen College spent £120 to acquire the extensive collection left by John Jewel, bishop of Salisbury (d. 1571).[49] Although the colleges were now buying large quantities of books with their own funds, valuable bequests of such items occurred at regular intervals, without which the various collections could not have expanded as rapidly as they did.

Rich clerics were particularly active in this form of educational philanthropy. In 1561 an Essex vicar, John Dotyn, bequeathed a substantial collection of books to Exeter College, Oxford, many of them early printed works on medicine. In 1575 Archbishop Parker left 433 volumes to his old Cambridge college, Corpus Christi. The Parker bequest was especially rich in medieval manuscripts and included nearly 150 from the twelfth century or before. It also contained 21 volumes of miscellaneous state papers relating to Henry VIII's break from Rome and the early history of the Church of England. During the last quarter of the sixteenth century, Parker's two successors on the throne of St. Augustine contributed to the further growth of two different college collections. In 1583, Archbishop Grindal bequeathed the bulk of his substantial library to Queen's College, Oxford, although some of his books found their way to Pembroke Hall, Cambridge, where one of his chaplains had studied a generation before. Sometime during the 1590s— probably in 1599—the next primate, John Whitgift, arranged the transfer of 72 valuable manuscripts from the cathedral *scriptorium* at Canterbury, where they were seldom used, to the library of Trinity College, Cambridge. On his death in 1604, Archbishop Whitgift bequeathed 154 more "splendid medieval manuscripts" to the officials of Trinity College, even though he reserved nearly all his printed books to form the nucleus of a library at Lambeth Palace.[50]

Rich gentlemen and government officials were also important donors of books during these years. In 1566 Sir William Petre gave Exeter College, Oxford, to which he had already granted lands worth as much as the original endowment, the handsome European editions of the writings of St. Augustine and St. Jerome, which had appeared in 1543 and 1546, respectively. Meanwhile nearby Magdalen College had received a large gift of books from Henry Hastings, third earl of Huntingdon, who had sent a younger brother to study there in 1560. Huntingdon's gift included the works of Gregory Nazianzen in Latin and Greek, which had recently become available in print. During the 1590s Sir Thomas Tresham, a Northamptonshire squire of Catholic sympathies, donated 190 volumes to St. John's College, Oxford, while that same society benefited from a bequest of 256 books received in 1600 from the estate of Henry Price. About the same time, William Smart of Ipswich presented more than 100 books that had once belonged to the abbey of Bury St. Edmunds to Pembroke Hall, Cambridge.[51]

If scores of donors aided the college libraries of the time, benefactors of all ranks and stations gave energetic support to the campaigns to reestablish the university-wide collections. As noted in earlier chapters, the Oxford and Cambridge libraries had suffered repeated depredations between 1535 and 1558, as zealous religious reformers removed and destroyed books that gave them offense. By 1556 Duke Humphrey's Library at Oxford was so barren and depleted that Convocation ordered the sale of all the desks and fittings in the room. At Cambridge the destruction was on a lesser scale, although improper care of the books from the 1520s took a heavy toll, and by 1553 a collection that had consisted of 500 to 600 volumes during the 1480s had declined to less than 180. Eventually there was almost bound to be an effort to rebuild both university libraries, especially when the college holdings began to expand at a steady rate.

During the early 1570s a successful campaign at Cambridge began under the direction of Dr. Perne, the energetic master of Peterhouse for many years. The Peterhouse collection had escaped serious harm during earlier upheavals, so Dr. Perne felt free to devote his time to the needs of the whole university. After a 1573 survey revealed that the Cambridge University Library currently had only 175 volumes, Dr. Perne and several other college heads launched a drive to secure whatever donations might be procured. On 16 May 1574, Bishop Pilkington of

Durham sent twenty books from his collection, and eight days later Archbishop Parker donated 25 manuscripts and 75 printed works. Within another few months Lord Keeper Bacon presented 73 books, mostly on geography, mathematics, and music, while that same day Bishop Horne of Winchester sent fifty folios, which were mainly early printed editions of the Church Fathers. Because of the gratifying outcome of the campaign launched in 1574, a keeper of the library was appointed in 1577, on Dr. Perne's suggestion. Predictably, the first keeper was a fellow of Peterhouse, a Mr. W. James, whose annual stipend of £10 was increased to £12 in 1589 through a provision of Dr. Perne's will. At Dr. Perne's death, the library was a grateful recipient of 120 of his books, the remainder being used to enlarge the collection at Peterhouse.[52]

During the last years of the sixteenth century, the Cambridge University Library showed continued growth. Before the end of the 1580s both Bishop Barnes of Durham and Bishop Chaderton of Chester presented many valuable printed works, whereas Lord Burghley sent dozens of Greek and Latin books, primarily on law and medicine. As early as 1587, John, Lord Lumley promised to give duplicates from his great collection of 2,800 volumes, although he did not do so until 1598, when he finally sent 89 folios. Meanwhile, in 1591, Thomas Lorkin, the Regius professor of medicine at Cambridge, had bequeathed his collection of 140 medical books, which were unaccountably withheld by his executor for three years, however. As a result of these and many similar donations, the Cambridge University Library had approximately 950 books by 1600, a respectable if not commanding total.[53]

Even more successful than the campaign at Cambridge was the attempt to reestablish a true university library at Oxford. The leader of this undertaking was the distinguished diplomat Sir Thomas Bodley (1545-1613), whose name is memorialized by the great Bodleian Library of today. Born at Exeter and educated at Magdalen College, Bodley compiled an outstanding undergraduate record and was eventually elected to the position of university orator. Between 1576 and 1580 he traveled extensively on the continent, and shortly thereafter he entered the diplomatic corps, making an enviable record for himself in that field between 1585 and 1595. During the mid 1590s, he was closely associated with the political faction led by the earl of Essex, who solicited his appointment as principal Secretary of

State in 1596. When Bodley failed to receive that important office, he retired from public life, and within a short time he decided to launch a great educational enterprise at Oxford. On 23 February 1598, he offered in a famous letter to the vice-chancellor to restore the old library chamber, empty for over four decades to its former state, and "to make it fitte, and handsome with seates, and shelfes, and deskes, and all that may be needfull, to stirre up other mens benevolence, to helpe to furnish it with books." Bodley's proposal was quickly accepted and a committee of six men appointed to assist him. The building of desks and book presses began within a few months, and by 1600 the former library had been handsomely refurbished. During that year a senior fellow of New College, Thomas James, was named its first librarian, the acquisition of books and manuscripts being already well advanced.[54]

Bodley's efforts on behalf of a university-wide collection at Oxford generated considerable enthusiasm, and almost at once donors appeared from all sides and made generous contributions. Lord Lumley, who had honored his promise to the Cambridge University Library in 1598, sent 34 folios to the Bodleian the next year. Lords Cobham, Buckhurst, Lisle, Montacute, and Mountjoy also made substantial gifts, while in 1600 George, Lord Hunsdon donated 215 books. Bodley's old political supporter, the earl of Essex, sent 190 volumes in 1600. Four other members of the elite made notable contributions during this early period. By 1602 Sir Walter Cope, Sir Francis Vere, Sir John Croke, and Philip Scudamore had presented 191 books and manuscripts between them.[55]

Meanwhile, at Oxford itself, the campaign organized by Bodley produced an outpouring of contributions. Among the leading supporters of the project was Thomas Allen of Gloucester Hall, who belonged to the committee appointed in 1598 to advise Bodley. Not only did Allen donate twenty choice manuscripts from his own collection, but he also addressed appeals to prominent members of the political nation, including the "wizard earl" of Northumberland and Sir Walter Raleigh, who sent monetary contributions of £100 and £50, respectively.[56] Allen's associate at Gloucester Hall, William Gent, who also belonged to the advisory committee, was an even more generous contributor to the undertaking. In 1600 Gent presented works by Copernicus, Tartaglia, Archimedes, Regimontanus, Durer, Finé, Gesner, and Agricola, as well as a large number of medical tracts. By the time he died in 1613, Gent had given over 400 works to enrich the burgeoning collection. Other Oxford scholars who made substantial gifts at this early stage included Henry Stanford of Trinity College, John Fortescue of Corpus Christi, Anthony Blencowe of Oriel, and the first librarian himself, Thomas James. Together these four men donated 142 books and manuscripts.[57]

Several prominent clerics supported the campaign in similar ways. The archbishop of York, Tobias Matthew, made a substantial gift of books, while Bishop Westphaling of Hereford sent £20 to be used for the purchase of printed works or manuscripts. Shortly before his death in 1602, Dean Nowell of St. Paul's Cathedral made a comparable monetary contribution, and about that time the dean and chapter of St. George's Chapel, Windsor, did the same. The founder's brother, Laurence Bodley, a canon of Exeter Cathedral, presented thirty-seven folios, while his fellow canons at Exeter voted to send eighty-one of their library's choicest manuscripts, including a rare and extremely valuable Anglo-Saxon missal. In all these ways the Bodleian Library acquired an impressive collection of approximately 2,500 works by the time of its official opening in November 1602.[58]

In the years after 1602 the flow of books to the Bodleian did not cease. On the contrary it seems to have quickened; for when the first catalogue was compiled in 1605, it included nearly 6,000 titles. Moreover, by the time the second catalogue appeared in 1620, the collection had grown to approximately 16,000 works, making it easily the largest in the country.[59] It is true that much of the continued growth was owing to an agreement Bodley negotiated with the Stationers' Company of London in 1610. The Stationers had enjoyed a near-monopoly over book publishing in England since 1557, and in 1610 they consented to donate a copy of every book printed each year by all their members. In this way the Bodleian became the first library of deposit in the British Isles, if not in the world, and its holdings increased automatically as a consequence.[60]

By the outbreak of the Civil War, the Bodleian had attracted many other private donations, and by that juncture it was the largest library in Europe, with the possible exception of the Vatican Library in Rome, which dated from the mid-fifteenth century. The Bodleian's rapid expansion during the decades after its conception and establishment in 1598 would have been impossible without the enthusiastic support of all segments of English society for higher education in general and for Oxford University in particular.

9

Society, Religion, and the Grammar Schools, 1558-1603

❧ Just as Oxford and Cambridge were actively supported by all social groups except the very poor, so too were the grammar schools, which prepared boys for admission to the universities. During the Elizabethan period, more than £250,000 was contributed to school endowments and 130 new institutions were established throughout the realm. As a consequence, some 360 grammar schools in all existed by the time of the queen's death in 1603.

Several of the new grammar schools of the age resulted from community-wide efforts. Such was the case at Sandwich, where in 1563 the mayor and leading inhabitants organized a campaign that netted over £285 for the construction of a schoolhouse, a local lawyer having pledged to contribute lands for its support. At Richmond in the North Riding of Yorkshire, there was also a communal effort to establish a grammar school, which was officially founded in 1567. At nearby Halifax a campaign to raise funds for a school began in 1585, although that campaign proceeded slowly until a new vicar arrived in 1593 and infused it with new life. By 1601 over £265 had been raised for the Halifax school, which had begun to function the previous year. At nearby Wakefield there was also a successful drive, orga-

nized in 1591 by a rich wool merchant, to raise funds for a
school, while at Willingham, Cambridgeshire in 1593, 102 donors
subscribed just over 20s. each towards the establishment of an
endowed school.[1]

If several new grammar schools were founded in this way,
the great majority were established through individual action,
as in the past. No single group or social class played a dominant
role in this important enterprise. Grocers, mercers, and fish-
mongers; drapers, yeoman farmers, and lawyers; nobles, landed
gentlemen, and women; bishops and country parsons: all made
important contributions to the rapid increase in the number of
grammar schools after Elizabeth's accession to the throne. Since
130 endowed schools were founded between 1558 and 1603,
it would be impossible to discuss them all. Particulars will
therefore be given for only one of exceptional importance—
Westminster School, which was founded (or more accurately
reestablished) by Queen Elizabeth and indirectly exercised a
strong influence over the better grammar schools of the age, as
we shall see.

Although not a great patron, comparable to Lady Margaret
Beaufort or Henry VIII, Queen Elizabeth did give considerable
support to educational causes. During the 1580s, as noted in
the previous chapter, she established ten scholarships for poor
boys at the universities, while in 1571 she provided the site and
property of an Oxford hall to help with the establishment of
Jesus College. Meanwhile she had resurrected and given lands
worth £320 to the former chantry school at Wimborne Minster,
Dorset, which Lady Margaret had originally founded. After a
progress through Kent in 1574, she refounded the monastic
school that had once existed in the town of Faversham. During
the course of her reign she also assisted more than a dozen
other grammar schools, and not long before her death she
donated £200 to Trinity College, Dublin, which had been founded
in 1591. None of these educational works ranks, however, with
her one major contribution—the reestablishment of Westminster
School in 1560.

Shortly after her accession in 1558, Elizabeth dissolved
Westminster Abbey, which had been reconverted into a true
monastic society by Mary, and assigned it the status of a collegiate church, as Henry VIII had done two decades before. Further,
in June 1560 Elizabeth issued letters patent for the reestablishment of a school of the same size as the one that had functioned

in the Abbey's precincts between 1543 and 1555. To be financed out of the revenues of the deanery and chapter, this school was to consist of up to 120 students, of whom forty would be known as "Queen's Scholars." All poor boys of limited means, these students were to be admitted free of charge and would receive yearly payments of £4 7s. 6d. for their ordinary expenses. The other pupils would be required to pay whatever fees the school charged, although they could board at the school in the dormitory known as the Long Room, the old monastic granary that was used for that purpose until the eighteenth century. As the classroom the great monastic dorter was adapted, and in that single chamber all the boys were taught until 1884.[2]

Statutes for Westminster School were issued in 1560 by Dr. William Bill, dean of the Abbey as well as provost of Eton and master of Trinity College, Cambridge. The schoolmaster was to receive a yearly stipend of £19 11s. 8d., while his usher or assistant was to be paid £14 11s. 8d. and the master of the singing boys £11 11s. 8d. In deference to the queen's wishes, the schoolmaster was always to be an ordained cleric, and by means of six scholarships the school was academically linked to her father's great university foundations, Christ Church and Trinity College, both being required to elect three promising graduates of Westminster School to existing scholarships each year. For the curriculum of the school, Dr. Bill adopted with minor changes the course of study that had long been used at Eton.[3]

Dr. Bill died in 1561, after getting the school off to a strong start. To succeed him as dean of Westminster, the queen appointed Gabriel Goodman, a protégé of Sir William Cecil, who had an abiding interest in the school. Goodman remained at the Abbey for forty years, and under his watchful eye, the school became one of the finest in the land. It produced scores of outstanding graduates, including Richard Hakluyt, Ben Jonson, John Dryden, John Locke, and Sir Christopher Wren.

The first great teacher associated with Westminster School was Edward Grant. An accomplished Greek and Latin scholar, Grant received an A.B. from St. John's College, Cambridge, in 1567 and an M.A. from a yet-undetermined Oxford college six years later. He first became associated with Westminster School in 1570, when he was appointed assistant headmaster. Within two more years he was elevated to the headship, a position he occupied until 1593. In 1577 he became a prebendary of the Abbey, and before his death in 1601 he was named its sub-dean.

As early as 1575 Grant produced an outstanding Greek grammar for his pupils' use. Dedicated to Cecil and entitled *Graecae Linguae Spiciligium,* this was the first such work to be published by an Englishman since the time of Richard Croke two generations earlier. It was a fairly large quarto of 204 leaves and has been described by one authority as:

> One of the neatest grammars I have ever seen of any language. . . . It is an example of the marvellous results obtained by applying the form of the Latin grammar to the presentation of the grammatical forms of another language.[4]

Even before the publication of Grant's textbook in 1575, Greek had been taught in several grammar schools of the realm. Between 1510 and 1522, William Lily had offered instruction in that language to the students of St. Paul's School, but by common agreement the first English schoolmaster to teach Greek was William Horman, headmaster first at Eton (1485-94) and then at Winchester (1494-1502). Although the evidence is far from conclusive, Horman's *Vulgaria* of 1519 included a few grammatical exercises he had probably assigned to his pupils before 1502. Among these were Greek phrases and a series of references to Greek writings and plays. Horman seems to have established a tradition of Greek-teaching that continued at Eton for several decades after his departure in 1494. During Queen Mary's reign, Sir Thomas Pope, who had been a student there during the early 1520s, wrote, "I remember when I was a young scholler at Eton the Greke tongue was growing apace; the study of which is now . . . much decaid."[5]

During the mid-sixteenth century, there were periodic attempts to include the teaching of Greek in the curriculum of the better grammar schools of the realm. For example, in the 1544 statutes of the grammar school attached three years before to Chester Cathedral, Henry VIII decreed that Greek as well as Latin should be taught to all the boys enrolled in that institution.[6] However, as long as there was no suitable textbook available, comparable to Lily's Latin grammar of 1515, Greek studies could not become permanently established at the grammar-school level. The appearance of Grant's long-needed textbook in 1575 changed the situation dramatically. For the first time schoolmasters throughout the realm had a work they could use to instruct schoolboys, and the teaching of Greek made rapid strides thereafter. Moreover, Grant's textbook provided the basis for an even more successful Greek grammar published in 1597 by the next headmaster of Westminster School, William Camden. Camden's textbook bore the title *Institutio Graecae Grammatices Compendaria,* and it was such an outstanding work that it was quickly adopted in all the better grammar schools of the kingdom. It remained the standard Greek textbook for English schoolboys until 1663, when yet another improved grammar was published by a later headmaster of that same school, Richard Busby.

At the same time Greek was being added to the curriculum of the better grammar schools, a greater religious component was developing also. The canons issued for the Church of England in 1571 required all schoolmasters to teach their pupils appropriate selections from the Bible. In addition, the new canons directed all schoolmasters to accompany their boys to church whenever a sermon was scheduled and to offer instruction in the tenets of the faith from an approved catechism. The catechism that gained quick acceptance after 1571 was a Latin work published the previous year by Alexander Nowell, dean of St. Paul's. Nowell's catechism was so popular that an English translation was almost immediately prepared by Thomas Norton, while in 1573 a Greek version was published by William Whitaker. Later in the reign Nowell's work was abridged into both a *Smaller* and a *Middle Catechism.* Over the years so many schoolboys were drilled by Nowell's precepts that it would be impossible to calculate the number.[7]

Whether the average schoolmaster of the period objected to the growing stress on religious instruction seems doubtful. Products of a society that emphasized daily worship by the family as well as regular church attendance on Sundays, they probably *welcomed* the addition of a larger religious element to the curriculum, which had hitherto been noted for its monotonous dependence on Latin grammar and literature. As a consequence there is no proof that any teacher after 1571 voiced opposition to his growing religious responsibilities; nor were they any complaints, apparently, when school statutes began to delineate those responsibilities more carefully and precisely.

At Maidstone, Kent, for example, the original statutes of 1560 had stipulated only that all students enrolled in the local grammar school were to attend the nearby parish church on Sundays and holy days throughout the year, "upon payn of due correction" for each unjustified absence. However, when revised statutes for the Maidstone school were issued in 1575, they were made much fuller on that score. Indeed, the tenth clause of the revised statutes decreed that, "The Master shall once in the weeke call all his Scollers to accompt howe they have frequented Divine Service and for their behavioure in Church at sermon tyme." Further, the first clause of those same revised statutes specified that:

> Acknowledging God to be the author of all good giftes, the Master with all his Scollers or the most parte of them shall every day at vii of the clock in the mornyng, humbly knelyng uppon their knees, make their prayers to Almightie God in manner & forme thought good by the Master so [long as] yt not be contrary to the lawes of this Realm.[8]

The same tendency towards a more careful delineation of the schoolmaster's religious duties is evident in the statutes of the grammar schools at Bury St. Edmunds and Wakefield. At Bury the original statutes of 1550 were revised in 1583 and made far more complete. According to the revised statutes:

> The boys shall learn thoroughly by heart, as well in Latin as in English, the Articles of Religion, the Lord's Prayer, the Ten Commandments, and other such Institutes of the Christian Faith as may be though desirable, and shall be taught therein every day of the week until their knowledge be perfect.[9]

At the Wakefield school, which accepted its first students in 1591, the master was required by the statutes to swear that, "The youth of this schole I shall diligentlie instruct in religion, learning, and good manners." More precisely, the Wakefield schoolmaster had to drill his pupils on the basic principles of the faith every Saturday between 1:00 and 2:00 P.M. and see that the boys attended church on Sundays and listened attentively to the sermon. On Mondays he was to question them at length about what the preacher had said the previous day, punishing those who had been absent or inattentive, "either by word, or by the rod, as the quality of the offence deserveth."[10] Although religion had always been taught in the country's schools, it had never enjoyed the prominence it attained after 1571, when the Geneva Bible of 1560, the Bishops' Bible of 1568, Nowell's catechism of 1570, and various other works of that nature were readily available for teaching purposes.

Because of the increasing time given to religion by the grammar schools, the national government was bound to seek a way to supervise the activities of schoolmasters. In actual fact, such a mechanism had long been at hand. Since the Synod of Westminster of 1200, successive monarchs had relied on the bishops and their deputies to licence men to teach within individual dioceses. Without an episcopal licence, which was granted after an interview or oral examination, no one could legally teach or keep a school. During the 1550s, several of Mary's prelates, including Bonner of London and Pole of Canterbury, had issued injunctions in an effort to strengthen the licencing process. As for Mary herself, she had instructed the episcopal bench as early as 1554 to "examine all schoolmasters and teachers of children and, finding them suspect in any ways, to remove them and place Catholic men in their rooms."[11] This policy of using the clerical hierarchy to oversee and control the religious beliefs of grammar-school teachers was continued after Mary's death. During the years 1558–1603, the episcopal licence was in fact the chief instrument used to enforce the Elizabethan settlement of religion in the country's grammar schools. John Lawson has therefore written without exaggeration:

> The grammar schools must have played a significant part in achieving the transition of England from Catholicism to Protestantism in the short space of three or four decades, though it is a part seldom acknowledged by historians of the period.[12]

Queen Elizabeth clearly expected all schoolmasters to acknowledge her supremacy over the church and be practising Anglicans. Shortly after her accession, she forbade men to teach without a licence, signifying a bishop's approval of their "right understanding of God's true religion," their "sober and honest conversation," and their "learning and dexterity in teaching."[13] These carefully worded phrases enabled the bishops to purge the grammar schools not only of Catholic sympathizers but also of teachers they considered morally or academically unfit to instruct schoolboys. How the bishops used the power conferred on them by the monarch naturally varied from diocese to diocese. One prelate who had no qualms about wielding his full authority was Thomas Young, archbishop of York from 1561 until 1568.

During his first year in office, Archbishop Young deprived a Yorkshire schoolmaster of eighteen years, Stephen Ellis of Skipton in Craven, a "good grammarian" who had called attention to himself by clinging too long and too loudly to the Old Faith. Presumably the beliefs of Ellis's successor, Robert Bolton, were more satisfactory to the authorities, since he remained in office until his appointment to be vicar of Carleton in 1577.[14] After a parliamentary act of 1563 required all schoolmasters to take the earlier Oath of Supremacy, Archbishop Young increased his inquiries into the convictions of schoolmasters throughout his diocese. In 1564 he asked detailed questions of at least fifty-seven men and refused to licence a number of them on religious grounds. Several others he restricted to the teaching of English grammar, since he considered them unqualified to offer instruction in Latin.[15]

If Archbishop Young was the most diligent prelate at the beginning of the reign, William Chaderton and William Overton were probably the most watchful at the end. Two years after becoming bishop of Chester in 1579, Chaderton addressed probing questions to his diocesan clergy about the men who taught in schools within their parishes. Chaderton wished to know:

> ... what schoolmasters have you within your parish or chapelry that teach openly or privately in any school, gentleman's house or elsewhere; and whether they be of good and sincere religion and licensed by the bishop of the diocese to teach in writing under his seal, and whether they be diligent in teaching and bringing up of youth and to instruct them in goodness and virtue, and especially in Master Nowell's Catechism lately set forth, and whether they teach anything contrary to the religion now set forth, or do not cause their children to resort to church to the divine service and sermons.[16]

Even more zealous than Chaderton was William Overton, bishop of Lichfield and Coventry from 1578 until 1609. In 1584 Bishop Overton went to the extreme length of canceling all existing licences after discovering "obstinate untowardness in religion in divers young gentlemen" and in the schoolmasters who had instructed them. A schoolmaster seeking the recovery of his licence had to appear before the bishop's court at Lichfield and be carefully examined about his "ability for learning and sound-ness of religion." A number of men were unable to satisfy Overton or his deputies on those two counts and failed to secure the return of their licences. Others regained authority to teach, but only in certain specified districts and not throughout the entire diocese.[17]

The concern about religious and moral instruction in the grammar schools did not cease upon Elizabeth's death and James I's accession to the throne. Indeed, the canons issued for the church in 1604 decreed that the local curate was to have first claim to the post of parish schoolmaster, although his clerical status did not absolve him of the requirement to secure a licence to teach. Further, a parliamentary act of that same year raised the penalty for keeping a school without proper authoriza-tion to 40s. a day. Despite such harsh measures as these, the government was unable to keep wealthy Catholic families from securing instruction in the Old Faith for their children. Some Catholic parents, especially in remoter districts of the north and west, engaged tutors who presided over illicit household schools, while others sent their teenage sons to a Jesuit academy at St. Omer, in the Low Countries. This school had opened in 1592 and was intended to serve as a preparatory division for Cardinal Allen's nearby seminary at Douai for missionary priests. By 1599 the St. Omer academy, which accepted boys from the age of fourteen, had 100 English students enrolled, while by 1635 the English contingent had almost doubled.[18]

Although the bishops never stamped out Catholic education completely, their watchfulness contributed to the rising stan-dards that were so evident in the grammar schools of the period. From time to time the bishops refused to licence teachers they considered unqualified to offer instruction in Latin grammar, and they actively promoted the employment of men with univer-sity degrees since such men were likely to be both "religiously sound" and academically well prepared. As a consequence a larger percentage of schoolmasters were university graduates by the end of the Tudor era than had been the case a century earlier, at least throughout the southwestern counties.[19] Writ-ing about the schools of Cambridgeshire between 1574 and 1628, Margaret Spufford contends that:

> . . . the general quality of the masters teaching in them was extraordinarily high. Nearly two-thirds of the men

licensed to teach grammar are known to have been [university] graduates. A number of the remainder may, of course, have qualified as well.[20]

In the London area the proportion was never as high, although it rose steadily over the period. During the 1580s approximately 27 percent of all the teachers in the diocese of London were Oxford and Cambridge men, but by the 1630s almost 60 percent were. The same phenomenon was evident in a rural county like Leicestershire, where during the years 1570–1660 "standards in the schools generally rose."[21]

It would naturally be wrong to attribute all the improvement that occurred to the bishops. Other forces at work during the age contributed to the same end. For example, more and more school founders believed that the master should normally be a university graduate. When in 1553 the rich London skinner, Sir Andrew Judd, established the Tonbridge Grammar School, he decreed that the master must always be of A.B. standing and, if possible the holder of an M.A. as well. Between 1553 and 1640 all seven of the men who presided over the Tonbridge school were in fact individuals with M.A. degrees.[22] During the mid 1580s the Reverend Robert Johnson, archdeacon of Leicester and rector of a Rutlandshire church, was even more explicit about the qualifications of the masters who were to preside over the two schools he had recently established within his county. The Reverend Johnson actually decreed that each of those schoolmasters:

> ... shall be at the time of his election, and so continue, an honest and discreet man, Master of Arts, and diligent in his place, painful in the educating of children in good learning and religion, such as can make a Greek and Latin verse.[23]

Similar provisions were included in the statutes of the Charter-house School, London, which was established with funds left by the lawyer and coal magnate Sir Thomas Sutton (d. 1611). The Charterhouse School statutes stated with rare precision:

> The school-master shall be Twenty-seven years of age at least, a Master of Arts, of good reputation, both for his life and learning in the Latin and Greek tongue. The Usher shall likewise be well qualified for his place,

having taken [the] degree of Bachelor of Arts two years at least before his election, aged Twenty-four years.[24]

Considerably more school founders of the era required the master to be an Anglican clergyman. This was the case not only at Westminster School in 1560 but also at New Woodstock, where in 1580 a Mr. Cornwall bequeathed funds for a grammar school to be run by an ordained cleric. The same requirement prevailed at Gainsborough and Tiverton. Indeed, at the latter place every schoolmaster was an Anglican priest from 1604, when the school finally opened, until 1874. The same arrangement had developed over fifty years earlier at Great Yarmouth, where there was an unbroken succession of clerical schoolmasters from 1551 until 1903.[25] Numerous other examples of this sort might be cited, but the point that really needs to be stressed here is that during the years 1558–1625, the percentage of clerics with academic degrees rose faster than that of schoolmasters. Thus school founders who decreed that the master must be in holy orders increased the odds that he would be a university graduate as well.

That a large majority of the schoolmasters of the era were clerics was also owing to the fact that clergymen themselves had extensive powers of appointment, since they often served as trustees of local grammar schools. At Barnstable the schoolmaster was chosen by the bishop of Exeter, while at Rochdale and Croydon the archbishop of Canterbury enjoyed the right to appoint. Vacancies at Heighington were filled by the dean and chapter of Durham Cathedral, while at Lowestoft the chancellor of the diocese of Norwich performed that function. In some sections members of the lower clergy exercised a comparable influence over the affairs of local grammar schools. At Tenterden the schoolmaster was chosen single-handedly by the vicar of the parish, while at Blakesley the resident vicar and the rectors of two neighboring churches were the permanent trustees of the grammar school, with power to select a new schoolmaster whenever vacancies occurred. Similar arrangements prevailed at Giggleswick, Cranbrook, Market Bosworth, Kirkby Lonsdale, and Dronfield, where in each case the local vicar was an *ex officio* member of the governing board of the town grammar school. In all these instances there are clear indications that clerics with rights of appointment were predisposed to nominate fellow clerics, particularly young men with recently awarded academic degrees.

Almost as important in this regard was the patronage exercised by certain university colleges. Over the years various
academic societies at Oxford and Cambridge had received the
right to appoint masters and ushers from the founders of new
grammar schools, and there can be little doubt that colleges
with such presentations exercised them almost exclusively on
behalf of their own graduates, especially those who had achieved
some academic distinction. By the 1590s St. John's, Cambridge,
had the right to appoint more schoolmasters than any other
college at either university. It not only named the masters
at Pocklington, Shrewsbury, Sedbergh, and Rivington, but it
also had an important consultative role in the selection of the
schoolmasters at Stamford and Aldenham. In comparison, no
other college seems to have controlled more than four such
appointments. New College, Oxford, chose the schoolmasters at
Winchester, Bedford, Rycote, and East Adderbury, while Trinity College, Cambridge, enjoyed three such presentations — at
Uttoexeter, Stevenage, and Stowe. Corpus Christi, Oxford, exercised that power at Manchester and Cheltenham, but most
colleges enjoyed only one such nomination. All Souls, Oxford,
made the selection at Faversham, and nearby Queen's at St.
Bees, while Emmanuel, Cambridge, appointed both the master
and usher at Bungay. In all these cases the colleges tended to
give first consideration to their own graduates, who were frequently already men of the cloth.

In order to attract and hold university graduates, whether laymen
or clerics, the schools of the Elizabethan period had to pay
higher salaries than their pre-Reformation counterparts. To be
sure, many schoolmasters received stipends of only £12 or £13
a year. But the majority made in the neighborhood of £20 or
£25 annually, while a select few, such as those at Shrewsbury
and St. Paul's, were paid £35 or more. There was, moreover, a
strong tendency after 1575 for schoolmasters' salaries to rise.
At Sutton Valence, Kent, where a school was established in
1578, the master originally received £20 per year plus a free
house and garden plot. Yet within a few years the Clothworkers'
Company of London agreed to assume responsibility for the
school and increased the master's yearly stipend to £30. Even
more dramatic were the additions made to the schoolmaster's
salary at Norwich. From 1562 until 1602 the master of the
Norwich Grammar School received £20 a year, but between
1602 and 1610 he was paid £26 13s. 4d. annually. During the

years 1610–36 his salary was £40, and after 1636 it was a generous £50. Thus, schoolmasters were better paid than is generally realized, although in a few places, especially small northern towns, their compensation remained woefully small.[26]

By comparison, the salaries of their teaching assistants tended to lag far behind, and in most cases the ushers were paid between £9 and £16 less per year than what the masters received. During the Elizabethan period, almost two-thirds of all ushers made less than £10 a year, and as late as 1596 the usher of the Boston Grammar School received a pittance of £3 yearly. At Pontefract from 1583, where the master's salary was £20, the usher was paid £5 7s. 2d.; while at nearby Wakefield during the 1590s, the stipends of the master and usher were £26 13s. 4d. and £10, respectively.[27]

As a consequence of this large differential in pay, the chance of obtaining well-educated ushers with university degrees was slight at best. In most cases ushers were barely equipped to perform their duties, and there was often friction between a poorly paid usher and his better-rewarded superior. In addition, many ushers held office for only a year or two before seeking better-paid employment, and schoolmasters therefore had to train assistants to their specifications at regular and frequent intervals. Moreover, schoolmasters often had to contend with unresponsive older students, since the ushers were ineffective in preparing the pupils for advanced work.

A contentious relationship with their ushers was only one of many difficulties that confronted most schoolmasters. Indeed, the average schoolmaster of the era worked under such trying conditions that many men regarded the prospect of a teaching career with horror. When in 1522 a Cambridge scholar was offered one of the best teaching posts in the realm, the mastership of St. Paul's School, he refused even to consider it and asked rhetorically, "Who would put up with the life of a schoolmaster who could get a living in any other way?"[28] Only a few years earlier, another individual, with whom Erasmus had a memorable conversation, characterized his position at the helm of a local grammar school as "tragic and deplorable"; to which the Dutch scholar made the well-meaning but naive reply that "schoolmastering is the noblest of occupations: to be a schoolmaster is next to being a king."[29] Only a few teachers are likely to have agreed with Erasmus. Their status in society was too low and the daily problems confronting them too great.

In the first place, most Elizabethan schools accepted too many pupils in relation to the number of teachers they employed. Today a teacher is rarely assigned more than 25 to 30 students at most, but four centuries ago a single teacher might well be responsible for 50, 60, or even 70 pupils. Rarely did a school with fewer than 50 students employ an usher to help in teaching the basics of grammar to the younger pupils. In a school of 50 to 100 students, the master would probably have one assistant; and in a school of more than 100 students, he might have an extra helper for each additional 50 to 60 boys, but this was not always the case. For example, Merchant Taylors' School in London usually had at least 250 boys enrolled, but its teaching staff consisted of only a master and three ushers. Shrewsbury School was an even larger institution, probably the largest in the country during the Elizabethan period. In 1581 there were 360 students in attendance at Shrewsbury, who were instructed by the master and four ushers. But this meant that each teacher on average was responsible for 72 students at a school that was widely considered the finest in the land.[30]

A second major difficulty that hampered most schoolmasters was the "open classroom situation" in which they all taught. Elizabethan grammar schools were in essence one-room schoolhouses, although 100 to 350 students might well be enrolled. All the boys sat on uncomfortable wooden benches in a single classroom that was usually between 20 and 30 feet wide and 60 to 80 feet long. At Eton, one of the best schools of the period, the classroom measured 24 by 76 feet, while at Shrewsbury, it was 21 feet wide and 78 feet long.[31] These large, open classrooms were hardly suitable for the kind of teaching that took place in them. As any language teacher knows, the rules of grammar are difficult to explain and make interesting under the best of circumstances. But in a large open space containing 100 boys or more at different academic levels, it was virtually impossible. The students' attention was constantly diverted by what was happening elsewhere in the room; and there was thus a tendency to erect partitions, put up curtains, or create barriers in some way. At Shrewsbury by the early seventeenth century, wooden screens were in general use. In a book written in the mid 1630s but not published until 1660, Charles Hoole suggested that all schoolrooms "be so contrived with folding doors betwixt every Form, as that upon occasion it may be laid open into one roome, or parted into six, for more privacie or hearing every Form without noyse, or hinderance one of another."[32] Apparently the first school building that had a separate classroom for each form was the one Thomas Farnaby created in London during the 1620s by merging several houses in Goldsmiths' Alley. Farnaby's school did so well that it made him a rich man, one of the few teachers of the age to enjoy material success.[33] One cannot help but feel that an important reason for the great success of Farnaby's school was that he of necessity rejected the open classroom for the teaching of subjects that do not require—indeed, do best without—group interaction.

A third difficulty that hampered most schoolmasters was the exceptionally long hours they worked. The school day usually began at 6 or 7 A.M. and lasted until 5 or 6 P.M., although there was a midday break for dinner and fifteen-minute recesses at 9 A.M. and 3 P.M. At Wakefield Grammar School in 1607, morning classes extended from 6:00 until 11:00 A.M., while the afternoon session lasted from 1:00 to 6 P.M. At boarding schools like Eton and Winchester, the boys were required to rise at 5 A.M. and attend prayers in the chapel at 5:30 before classes commenced at 6 o'clock. Because most schools attempted to avoid unnecessary use of expensive candles, the day was usually two hours shorter during the dark winter months, when it began at sunrise and ended at 5 P.M. However, it was not at all unusual for teachers and pupils to spend ten hours a day at school, six days a week.

Such long hours are likely to have caused fatigue as well as a somewhat cavalier attitude towards teaching and learning alike. The boys' attention probably strayed increasingly as the day wore on, causing disciplinary problems to mount and the teachers' nerves to become jagged. As a consequence many schoolmasters made excessive use of paddles and whips, since the age did not frown on the application of corporal punishment to wayward schoolboys. More than a few teachers of the period were widely known as ferocious birchers of "their children." Nicholas Udall, who was headmaster at Eton during the 1540s, and his most celebrated pupil, Richard Mulcaster, who became an eminent schoolmaster in London after 1561, both acquired somewhat odious reputations for the severity of the whippings they applied. Occasionally a schoolmaster lost all self-control and punished a student unmercifully, causing permanent injury. This happened in 1582 at Braintree, Essex, where a young boy named William Bedell was brutally attacked by his enraged schoolmaster. Not only was young Bedell knocked down a flight of stairs, but he was also hit so violently on the side of his head "that the blood gushed out of his ear, and his hearing was in consequence so impaired that he became in process of time wholly deaf on that side."[34] Such violent school-masters were rarely dismissed, however. At Clitheroe in 1619 there was a spirited campaign to secure the schoolmaster's discharge because he was "of a hot stomach and beats men's children most cruelly." But that campaign, like nearly all compa-rable ones of the period, failed to achieve its goal.[35]

A final difficulty that confronted many schoolmasters was rigid and unimaginative school trustees who insisted on an inflexible adherence to the founders' statutes. A case in point is the experience of Thomas Neale, who was master of the Aldenham School in Hertfordshire from 1599 until 1623. A dedicated teacher with a degree from Cambridge, Neale encountered repeated criticisms from the Brewers' Company of London during his last decade at Aldenham. The school's offi-cial trustee after its founder's death in 1600, the Brewers' Com-pany demanded that Neale devote all his time to teaching his pupils the finer points of Latin grammar, even though Aldenham was a poor farming community with little need for the type of classical instruction decreed by the school's statutes. By the early 1620s Neale seems to have devised a course of study more appropriate for the average boy who came to work under him for a year or two, although he never refused to teach Latin grammar to the occasional student with an aptitude for it. This policy of the schoolmaster's infuriated the Company's leaders, particularly when they learned in 1623 that only one of his pupils was currently studying Latin. On 19 September Neale was abruptly told that he would be dismissed within ten more days. Yet because he was respected throughout the area for his learning and piety, he was soon named vicar of Ridge, a few miles away.[36]

Even Richard Mulcaster, one of the greatest teachers of the age despite his excessive use of corporal punishment, was frus-trated by the opposition of the Merchant Taylors' Company while he headed its large school between 1561 and 1586. The puritan-minded leaders of the Company disliked Mulcaster's stress on the performance of ancient Latin plays by the boys of the school. Moreover, they refused to take responsibility for the £10 yearly supplement that one of the school's original pro-ponents, Richard Hilles, had paid Mulcaster out of his own pocket from the time the school opened in 1561 until his death in 1577 or 1578. With his income almost halved, Mulcaster found himself in dire straits and felt compelled to take boarders into his own house. Still unable to manage, he admitted more boys into the school than the 250 permitted by the statutes in order to obtain additional entrance fees. This sparked bitter criticisms of his actions by the Company, and when he finally resigned in 1586 out of financial necessity, he expressed his animosity towards the Company in the bitter but understandable phrase, *"Fidelius servus, perpetuus asinus."*[37]

In view of the many problems they faced, it is hardly surprising that many schoolmasters tired of teaching after a few years and suffered the condition we know today as "burnout." William Camden, an unusually dedicated and conscientious teacher, eventually lost all enthusiasm for the work and resigned the headship of Westminster School after a teaching career that spanned less than three decades. Thereafter Camden supported himself as Clarenceux King of Arms in the College of Heralds until he died in 1623. Thomas Asheton, who did such an outstanding job at Shrewsbury School from 1561 until 1571 that he is often considered its real founder, also resigned his post some years before his death, while Christopher Johnson, the first headmaster of the reestablished Westminster School, voluntarily stepped down to become a doctor in the capital.

Many of the men who gave up teaching careers did so to accept positions in the church, which were usually better paid, commanded greater respect, and led to higher levels of satisfaction. John Argall, who held an Oxford M.A., was master of the grammar school at Abingdon, Berkshire, from 1565 until 1571, when he resigned to become vicar of Chalgrove, Oxfordshire. A slightly younger Oxford M.A., Charles Butler, presided over the grammar school at Basingstoke, Hampshire, from 1587 until 1594, when he too departed in order to accept a vicarage. During the reign of James I, Luke Mason, who was the schoolmaster at Newark from 1615 until 1618, and William Lance, master of the famous Harrow School in western Middlesex during the years 1615-21, both resigned their positions in order to accept clerical livings.

If many men dealt with the frustrations of teaching by seeking other livelihoods, the majority remained in the profession and coped with their problems as best they could. Indeed, most schoolmasters continued at their posts year after year, without relief of any sort or even the prospect of an occasional return to the university for renewed study. In view of this, it is remark-able that there were as many dedicated and conscientious teachers as there were, and we should therefore disregard the famous statement of Henry Peacham that "for one discreet and able teacher, you shall find twenty ignorant and careless, and . . . whereas they make one scholar they mar ten."[38]

That Peacham exaggerated the situation is proved by the large number of teachers who gave careful thought to what they did in the classroom, in an effort to make learning both an enjoyable and a rewarding experience. Two schoolmasters of that type, whose students clearly profited from their capable instruction, were William Camden and Hugh Robinson. Camden presided over Westminster School from 1593 until 1599 after being an usher there for twenty years. As noted earlier in this chapter, he produced an improved Greek textbook for his boys' use, and he also gave considerable time to the teaching of history, his own special interest. One of Camden's many pupils was the great Jacobean poet and playwright Ben Jonson, who was deeply grateful for his excellent teaching. Indeed, Johnson expressed his appreciation to old schoolmaster in the moving couplet:

> Camden most revered head to whom I owe
> All that I am in arts, all that I know.

The slightly younger Hugh Robinson was headmaster at Win-chester from 1613 until 1626. He published several textbooks for his students to use, the most important of which was his *Rhetorica Brevis* of 1616. This work was assigned to boys in the fifth and sixth forms at Winchester, and it was so successful that it was often used by poets and writers during the seven-teenth and eighteenth centuries.[39]

Perhaps the most dedicated teacher of the period was Richard Mulcaster, who, as already noted, presided over Merchant Taylors' School for twenty-five years and then, after a decade of private teaching, was headmaster of St. Paul's School from 1596 until 1608. A man of great ability, Mulcaster adopted a broader approach towards secondary education than any of his contem-poraries, with the possible exception of Camden. He recog-nized the need to teach arithmetic and geometry to schoolboys, and he additionally considered music a serious part of education, insisting that his pupils be able to perform vocal and instrumen-tal parts at sight. Never a pedant, he also emphasized the importance of drawing and what is today known as physical education. To him a boy should be able to fence, wrestle, and run; to dance, ride, and hunt; in short, to do all those things that increased bodily strength and coordination and which contemporary opinion deemed important.[40]

During the early 1580s, Mulcaster revealed much about himself and his beliefs in two important books, the *Positions* of 1581 and *The First Part of the Elementarie* of 1582. It would be impossible to do justice to the richness of Mulcaster's thought as demonstrated by these two works in a brief paragraph or two. But perhaps we can note a few of his suggestions for the improvement of education and how he hoped "to helpe the hole trade of teaching, even from the verie foundation that is . . . which is the verie infantes train, from his first entrie untill he be thought fit to passe thence to the Grammar schoole."[41] Mulcaster believed in the need for periodic conferences between parents and teachers, particularly when students were not progressing satisfactorily. In addition he advocated regular discussions between the masters and ushers of the larger schools, comparable to the staff meetings of today, which he felt would be helpful. He recognized the usefulness of special methods courses for future teachers and believed that the best qualified persons should be responsible for instructing the youngest students.

As already noted, Mulcaster emphasized the importance of teaching arithmetic and geometry. In fact, he urged that instruction in mathematics begin at the earliest possible age, and he hoped to see the establishment of a special department of mathematics at the universities one day. Fully conscious of how the English language had attained greater expressiveness during his lifetime, he called for all schoolchildren to be instructed in the proper use of their own native tongue. He proposed that the length of the school day, which generally extended to ten or eleven hours, be reduced by at least two hours, and he insisted that teachers be assigned fewer than the fifty to seventy-five students they currently superintended. A strong advocate of "educational mixing," he tried to discourage the growth of elitist schools that catered to the sons of rich families only, and he favored some education for all boys and girls, regardless of how humble their social circumstances. Almost all of Mulcaster's ideas were positive and constructive. Among the few that were not was his belief that the education of boys should always take precedence over that of girls and his contention that English students should be forbidden to attend foreign schools. Presumably he was afraid that English children educated on the continent would be confirmed in the Catholicism of their parents or come under strong Catholic pressures to renounce Protestantism.

Mulcaster was only one of several schoolmasters who wrote important tracts on education and how to improve the teaching methods of the time. Among the other works in this genre were John Hart's *Method or Comfortable Beginning for all Unlearned Whereby they may be Taught to Read English* and Edmund Coote's *Englische Scholemaister,* which appeared in 1570 and 1596, respectively. Hart's book was of no real significance for professional teachers, since it was essentially a self-help manual designed to aid the poor, who used it to develop basic reading skills. But Coote's was an influential book that remained available for generations. Only ninety-six pages in length, it was reprinted twenty-four times by 1636 and another twenty-three times by 1696. Reissued as late as 1737, *The Englische Scholemaister* was intended not only for teachers in the grammar schools but also for merchants and craftsmen who needed help in instructing their apprentices and household servants. The book was mainly concerned with ways to acquire reading skills and began by demonstrating the proper method of teaching the alphabet. It also contained sections on religion and Christian precepts. A short but thorough catechism on pages thirty-seven to forty-four was followed by eleven psalms and a number of prayers, including a thanksgiving to be said after meals. *The Englische Scholemaister* was thus a combined devotional and educational work, which helps to explain its extraordinary appeal to the people of the time.[42]

Almost as important an educational writer as Coote, William Kempe was headmaster of the Plymouth Grammar School during the last years of the sixteenth century. Kempe was familiar not only with the theories of Mulcaster and Roger Ascham, who wrote several important works before his death in 1568, but also with those of such continental writers as Joachim Sturm and Pierre de la Ramée. Like most Elizabethan teachers, Kempe stressed the study of both Cicero and Terence as models of fine Latin style; and because he believed most boys would profit from additional schooling, he proposed a comprehensive curriculum in eight forms rather than the usual six. Like Mulcaster earlier, Kempe preached that schoolboys should be well-versed in mathematics. In 1588 he published an important book,

Education of Children in Learning, in which he advocated that mathematical and reasoning skills be taught to boys before their sixteenth year, so they would be able "to wade without a schoolmaster through deeper mysteries of learning" when they were older. In addition he held that learning alone civilizes mankind and provides the Christian knowledge which is essential for salvation. Hence, the entire English people should promote education in every way possible in order to strengthen the realm and advance the Kingdom of God. In 1592 Kempe published a second important work, *The Art of Arithmetike in Whole Numbers and Fractions,* which was basically a translation of an earlier French book on that subject. Kempe dedicated this second work to Sir Francis Drake, of whom he was an ardent admirer.[43]

John Brinsley, a man of equally strong religious convictions, presided over the grammar school at Ashby de la Zouch, Leicestershire, from 1599 until 1619, when his radical puritanism caused the bishop of Lincoln to secure his ouster. Brinsley also published two important books, the first of which appeared in 1612 and was entitled *Ludus Literarius, or the Grammar Schoole.* He constructed this tract in the form of a dialogue between two experienced schoolmasters, whose reflections and observations were intended to help "the younger sort of Teachers, and . . . all Schollers." Although a practical book with sections devoted to school governance and similar matters, *Ludus Literarius* was primarily a manual of style, and its chapter headings included: (1) "How to make Epistles, imitating *Tully*"; (2) "How to enter and make Verses with delight and certainty, without bodging"; and (3) How to attaine most speedily unto the knowledge of the Greek tongue."[44] Of greater practical significance was Brinsley's second book, *A Consolation for our Grammar Schooles,* which was published in 1622 with help from the Virginia Company of London. In this work Brinsley gave forceful expression to his belief in the supreme importance of correct procedures for the teaching of reading and other basic skills. He also acknowledged the significance of motivation, especially in the instruction of younger students, and sought to make learning an enjoyable experience, almost like play. In *A Consolation,* Brinsley's deep religious faith and unquestioning trust in the value of education were totally apparent. He wrote in fact that "Good learning is indeed the heavenly light, the truest honour, the best riches, the sweetest pleasure." He additionally held that God had selected the grammar schools "to be His nurseries of all learning and virtue," so that in time "men of true wisedom & godlinesse . . . [would] both rule and obey everie where."[45]

To be sure, the average schoolmaster of the age wrote no books but performed his duties in a quiet and dependable manner. One such individual was John Brounsworde (d. 1589), whose memory was cherished for decades by his former students. After heading the Wilmslow Grammar School during the 1550s, Brounsworde was schoolmaster at Macclesfield from 1566 until 1588. Widely hailed as "a distinguished scholar," he was eventually honored by his students, who had a brass plaque commemorating his life and teaching installed on a wall of the local parish church.[46] Two other teachers of this dedicated and reliable sort were John Livesay and Robert Fowbery. Educated at Oxford, where he received an A.B. during the 1570s, Livesay presided over the grammar school at Skipton in Craven from 1577 until 1617. A compassionate man, apparently, he bequeathed £8 to the local poor when he died, even though his yearly stipend had been only £14 0s. 2d.[47] Robert Fowbery, who had begun a degree at Cambridge although he never completed it, was the schoolmaster at Hull from 1593 until 1613. He became widely known for his "painfull and good manner of teaching," and in 1613 he received an invitation to head the grammar school at Newcastle-on-Tyne, where he remained until his death ten years later.[48]

Only three more examples of these selfless and seldom-remembered schoolmasters can be given here. John Twyne, a respected Oxford scholar, was headmaster of the King's School, Canterbury, for twenty years and attracted so many pupils through his excellent teaching that he became a rich man. On his death in 1581, he left an unprinted work, *De Rebus Albionicis atque Anglicis,* which was published by his heirs and gave reasons for doubting Geoffrey of Monmouth's fanciful account of early British history. A great reader and an avid archaeologist, Twyne also left a large collection of Romano-British pottery, glass, and coins, which he evidently used to instruct his students.[49] Although not as financially successful as Twyne, Peter Carter seems to have been an equally committed teacher. After receiving a Cambridge M.A. in 1557, Carter became schoolmaster at Whalley, Lancashire, which was probably his native village. Successively the head of several other schools in the northwest before his death in 1590, he devised an unusually popular work on logic, *Annotations in Dialectica,* which was published eleven

times between 1563 and 1640.[50] Two decades younger than
Carter, Richard Knolles (1550-1611) headed the Sandwich Grammar School during the last years of his life. Knolles had a
passion for history and eventually published *A Generall Historie
of the Turkes,* which was reprinted many times after 1603.
Among the numerous admirers of that pioneering book were
Samuel Johnson, Lord Byron, and Samuel Taylor Coleridge,
who were obviously not repelled by its great length of 1,300
pages, although Edward Gibbon criticized it as prolix and
uncritical.[51]

The existence of such dedicated teachers as Kempe, Livesay,
Fowbery, Twyne, Carter, and Knolles, not to mention Camden,
Mulcaster, Brinsley, and scores of others, raises doubts about
the traditional view of the Elizabethan grammar schools as
backward and even reactionary institutions. Certainly there
were lazy and ineffective teachers in some places, and many
were guilty of resorting to brutal methods of corporal punishment.
But for every schoolmaster known for his occasional acts of
violence there were at least three times as many who were
diligent and conscientious, without any record of mistreating
their students. Moreover, it should always be remembered that
whatever happens in the schools of an age is a reflection of
what the wider society believes is appropriate and required,
and the years 1558-1603 are no exception. That the beating of
wayward schoolboys was considered an acceptable if not necessary practice helps to explain the harsh punishments in the
schools. This in turn helps to account for the image of Elizabethan schoolmasters as merciless pedants, an image most writers
are still reluctant to modify in any way. All in all it seems safe to
conclude that the schoolmasters of that period have received
considerably less justice from historians than any comparable
group in society.

10

Women,
Lawyers, and Clerics

By the reign of James I, education and literacy were more common among the English people than ever before. That this was so was a result not only of the steady growth of educational opportunity during the previous 250 years but also of the increasing support for educational institutions among all social classes except the very poor. According to the findings of Professor W. K. Jordan, the most thorough student of English philanthropy between 1480 and 1660, the degree of support for educational institutions had grown steadily during the Elizabethan period but reached its greatest extent between 1601 and 1640. Professor Jordan investigated patterns of charitable giving in London, Bristol, and eight sample counties (Kent, Lancashire, Worcestershire, Yorkshire, Buckinghamshire, Hampshire, Somerset, and Norfolk). He found that during the years 1561–1600, some £139,947 was contributed by donors in those ten locales to assist new or existing institutions. During the later period, 1601–40, however, educational giving in those areas increased by over 250 percent and reached the commanding figure of £383,594.[1]

Because of the unusually strong financial commitment to educational institutions during the reigns of James I and Charles I, hundreds of new fellowships and scholarships were established at the universities, as well as several endowed professorships and two new Oxford colleges (Wadham and Pembroke). In addition, dozens of new grammar schools appeared in all sections of the realm, making it possible for additional boys to secure fairly rigorous intellectual training. All these types of educational giving were well established and marked a further extension of patterns developed during previous eras. In one important respect, however, an innovation of great potential importance occurred during the last decades before the Civil War — the foundation of the first schools intended solely for the education of girls.

As noted in chapter 6, female education had been seriously affected during the last decade of Henry VIII by the dissolution of all the nunneries and the nearly 100 schools maintained by them. Because the grammar schools of the era rarely admitted girls, a separate system of secondary schools for young females was badly needed, and as early as the 1550s Thomas Becon had proposed the establishment of such a system in his *New Catechism*.[2] Unfortunately, it was not until midway in the reign of James I that the first of the many new female academies were founded.

The first institution that catered exclusively to girls was the academy known as the Ladies Hall at Deptford, Kent. Exactly when this school was founded, and by whom, is unclear, but it was firmly established by 1617, when a dozen of its students, all attired in matching green gowns and shoes, participated in a masque for the entertainment of Queen Anne and her attendants at nearby Greenwich. After the establishment of the Ladies Hall, such boarding schools for girls proliferated, particularly in the southeast and the more heavily populated sections of the midlands and west. In 1624 Nicholas Ferrar opened a female academy at Little Gidding, and three years later an alderman of Bristol, John Whitson, left funds to maintain a school that would teach forty poor girls the techniques of reading and "plain needlework." Within a few more years, small female academies were also in existence at Oxford, Burchester, Westerham, Leicester, Manchester, Lydbury, and Exeter. To serve the needs of the London merchant elite, a number of such schools appeared in the suburbs of Hackney, Putney, and Chelsea. Of those three suburbs, the Middlesex village of Hackney was the most favored, and during the middle third of the century it had at least three competing academies. The largest and most important of the Hackney schools was the one directed by Mr. and Mrs. Robert Perwick, which flourished between 1643 and 1660 and generally had at least 100 girls enrolled.[3]

Unfortunately, the Perwicks seem to have stressed dancing and the various forms of vocal and instrumental music. There is little evidence that they gave more than scant attention to serious academic subjects, since needlework, cooking, and "good housewifery" were also important parts of the curriculum. Doubtless there was a greater stress on academics at the competing Hackney school run by Mrs. Salmon, which was in existence by 1639 and where Katherine Phillips, "the matchless Orinda" of later years, studied for a time. A girl with real poetic gifts, Katherine Phillips is known to have written original verses while at Mrs. Salmon's school and to have mastered French and Italian as well as bookkeeping during her stay there.[4]

The most capable person associated with women's education during the mid-seventeenth century was probably Bathusa Pell, the talented daughter of a Sussex clergyman. Born in 1612, Bathusa Pell seems to have learned most of what she knew not from her father, who died when she was less than six, but from her brother John, who was a year or two older. John Pell received his earliest education at the Steyning Grammar School in Sussex, from which he proceeded at the age of thirteen to Trinity College, Cambridge, where he had completed an M.A. degree by 1630. He soon became a well-known mathematician, but his greatest talent was for languages: by the age of twenty he is said to have mastered French, Italian, German, Dutch, Hebrew, Arabic, and of course Greek and Latin. Doubtless he gave lessons to his gifted sister Bathusa during vacations, for she had a good command of French, Italian, and the three biblical languages by the age of fifteen. She subsequently became one of the most accomplished women of the period and in later years exchanged letters in Greek with several eminent persons on the continent, including the scholarly Dutchwoman Anna van Schurman.[5]

At some time during the early 1630s, Bathusa Pell married a Mr. Makin, about whom nothing is known. Perhaps he was a lawyer or a merchant who died within a few years. Whatever the case, he did not hinder her continued intellectual growth, and by the late 1630s she was known as a person of wide learning. In 1641 she was appointed chief tutor to the six-year-old Princess Elizabeth, the second daughter of Charles I and Henrietta Maria. Apparently the little princess flourished under Mrs. Makin's tutelage, for she developed a love of reading and supposedly mastered five languages by the age of eight! However, once the princess died of a brief illness in 1650, Mrs. Makin opened a boarding school for girls at Putney, which she moved within a few years to Tottenham. For a yearly fee of £20, she offered instruction in Greek, Latin, Hebrew, French, Italian, and Spanish. She also taught the older girls singing, dancing, arithmetic, geography, and history.[6]

Mrs. Makin was not the only person of the age who believed females should receive the same rigorous intellectual training as boys. Among others who held that view was William Austin (1587–1634), a prospective member of the Royal Academy of Letters that Charles I proposed but never had sufficient money to establish. A sincere admirer of women's abilities, Austin argued in his book *Haec Homo, wherein the Excellency of the Creation of Women is described*, that " . . . *homo* stands equally for man and woman" and that the souls of each "are equal before God." Just as Becon had held during the 1550s, Austin believed that the spiritual equality of the sexes required the establishment of an adequate system of schools for girls. Austin's book must have struck a responsive chord, for when his widow Anne published it in 1638, it proved so popular that it was reprinted the next year.[7]

Despite the strong support for female education during the early Stuart period, the view has become established during the last decade that the sixteenth-century stress on women's training had become perceptibly weaker by the last years of Queen Elizabeth. In 1975 Pearl Hogrefe gave reasons for the declining interest in female education that she thought was evident by 1590 but became pronounced only after James I's accession in 1603.[8] In 1979 Alison Plowden extended that view by commenting:

> . . . by the end of the Elizabethan period it was becoming fashionable to poke fun at female learning. This decline was partly due to the fact that there was no royal schoolroom to give a lead, no young princesses to be imitated, and the Court, although it remained a brilliant social and political centre, was no longer a centre of higher thought.[9]

In 1984 Lady Antonia Fraser embraced the new orthodoxy and gave strong support to the idea that there was a marked weakening of the earlier concern for female education during the last two decades of Queen Elizabeth's reign.[10]

The notion that women's education entered a period of decline after about 1588 is undoubtedly an exaggeration of the facts; it depends largely on the mistaken view that English girls no longer studied foreign languages, as their privileged predecessors of the mid-sixteenth century had done. All the proponents of this opinion give considerable attention to the education of Anne Clifford, the capable daughter of the third earl of Cumberland, who had taken a Cambridge M.A. before transferring to Oxford in 1577 in order to study geography. Born in 1590, Anne Clifford had a lively and inquiring mind, as almost everyone observed who met her after she became countess of Dorset. It is true that her somewhat eccentric father forbade her to study foreign languages, simply because he himself disliked them and considered them a waste of time. Yet if he restricted her education in that way, he nevertheless engaged an excellent tutor for her, the poet and historian Samuel Daniel. Under Daniel's supervision, Anne Clifford studied history in considerable detail and also read a wide variety of other works, including Gerard's *Herbal,* Sidney's *Arcadia,* and most of the poetry of Spenser. In addition she studied much foreign literature in English translation, including Cervantes' *Don Quixote* and Montaigne's *Essays.* In time she became passionately devoted to reading, and being fascinated by "all things worth knowing," she acquired such a fund of learning that she could easily converse on almost any topic. John Donne, the scholarly dean of St. Paul's Cathedral during the 1620s, had such respect for her abilities that he asserted she could "discourse of all things, from Predestination down to sleasilk."[11]

Anne Clifford was only one of several girls during the period who acquired excellent educations despite parental objections of one kind or another. Another talented girl of the era who faced opposition rather than encouragement at home was Elizabeth Tanfield (1585–1639), whose ability was recognized quite early. Elizabeth learned to read at the age of three and began to study French the next year. Her father, a leading judge of the late Elizabethan period, was proud of her cleverness and occasionally took her to court when he was hearing routine cases. But Lady Tanfield, a severe and unaccommodating person who was barely literate, had completely different feelings. She did everything she could to destroy the girl's love of reading, even hiding her books and forbidding the servants to supply her with candles, so as to keep her from reading in her room at night. At the age of fifteen Elizabeth escaped her mother's reach by

marrying Henry Carey, the future Viscount Falkland, who had a
serious interest in history and literature. He encouraged her to
develop the potential her mother had always sought to suppress,
and she soon blossomed. Within a short time she had mastered
Latin and Hebrew as well as such modern languages as French,
Italian, and Spanish. In 1602 or 1603 she wrote a play set in
ancient Syracuse and dedicated to her husband, which has
unfortunately disappeared. But shortly afterwards she completed a second play, *The Tragedy of Mariam, The Fair Queen
of Jewery*, which can be studied in a modern edition of 1907.
The central figure in that melodrama was King Herod's wife
Mariam, who consistently opposed his tyranny, despite her
realization that such actions would eventually prompt her own
death. In later years Lady Falkland wrote much poetry, including a *Life of Tamburlaine* and many short verses that she
destroyed because of their imperfections. She also translated
the epistles of Seneca and read virtually everything she could
procure, including chronicles and histories of all sorts.[12]

Among landed families of slightly less wealth, the best educated girl of the era was undoubtedly Lucy Apsley, daughter of a
Sussex gentleman who was also Lieutenant of the Tower of
London. Born in 1620, Lucy had a French governess from the
time she was weaned and grew up to be bilingual. She learned
how to read at the age of four, and because of her excellent
memory, she was able to repeat the sermons she heard at
church on Sundays, to her parents' wonder and amusement. As
she herself later wrote about her total recall of the sermons she
heard given, " . . . while I was very young, [I] could remember
and repeat them exactly, & being caressed, the love of praise
tickled me, and made me attend more heedfully."[13] Lucy's education was supervised by the family chaplain, whom she herself
derided as "a pitiful, dull fellow." Fortunately she had several
capable tutors to instruct her in their specialties, and on this
score she later commented:

> When I was about 7 years of age, I remember I had at
> one time eight tutors in several qualities, languages,
> music, dancing, writing, & needlework; but my genius
> was quite averse from all but my book. . . . After dinner
> & supper I still had an hour allowed me to play, & then I
> would steal into some hole or another to read. My father
> would have me learn Latin, & I was so apt that I
> outstripped my brothers who were at school. . . . [14]

Many more examples of early seventeenth-century girls who learned foreign languages could easily be given. Sir Thomas Fairfax, John Milton, and Oliver Cromwell all provided classical training, which naturally included instruction in Greek and Latin, for their daughters. So too did David Allen, rector of Ludborough, Lincolnshire during the early Stuart period. Allen's daughter Rachel eventually became famous throughout the region for her mastery of the three biblical languages.[15] Finally, there is the case of Bathshua Reynolds, who helped to direct a school established and run by her father. The young Simonds D'Ewes became a pupil in that school in 1615, at the age of thirteen. In his later autobiography, D'Ewes revealed great admiration for the abilities of Bathusa Reynolds, maintaining that she

> ... had an exact knowledge in the Greek, Latin, and French tongues, with some insight into Hebrew and Syriac; much more learning she had doubtless than her father, who was a mere pretender to it; and by the fame of her abilities which she had acquired from others, he got many scholars which else would never have repaired to him.[16]

There were thus many more well-educated females—and females trained in foreign languages—than the proponents of a decline in women's education after 1588 are willing to admit. Nevertheless, it is easy to see why that erroneous interpretation has developed. In the first place, the disparity between male and female education, which had grown throughout the sixteenth century, continued to increase during the years 1603–40. Large numbers of well-endowed grammar schools for boys appeared in all parts of the realm during the reigns of James I and Charles I, but the new female academies of the era were usually poorly funded and rarely survived for more than twenty years. Except in a few instances, the latter institutions failed to provide truly rigorous training for their students and tended to be more like "finishing schools," with considerable time devoted to etiquette and the social graces. Certainly none of the female academies developed into permanent boarding schools, comparable to Eton, Rugby, Winchester, St. Paul's, or Harrow. Second, women still had no option of attending the universities or the Inns of Court; so for instruction beyond the secondary level, they were dependent on whatever tuition a father or a brother, a cousin or local clergyman, could provide. For a gifted woman like Bathusa Pell, whose brother John was an outstanding student, this unequal system posed no real problem. But relatively few girls were in such a fortunate situation, and there is no way of knowing how many poor but talented girls were restricted to the acquisition of rudimentary educational skills as a result. For girls without capable and inexpensive or free male assistance, which was undoubtedly the norm, the growing disparity between male and female education was one of the most unfortunate developments of the period, since it reinforced traditional views of male superiority and made it harder than ever for women to realize their full potential. Third, many people of the period continued to believe that women needed far less education than men, and this mistaken attitude led to an ill-conceived two-track educational program in a number of the schools established during the years 1603-40.

Between James I's accession and the eve of the Civil War, over a dozen schools were founded for the education of poor children of both sexes, most of these schools being largely vocational in nature. One of the first benefactors to establish a school of this sort was Dame Alice Owen, who in 1613 founded "Lady Owen's School" for thirty children of lower-class families in Clerkenwell and Islington parishes. In 1623 Lady Anne Townshend, a granddaughter of Sir Nicholas Bacon, gave £500 to endow a similar school for the training of poor boys and girls in Heydon and four adjacent parishes; while in 1629 Archbishop Samuel Harsnet of York established a school at Chigwell, Essex in which there were usually an equal number of poor children of both sexes. Finally, at Kirk Leatham, Yorkshire, during the 1630s, the owners of the local alum works agreed to pay £12 a year to a schoolmaster who would instruct their laborers' children, boys and girls alike, without charging fees of any kind.[17]

Unfortunately, there tended to be a significant difference in the training given to male and female pupils in these new schools. The boys were generally taught reading and arithmetic, and on occasion some history as well as writing and even a bit of French or Latin. But aside from reading, the girls learned only how to spin, knit, and make bean-lace. At the Free School established in 1628 at Great Marlow, Buckinghamshire, some twenty-four girls were taught to spin, knit, and make various kinds of lace but not, apparently, how to read, while an equal number of boys were given instruction in reading and the principles of arithmetic. This sort of educational disparity continued for generations to come. As late as 1791, the Reverend William Gilpin established a school for poor boys and girls whose parents lived within his Hampshire parish. In the Reverend Gilpin's school, the boys were taught reading, writing, and arithmetic, but the girls were only taught how to read, sew, and knit.[18]

There is a fourth and final reason for the erroneous view that women's education entered a period of decline during the late Tudor or the early Stuart period. It is often held, and not without justification, that the influence of James I was harmful to the cause of rigorous female instruction. As is well known, James I did not like women, and as soon as he was settled on the English throne, he established his frivolous wife Anne of Denmark in a separate residence at Somerset House and never lived with her again. When she died in 1619, he claimed to be too ill to attend her funeral and sent their son Prince Charles to serve in his stead as Chief Mourner. There is a story, perhaps apocryphal, that when a proud courtier presented his daughter to the king and boasted of her learning, James responded impatiently, "But does she spin?" Whether that story is true or not, the monarch's attitudes still set a powerful example at this time, and it is indisputable that well-educated women rarely graced James's court, thereby triggering a disregard for serious female instruction in some quarters.

In fairness to James's memory, however, it should be noted that he did not neglect the training of his only daughter Elizabeth, although this may not have been recognized at the time. After 1603 James sent Elizabeth and a youthful companion, a daughter of Sir Robert Carey, to live with Lord and Lady Harington at Coombe Abbey, Warwickshire. Lord Harington, a serious man with an extensive library, supervised the education of the two girls, who studied French, Latin, and Italian, as well as history, geography, and literature. They received instruction in music from the famous composer Dr. John Bull and in calligraphy from a Mr. Beauchamp, one of the leading writing masters of the time. The two girls even studied a bit of science while at Coombe Abbey. They peered at insects through a primitive microscope, and because Elizabeth loved animals, she was given a small farm to manage, which was stocked with miniature sheep and cattle.[19]

Just as a few scholars hold that women's education declined from about the year of the Armada, several historians contend that legal education at the Inns of Court was of a lower quality by the end of the Tudor period than it had been during earlier eras. Indeed, W. S. Holdsworth maintains that the Inns began to decay during the last years of Henry VIII, while Kenneth Charlton is convinced that a period of stagnation set in even earlier, shortly before the fifteenth century closed.[20] Other able historians dispute such an interpretation, however, and assert that there was no decline in the Inns' educational standards before the Civil War of the 1640s. R. J. Fletcher espoused that view, and in his introduction to the *Pension Book of Gray's Inn,* he wrote that "[t]he reigns of Elizabeth and her successor were the palmy days of the old system of legal education. The Readings were regularly held . . . and daily during term and the learning vacations there were moots and bolts."[21] A. W. B. Simpson supports this opinion and holds that, at Gray's Inn at least, the instruction continued at a high level until the outbreak of the Civil War. However, that bitter conflict "plunged the educational system of the Inn into a state of disorder from which it never recovered."[22]

This is not the place for an account of the complex issues involved in that scholarly debate. Yet it should be acknowledged that there is much circumstantial evidence to support the view that by the 1590s the system of legal education was not what it had been a century earlier. The Inns had expanded from societies of about 100 members each to institutions with approximately 250 residents, causing a sharp increase in disciplinary problems. The violent and unrestrained behavior of the younger members, which had been a difficult matter even before the Reformation, had grown in incidence and seriousness, with duels and other physical combats often disrupting the peace of each society. A growing number of aristocratic boys with no desire to become professional lawyers were enrolling, and they saw no need for regular attendance at the Readings, mock trials, and other exercises that still occurred at regular intervals. Senior members of the Inns were increasingly preoccupied with lucrative cases before the royal courts and preferred to pay nominal fines rather than take their turn as Reader. Finally, the number of plays, revels, and similar entertainments held each year had risen dramatically, suggesting a serious decline in scholarly zeal.

If all these factors suggest a half-hearted commitment to the pursuit of legal knowledge at the Inns by 1600, it is nevertheless true that many highly motivated students applied themselves diligently to their work during the early Stuart period. One such student was Simonds D'Ewes, who remained at the Middle Temple from 1620 until 1626, although his call to the bar occurred as early as 1623. In 1622 D'Ewes spent more than two weeks preparing the cases he had been assigned to plead during his first mock trial, and in April of the next year he wrote to his father Paul, who lived in nearby Chancery Lane, that "what with daylie study, dinner cases, supper discourses, [and] evening mootes, the whole time & minde are filled with the law." In a letter to a friend in 1626, D'Ewes again revealed how hard he usually worked, declaring that "my head hath been soe fulle of mootes as I scarce had time in the better part of a weeke to visit my father."[23]

Other surviving letters from the period reveal the existence of young men who were so immersed in their legal studies that they failed to communicate with worried parents over long periods.[24] The seriousness with which many students still approached their legal training is also suggested by the marginal notes and cross references that they scribbled in their notebooks from time to time. Dr. Louis Knafla has carefully examined the surviving books owned by Sir Thomas Egerton while he was a student at Lincoln's Inn during the 1560s. Because of the detailed notes and copious references Egerton jotted in his books, Dr. Knafla contends that Egerton pursued his legal studies with great diligence and acquired a profound understanding of the law's principles and details.[25] This proved of inestimable value to him when he, as James I's Lord Chancellor, was locked in a bitter struggle with Sir Edward Coke, England's leading jurist between 1605 and 1616.

Probably the most prolific legal scholar in English history, Sir Edward Coke had studied at the Inner Temple and was the most brilliant practitioner of the method of law reporting as pioneered by Edmund Plowden and Sir James Dyer a generation earlier. Between 1600 and 1616 Coke published thirteen volumes containing detailed accounts of 467 legal actions adjudicated since 1572. Once he became Chief Justice of the Common Please in 1605, Coke was determined to establish the sovereignty of the common law, even if he had to destroy the equitable jurisdiction of the prerogative courts in the process. Had Coke confronted an adversary of less knowledge and ability than Egerton, he might well have succeeded in his goal, which would have amounted to a serious setback for the cause of social justice in England. But because of Egerton's own mastery of the law, its history and philosophy, Coke's campaign was defeated and equity remained in existence.[26]

Two points about the Inns and the instruction they provided emerge from even a cursory examination of their development during the Elizabethan and early Stuart periods. First, the system of legal education was clearly evolving, although this should probably be regarded as a change of emphasis and direction rather than as an actual decline of quality; and second, the Inns were still healthy enough to be able to produce a stream of outstanding lawyers who, in addition to those already mentioned, included Sir Francis Bacon, Sir Henry Spelman, and the incomparable John Selden, a man of unrivaled knowledge and ability. What many writers have failed to stress are the reasons *why* the system of legal education evolved as it did and how it happened that no significant decline of quality occurred, even though the traditional exercises of earlier times were of decreasing importance after the 1580s.

First, it should be noted that even before Henry VIII's reign, an increasing number of the Inns' students spent a year or more at one of the universities before commencing their legal studies. This was as true of Richard Hankford and John Paston at the beginning of the fifteenth century as it was of Edmund Dudley and Sir Thomas More at the end. If a small number of pre-Reformation students entered the Inns with a year or so of university work behind them, considerably more did during later periods. Virtually all the outstanding lawyers of the century 1540–1640 attended a university first. Sir James Dyer studied at Broadgates Hall, Oxford, before enrolling at the Middle Temple, and Edmund Plowden is known to have spent three years at a still undetermined Cambridge college before entering the same Inn. Sir Thomas Egerton was an undergraduate at Brasenose College, Oxford, between 1556 and 1559, when he secured admission to Furnivall's Inn (one of the Inns of Chancery) in order to ready himself for the rigors of Lincoln's Inn. Examples of this sort could be multiplied almost endlessly, since by 1601 almost half of all the entrants of the four major Inns were Oxford and Cambridge men, whereas in 1561 only 13 percent had been.[27] Richard Crompton, son of a rich Bedfordshire gentleman, attended Brasenose College, Oxford, during the 1560s and then became a prominent member of the Middle Temple, where he twice served as Reader during the 1570s. Another Brasenose man, Sir John Savile of Halifax, Yorkshire, also enrolled at the Middle Temple, where he was an utter barrister from 1573 until he became a Baron of the Exchequer in 1598. Finally, Sir Thomas Coventry the Elder (d. 1606) was an undergraduate at Balliol College, Oxford, before he became a law student, qualified as a barrister, and capped a distinguished career as a justice of the Common Pleas.

Because many less famous men made the same academic progression from the universities to the Inns of Court, the academic skills of the younger students at the Inns were considerably improved by the last years of Queen Elizabeth. Moreover, the tutorial system of instruction had triumphed at Oxford and Cambridge by the final quarter of the sixteenth century, and as a consequence most entering students at the Inns were capable of working with a minimum of academic supervision.

As noted in chapter 1, the tutorial system received *de facto* recognition from the crown as early as 1548, while in Section 33 of the university ordinances issued during Mary's reign, the government had decreed that:

> No one . . . shall undertake the tutorship of any pupil without express leave from the [college] head himself, who before he grants it shall make diligent enquiry about the character of the pupil, and the qualifications of him who wishes to undertake the tutorship, whether he be fit and competent to instruct the pupil . . . and whether he has sufficient time to do it.[28]

Partly as a result of this, the tutors of the period 1558–1642 took their duties with great seriousness. They directed all their pupils' studies and even saw to it that all their fees were paid on time each month. Because of this close system of academic supervision, which had been adopted by almost all the colleges by 1575, general academic lectures were seldom attended, and most students became accustomed to working in independent fashion with little direction from anyone except their tutors. The study habits these young men developed at the universities inevitably influenced how they approached the common law once they enrolled at the Inns of Court. As a consequence of their earlier experience, they had the skill and the discipline to absorb large amounts of material on their own, without regular attendance at routine exercises, as had been expected of their medieval forebears.

Even before these important developments occurred, there

was a sharp increase in both the quality and the quantity of legal literature available for serious students to use. From the early 1490s until the late 1520s one of England's earliest printers, Richard Pynson, had concentrated on supplying the needs of England's legal fraternity. Yet it was apparently one of Pynson's competitors, Thomas Stanham, who in 1495 issued the first printed Year Book, which contained brief summaries of cases. A forerunner of the later detailed reports of Plowden and Dyer, the Year Books were published every year until 1535, when they lapsed, although one last volume of that sort appeared in 1568. The Year Books were an important reference tool for practising lawyers until they obtained something better.[29]

Meanwhile other, more specialized works flowed from the presses. Between 1523 and 1530, Christopher St. Germans of the Inner Temple published his *First and Second Dialogues between the Doctor and the Student,* which were reissued in a combined edition of 1532. Basically a treatise on the principles of equity, St. Germans' *Dialogues* remained a standard textbook until the appearance of Lord Nottingham's *Prolegomena* in the eighteenth century.[30] An important tract on the royal prerogative was published in 1548 by Henry Staunford, who became a justice of the Common Pleas six years later. Staunford also wrote a pioneering work on criminal procedure, *The Pleas of the Crown,* which appeared in 1560, after he had died.[31] Undoubtedly the most widely admired work of the age was Thomas Littleton's *Tenures,* a comprehensive tract on the principles of landownership. Written sometime during the reign of Edward IV, this important book had been printed twice by 1483. It passed through seventy more editions by 1628, when Sir Edward Coke included a valuable commentary on it in his *First Institute of the Laws of England.* Although Coke was obviously guilty of hyperbole, he reflected the contemporary opinion of Littleton's *Tenures* when he wrote, " 'This book is an ornament of the Common Law and the most perfect and absolute work that was ever written in any human science.' "[32]

So many other useful works appeared during the years 1550-1600 that it would be impossible to list them all. Perhaps the most important were: (1) Richard Tottel's *Abridgement of the Boke of Assizes* (1555), a short but popular compilation of medieval statutes and decrees; (2) John Rastell's *Exposition of Certain Difficult and Obscure Termes of the Lawes of this Realme* (1579), the first systematic guide to legal terminology; and (3) William Lambarde's *Eirenarcha* (1581), a pioneering account of the history and duties of the justices of the peace and one that was particularly valuable for lawyers because of its dependence on the statutes, cases, and literature pertaining to those unusually important local officials.[33] Of even greater utility, however, were the law reports of Plowden and Dyer, which initiated a new period in the development of legal literature. Although Dyer began to collect information about cases a decade before Plowden, his compilation did not appear until 1585, fourteen years after the latter published his celebrated *Commentaries*. Moreover, Plowden concentrated on many fewer cases than Dyer, whose book contained summaries of 668 different legal actions. Because Plowden's goal was "to elucidate as well as to report the authoritative legal opinions of his day," he limited himself to detailed analyses of only forty-three cases. As a consequence, the publication of his *Commentaries* created a sensation among students and barristers alike. The demand for it was so great that it was reissued in 1578, while the next year Plowden compiled a continuation in which he analyzed twenty additional cases. In 1585 a combined edition of both parts of the work appeared, with all sixty-three cases printed in an outsized folio of 1,134 pages. It was immediately hailed as a classic and was periodically reprinted until 1816.[34]

During the early Stuart period, legal writing was dominated by Sir Edward Coke, who not only published thirteen massive volumes of law reports, in which he analyzed 467 cases, but also compiled four large *Institutes of the Laws of England,* which appeared between 1628 and 1641, although Coke himself died in 1634. Many other useful works appeared during those same years, including several treatises comparing the principles of English common law with those of civil and canon law. Perhaps the most original tract of the early seventeenth century, however, was Powell's *Attorney's Academy,* a pioneering guide to courtroom procedure.

Because of the publication of all these important works at a time when most students at the Inns were academically qualified to use them, it seems obvious that, while the study of the law had evolved during the preceding century, the system of legal education had not really declined. Indeed, men far more learned than their medieval predecessors were being produced by the Inns in considerable numbers, although they were obtaining their technical knowledge in a somewhat different way. It is probably true that because of the rapid growth of the law and the massive accumulation of precedent during the century 1529-1629, the old methods of legal instruction were bound to change in any event. As it happened, the transition to a new system of legal education, more appropriate for students who had already been to a university, occurred effortlessly and almost without comment, since that change served the needs of students and barristers alike.

If this general argument is wrong, it is difficult to understand why the Inns enjoyed the respect they did from contemporaries. In 1600 Ben Jonson, who often satirized the lawyers' tricks and wiles, nevertheless characterized the Inns as "the noblest nurseries of humanity and liberty in this kingdom."[35] Many fathers must have agreed, since they continued to pay the steep admission fees that the Inns charged when their sons enrolled. At the Middle Temple during the first decade of James I, the entry fees varied between £3 6s. and £5,[36] which would have sufficed for an entire year's study at Oxford or Cambridge. In addition, many fathers granted their sons generous allowances, as much as £40 or even £50 a year while they were in residence. During the last decade of Queen Elizabeth, young John Kaye of Woodsome, Yorkshire, received almost £50 annually from his father during his five-year stay at the Middle Temple; whereas twenty years later George Radcliffe enjoyed an annual stipend of £40 while he was a resident of Gray's Inn. During his first three years at the Middle Temple, Simonds D'Ewes also enjoyed £40 annually from his father, although upon his call to the bar in 1623, young D'Ewes saw his allowance increased to £100 yearly.[37] Had the Inns been in a state of serious decay, it seems highly improbable that the fathers of the age would have paid such large amounts to have their sons trained there.

Although there are differing interpretations about the education of lawyers and women during the last years before the Civil War, virtually all historians agree that clerical training showed steady improvement between the 1580s and the 1640s. John Whitgift, who was Primate of All England from 1583, was an enthusiastic campaigner for higher clerical standards, especially for the average parish priest. Under Whitgift's leadership, the convocation of Canterbury ruled in 1585 that the lower clergy should study at least one chapter of both parts of the Bible every week. In addition, parish ministers were henceforth to complete written theological exercises, preferably in Latin, which were to be set for them once every quarter by the bishops.[38] Of far greater consequence for clerical learning was the steady rise in the percentage of rectors and vicars who were university graduates. In 1580 only 23 percent of all clerical incumbents in Worcester diocese held academic degrees, but by 1640 over 83 percent did. The same sort of improvement was noticeable among the holders of benefices in Leicestershire. In 1585 some 28 percent of all rectors and vicars in that county were university graduates, but by 1640 approximately 90 percent were. In the great bishopric of London, which generally attracted better qualified applicants than the outlying sections, those who were university men increased from 61 percent in 1583 to almost 90 percent by 1640.[39]

Just how much improvement took place by the eve of the Civil War can also be seen from the ecclesiastical appointments made by Sir Thomas Coventry the Younger, Lord Keeper of the Great Seal between 1625 and 1640. Traditionally the Lord Keeper nominated to all livings worth less than £20 a year that were in the gift of the crown or any of its wards. Between 1627 and 1640, Coventry made 1,380 presentations in all, and of the men he instituted to benefices, just over 88 percent were university graduates. Moreover, 1,126 of those individuals, or almost 81 percent, held M.A.s or even higher degrees.[40]

Exactly why such rapid progress occurred during those years is not entirely clear, although several interlocking factors seem to have been involved. Certainly the strong encouragement of Archbishop Whitgift and his three successors, Bancroft, Abbot, and Laud, played a part. The establishment of hundreds of new scholarships to assist poor boys who wished to study theology and prepare for clerical careers was also of undoubted importance. Additionally, the foundation of Emmanuel and Sidney Sussex Colleges as seminaries for the lower clergy was a matter of clear significance, especially since both those societies grew at a rapid rate.

Emmanuel College, for example, enjoyed steady growth after its establishment in 1584. This was largely owing to the outstanding leadership provided by its first master, Laurence Chaderton, who remained in office for 38 years and eventually became known as "the Pope of Cambridge Puritanism." Chaderton, who had earlier been an outstanding tutor of younger students while a fellow of nearby Christ's College, established an immediate clientele for Emmanuel, which had a roster of more than 200 undergraduates by the last years of James I. In 1622, seventy-nine freshmen enrolled, which was the largest group of new students admitted by any college at either university between the 1580s and the 1630s.[41] Almost as impressive as Emmanuel's rapid growth was that of Sidney Sussex, which in many respects was a smaller version of Emmanuel. Although legally established in 1596, Sidney Sussex did not admit its first eight members and begin its corporate life until two years later. Like Emmanuel, Sidney Sussex enjoyed inspired leadership from its first master, James Montagu, who eventually became a bishop as well as editor of James I's collected works. In 1599 Montagu increased the number of fellows at the college from eight to eighteen, and thereafter the society grew at an accelerated rate. It attracted so many undergraduates, many of whom were destined for the church, that by 1621 it had 140 members in all.[42]

Meanwhile two older colleges (one at either university) had developed a comparable stress on "godly teaching" and the training of young men for eventual parochial duties. At Cambridge, Gonville and Caius, despite some of its members' strong concern for science, was essentially a clerical seminary, since approximately 75 percent of its graduates during the years 1558-1625 became priests in the state church. Theological studies were especially stressed during the mastership of William Branthwaite, who presided over Gonville and Caius from 1607 until his death twelve years later. An accomplished Hebrew scholar, Branthwaite took his D.D. in 1598 and assisted in the preparation of the King James Bible of 1611. During his time the college attracted additional students of average means, especially the sons of men already in holy orders, so that by the late 1620s Gonville and Caius had "a predominantly middle class student body, one oriented mainly towards the church."[43] At Oxford during the final quarter of the sixteenth century, Henry Robinson presided over Queen's College with exceptional success from 1581 until 1599, when he resigned to become bishop of Carlisle. An outstanding administrator, Robinson strengthened the college finances, renovated the buildings, and enlarged the library by persuading Archbishop Grindal to bequeath his valuable collection of reformist tracts to the college in 1583. Yet Robinson's greatest concern was to supply a resident preaching ministry to evangelize the northwestern counties and other "dark corners of the land" where Catholicism remained strong. Robinson's work was effectively continued by the next provost of Queen's, Henry Airay (d. 1616), under whom the college enjoyed unprecedented prosperity. By 1612 the 33 resident members of 1552 had soared to 267, making Queen's the largest Oxford society of its day.[44]

There is a fourth and final reason for the steady rise of clerical standards that occurred from the 1580s—the energetic campaign to increase the remuneration of the parish priesthood as a way of attracting and holding learned men.

As early as 1577, William Harrison, archdeacon of Colchester, maintained that a yearly stipend of at least £30 was necessary for the support of a cleric who was a university graduate. Yet Archbishop Whitgift informed Queen Elizabeth in 1585 that hardly 600 of the 9,200-odd benefices in the realm were worth that amount, while over half were valued at less than £10 annually. Even worse, the new bishop of Carlisle, Henry Robinson, complained in 1599 that not a single vicar or curate in his diocese had an income in excess of ten marks a year.[45] A vivid description of such a poorly paid cleric is available in John Aubrey's *Brief Lives.* While discussing the great philosopher Thomas Hobbes (1588–1679), Aubrey made revealing comments about the philosopher's father, Thomas Hobbes the Elder, who for many years was rector of Westport, near Malmesbury. As a country parson the elder Hobbes received only ten marks a year, and partly in consequence he was noted for his "ignorance and clownery." Also according to Aubrey, old Mr. Hobbes "could only read the prayers of the Church and the homilies, and [he] disesteemed learning (his son Edmund told me so) as not knowing the sweetness of it." Although the rector was considered "a good Fellow" by most of his parishoners, he had a fierce temper, and on one occasion he assaulted a man at the church door who had offended him at an earlier time. That unseemly outburst caused him to flee his post, and a few years later he died in obscurity in the countryside east of London.[46]

Clearly, if parsons like Mr. Hobbes were to be avoided and more suitable and learned men retained, the stipends of parish ministers had to be increased. By the early years of Charles I much had been accomplished—although still more remained to be done. Because of the pioneering labors of Christopher Hill, Phyllis Hembry, and other scholars,[47] it is unnecessary to detail how the financial lot of the average parish priest was improved between the 1580s and the 1630s. Suffice it to say that clerical stipends were increased in three main ways: (1) through bequests from wealthy individuals who sympathized with the plight of the parochial clergy; (2) through voluntary action on the part of individuals or town corporations that pledged to pay an adequate stipend to a well-educated cleric or lecturer; and (3) through the reluctant acknowledgment by Whitgift and most of the clerical hierarchy that the evils of pluralism and absenteeism, which parliament had tried repeatedly to eliminate since 1529, could not be outlawed altogether. Only by allowing well-trained men to hold several benefices simultaneously in order to combine the income of those positions could the lesser clergy be significantly helped.

Of course the hierarchy's decision to tolerate pluralism doomed many other men to continued hardship, since pluralists were under an obligation to provide curates, or substitutes, to perform their duties in their stead, and it would naturally have been self-defeating for a rector or a vicar to pay his curates more than a minimum wage. Accordingly, most curates were poorly educated men who comprised an almost sub-clerical group that commanded little if any respect. Indeed, Richard Hooker had those men in mind when he maintained in 1598 that the lower clergy were "the scum and refuse of the whole land." Hooker's opinion was echoed less than two decades later by James I, who held in 1616 that ordinary churchmen were despised "by people of all degree from the highest to the lowest." Yet the rectors and vicars of the age, who often enjoyed two or more benefices and were increasingly known for their scholarly attainments, commanded considerable respect. As early as the mid 1570s, William Harrison characterized that portion of the parish priesthood as a sub-group of the gentry; while in 1600 Thomas Wilson ranked wealthier clerics alongside esquires and gentlemen as among "the lesser nobility" of the realm.[48]

If this two-tiered system was firmly in place by the early Stuart period and condemned most curates to lives of poverty and ignorance—at best curates were recent university graduates in desperate search of benefices of their own—there were numerous individuals among the higher ranks of the parish clergy who made important contributions to scholarship and learning. It would take a whole chapter, perhaps even a book, to describe the many different ways well-educated parish ministers influenced the cultural and intellectual life of the era. We must therefore be very selective and confine ourselves to a few telling examples.

One of the most interesting clerics of the early Stuart period was Edmund Gunter. Probably a native Londoner, Gunter was educated at Westminster School and then at Christ Church, Oxford, where he matriculated in 1600. After receiving an A.B., he studied for his B.D. and in 1615 took holy orders. In 1619 he was presented to the living of St. George's, Southwark, which he held until his death only seven years later. Exactly when Gunter became interested in mathematical and navigational problems in unclear; but before the end of 1618 he made notable improvements to the quadrant, designed a more efficient cross-staff, and demonstrated how to make back observations. Doubtless because of these achievements, he was named Gresham professor of astronomy in 1619. The next year he published a pioneering *Table of Artificial Sines and Tangents,* which consisted of logarithmic sines and tangents to seven decimal places. Gunter's other accomplishments were so numerous that they can only be mentioned in passing. While conducting experiments at Deptford, he accidentally discovered the variation of the magnetic needle. He also developed an accurate table of meridional parts for every tenth of a degree and was the first writer to employ the terms sine and cosine. He invented the decimal separator, devised the first efficient slide rule for rapid calculation, and developed a measuring chain that is still used by surveyors to this day.[49] Gunter's accomplishments were of such critical importance that his fame was widespread among later generations of Englishmen. During the Restoration John Aubrey commented of him that, "The world is much beholding to him for what he hath done well." Yet Aubrey, who entered Oxford sixteen years after Gunter died, also relates the amusing story that while the latter was a student at Christ Church, " . . . it fell to his lott to preach the Passion Sermon, which some old divines I knew did heare, but 'twas sayd of him then in the University that our Saviour never suffered so much since his Passion as in that sermon, it was such a lamentable one."[50]

Only a few years older than Gunter, Samuel Purchas made equally important contributions in regard to the history of exploration and discovery. Born at Thaxted, Essex, in 1577, Purchas was educated at St. John's College, Cambridge, where he received an M.A. in 1600 and later earned a B.D. After several years as a curate in southern Essex, he was named rector of Eastwood, only two miles from the port of Leigh, on the lower Thames. At that time Leigh was a great concourse for sailors and shippers, whose rousing tales fired the humble parson's imagination. In 1613 he published his first book, *Purchas his Pilgrimage,* which was essentially a compendium of history and geography as well as an account of the peoples and religions of the world. Imbued with much patriotic fervor, the book was so popular that it reappeared in 1614 and 1617, each time in substantially enlarged editions. Purchas dedicated the work to Archbishop Abbot, the author of the first real geography textbook, who was so impressed that he made Purchas one of his chaplains. The book also delighted the bishop of London, John King, who arranged for Purchas to become rector of St. Martin's, Ludgate in 1614. The book even won accolades from the elderly Richard Hakluyt, the pioneering writer on these matters, whose great work of 1589, *The Principal Navigations, Voyages, Traffics, and Discoveries of the English Nation*, has aptly been called "the prose epic" of the English people. Almost immediately a collaboration between Hakluyt and Purchas developed; and although there are signs that Hakluyt developed a dislike of Purchas's fawning and obsequious manner, it was natural that upon the former's death in 1616, his widow gave all his unpublished papers to the younger scholar, who used them to compile two additional works.[51]

In 1619 Purchas published a folio of 800 pages entitled *Purchas His Pilgrim: Microcosmus, or the Historie of Man.* Unquestionably the least important of his books, this was more a religious tract than a geographical or historical work, and G. B. Parks has dismissed it, perhaps too cavalierly, as an "extended sermon to work off the grief of family losses."[52] By the time *Purchas His Pilgrim* appeared, the parson was was well along on final book, *Hakluytus Posthumous, or Purchas his Pilgrimes, contayning a History of the World, in Sea Voyages, and Lande Travells by Englishmen and others.* This enormous work filled four large volumes and took four years to print. When it went on sale in 1625, it was offered at the high price of £3 8s. 6d., making it one of the most expensive books of the period. The first volume dealt sketchily and unsatisfactorily with Biblical history and portrayed all of man's earthly experiences as a religious pilgrimage. Fortunately, the later volumes were more successful and contained valuable accounts of the voyages of Columbus, Magellan, Hawkins, Cavendish, and Drake, of Chancellor, Frobisher, and many others. The book also included accurate information about the earliest attempts to develop commercial ties with India, China, Japan, and Russia. Purchas tried to weave all his material into a sustained narrative, as modern historians would do, but was far from successful, since he lacked the essential literary skills. Consequently his *Hakluytus Posthumous* is rarely read today, although Hakluyt's own *Principal Navigations*, which is little more than a pastiche from different hands, is still a work of living literature.[53]

One last clerical figure, William Oughtred (1575–1660), will be considered here. A native of Buckinghamshire, Oughtred received his early education at Eton, whence he proceeded to King's College, Cambridge. He received his A.B. and M.A. degrees in 1596 and 1599, respectively. He took holy orders in 1603, and from 1610 until his death fifty years later, he held the valuable living of Albury, Surrey, which was worth £100 annually. While still a Cambridge undergraduate, Oughtred demonstrated a talent for mathematics and navigation: as noted in chapter 8, his brilliant essay, "Easy Method of Geometricall Dialling," circulated widely and made him instantly famous. Once he was comfortably settled at Albury, dozens of students from European lands as well as England resorted to him in order to learn from the greatest mathematical teacher of the age. His fame became so great that the Grand Duke of Tuscany offered him a yearly pension of £500 if he would reside at his court and succeed the late Galileo Galilei (d. 1642) as official mathematician and philosopher. However, Oughtred's ardent Protestantism, and his likely knowledge of Galileo's problems with the Inquisition, caused him to have no interest in settling in a Catholic country.

Oughtred's many pupils included Lord William Howard, a younger son of the earl of Arundel and Surrey, probably the most cultivated English peer of the early seventeenth century. For Lord William's use, Oughtred wrote his best-known work, *Clavis Mathematicae,* in 1628. Published within three years, the *Clavis* was essentially a treatise on arithmetic and elementary algebra, although it incorporated several important advances in regard to mathematical notation. During his long career, Oughtred published several other notable books, including *Appendix to the Logarithmes* (1618), *Key of the Mathematicks* (1647), and *Trigonometria* (1657). His most capable students were undoubtedly John Wallis, Seth Ward, and Sir Christopher Wren, all of whom made outstanding contributions during the later seventeenth century.[54]

As in the case of Edmund Gunter, John Aubrey left an interesting description of Oughtred.

> He was a little man, had black haire, and black eies (with a great deal of spirit). His head was always working. He would draw lines and diagrams on the Dust.[55]

Although Oughtred's modern biographer contends that he was a conscientious parish minister, Aubrey's words convey an altogether different impression.

> I have heard his neighbour Ministers say that he was a pittiful Preacher; the reason was because he never studied it, but bent all his thought on the Mathematiques; but when he was in danger of being Sequestered [in 1645] for a Royalist, he fell to the study of divinity, and preacht (they sayd) admirably well, even in old age.[56]

Although Gunter, Purchas, and Oughtred were hardly typical of the parish clergy of early Stuart England, there were numerous other men on the scene of comparable learning and scholarly achievement: names like William Bedwell, William Barlowe, John Bois, George Herbert, and Robert Burton spring immediately to mind. Although space does not permit a discussion of the contributions made by all those men, the careful reader should already be aware of the degree to which clerical education had recovered and moved ahead since the disruptive changes of Henry VIII's time and the extent to which well-educated parish ministers were still among the intellectual leaders of English culture and society.

11

Zenith and Decline

By the eve of the Civil War, literacy and education were more widespread in England than in any other major European country. Unhappily, there is no satisfactory way to establish the precise literacy rate at that juncture, since the keeping of reliable statistics did not begin until a later time and even the examination of thousands of wills from the period to determine whether they had been signed or not is a flawed methodology. Reading was almost always taught prior to writing during those years, with the result that children who dropped out of school at an early age barely learned to write at all, while many elderly persons who could obviously read well during their final years signed their names in a slow and halting hand, suggesting that they lost experience in writing as they grew older. Besides, as Nicholas Tyacke has sensibly observed, "Marks made by testators may simply reflect illness, and in consequence are best ignored."[1]

Although the literacy rate of early Stuart times cannot be established with any precision, there are good reasons for believing that even among poor women, the most disadvantaged group in society, the ability to read, though not to write and certainly not to write well, had attained a respectable level, perhaps the 25 to 30 percent range. Of course most women did not learn to read while going to school but by using the self-help manuals that were now available in cheap editions. The most popular of those manuals, Edmund Coote's *Englische Scholemaister* of 1596, was reprinted over twenty times during the reigns of James I and Charles I. The 1636 copy in the British Library, which was one of the 2,000 or more copies that comprised the twenty-fifth impression, had so many girls' names scribbled throughout its pages in obviously different hands that that particular volume must have been used by a number of females to teach themselves, their sisters, friends, and others to read.

Because of the steady growth of literacy among all classes and groups, reading for edification and pleasure became one of the leading recreations of the period—and probably more so for women than for men, who engaged in blood sports and a much broader range of leisure activities than were condoned for females. During the two generations preceding the Civil War, many poor women obviously passed considerable time in reading, which was the cheapest and most socially acceptable form of entertainment available to them. That reading even among humble women became so widespread helps to explain why the production of books soared. In the year 1500, editions of fewer than fifty new books had been published in all. But by the 1580s the yearly total of new book titles had risen to slightly over 200, and by 1640 it was in the neighborhood of 600.[2] That women of all ranks and conditions were now dedicated readers also helps to explain why a few husbands of the age resented the increasing time their wives spent with books and occasionally took steps to compel them to spend their leisure hours in "more useful" activities.[3]

Among adult males the literacy rate was of course appreciably higher than for women because of the greater educational opportunities that were available for men and boys. In the London area and the southeast in general, the literacy rate for adult males may well have been as high as 60 to 65 percent, although in the outlying sections of the north and west it was clearly somewhat lower, perhaps only 35 to 40 percent.[4] That literacy was now widespread among adult males was also a result of the continuing stress on education and the establishment of additional grammar schools between 1603 and 1642. Although approximately 360 of those institutions had existed by the end of Queen Elizabeth's reign, several dozen more were founded within another generation, perhaps as many as 55 or 60. Yet the national population was increasing rapidly at the time, from slightly less than four million to almost six million by the eve of the Civil War; and it appears likely that the growing number of schools did not keep pace with the expanding pool of school-age boys who desired to gain admission to them. As a consequence, dangerously crowded conditions in the schools developed, which helps to explain John Milton's eloquent appeal of 1644 for additional teachers.[5]

The increasing student-teacher ratio in the schools probably had serious results in regard to discipline, since a substantial number of seventeenth-century teachers became known for their fierce tempers and harsh methods of punishment. In 1625 a clerical schoolmaster of Blackmore, Essex, the Reverend Andrew Walmesly, beat a ten-year-old pupil fifty times with an elm rod for being unable to recite his lesson properly.[6] Alexander Gill, Sr., who presided over St. Paul's School from 1608 until 1635, acquired a thoroughly evil reputation for the violence he inflicted on both current and former students, while Gill's son, Alexander, Jr., who succeeded him in the mastership of that large institution, was an obviously unbalanced man who behaved even more despotically. On one occasion the younger Gill dragged a student around so painfully by the ears that the usher in attendance felt compelled to protest. In 1640 the younger Gill was dismissed from his post, one of the few schoolmasters of the age to be so discharged.[7]

Probably because of those and other violent incidents, a clamor against the cruel punishments imposed in the schools developed. In 1622 Henry Peacham complained in his *Complete Gentleman* about the way boys were often "pulled by the ears, lashed over the face, beaten about the head with the great end of the rod, [and] smitten upon the lips for every offense with the ferula." Peacham, who was a schoolmaster himself, also maintained that "many of our masters for the most part so behave themselves that their very name is hateful to the scholar, who trembleth at their coming in, rejoiceth at their absence, and looketh his master, returned, in his face as his deadly enemy."[8] About the same time Mrs. Dorothy Leigh's gentle book on child-rearing practices, *The Mother's Blessing*, expressed similar views. According to Mrs. Leigh's small treatise, which passed through fifteen printings by 1630, patience and tenderness are essential during the schooling of young children, "for curtness hardens a child's heart and makes him weary of virtue."[9] During the next decade a Yorkshire schoolmaster, Charles Hoole, whose *New Discovery of the Old Art of Teaching School* had been completed by 1636, although it was not published until 1660, argued that schoolmasters should not punish boys for every error they made. Rather teachers should correct a student's mistakes in private, telling him kindly where he had gone astray, so as to save him from embarrassment before his fellow students. Only if a boy persisted in his errors should he be publicly reprimanded.[10]

Unfortunately, such progressive views were never adopted by more than a small minority, and most parents clung to the more traditional opinions expressed by Hezekiah Woodward. An Oxford graduate who directed an academy at Aldermanbury during the 1620s and 1630s, Woodward published an influential book in 1640 entitled *A Childes Patrimony,* in which he held that parental indulgence does a child greater harm than the devil.[11] Because teachers were expected to stand *in loco parentis* whenever classes were in session and often referred to their students as "their children," it seemed perfectly natural that they would discipline wayward schoolboys as most parents did. This helps to explain why brutal punishments remained typical of the English grammar schools for decades to come, although it also reveals why some parents after the Civil War refused to allow their sons to attend them.

Just as enrollments in the grammar schools increased to record levels during the generation preceding the outbreak of the Civil War, the universities reached the greatest size they would ever attain before the final years of Queen Victoria's reign, more than 250 years later. The expansion in student numbers during the late medieval period had been checked by the turmoil at Oxford and Cambridge between 1535 and 1555, but thereafter a period of steady growth occurred until about 1590, when economic conditions became seriously depressed and another downturn occurred until 1615. Then yet another period of rapid growth took place and lasted until the outbreak of the Civil War in 1642. By that juncture the academic population at Oxford had increased to approximately 2,900, while the number of students at Cambridge had expanded to 3,000 or more. During the 1630s, the two universities produced over 550 graduates each year, or more than twice as many as they had turned out between 1506 and 1535, the peak years of the late-medieval period.[12]

Most of the growth of the years 1615–42 can be attributed to the continuing stress on good teaching and the high esteem felt for most tutors of the age. One individual who remembered his college tutor with great fondness was Ralph Josselin, the son of an Essex yeoman farmer. Admitted to Jesus College, Cambridge, in 1630 or 1631, Josselin took his A.B. within four years and later served as vicar of Earls Colne for several decades. While at Cambridge he studied with Thomas Lant, whom he described in his autobiography as "my loving and I hope godly & honest *tutor;* he dealt lovingly with me." Apparently Lant did not push his pupil too hard, for Josselin acknowledged that he spent many winter mornings at the university "either in bed or by ye fire."[13]

If Lant was a lenient supervisor, other tutors of the age worked their students far harder and exercised a profound influence over their intellectual development. A good example of that kind of tutor was Richard Holdsworth, a prominent fellow of St. John's College, Cambridge, from 1613 until 1629. Highly regarded by his contemporaries, Holdsworth was described on at least one occasion as "truly religious and a great scholar." To assist his students he compiled a manual of instructions in which he distinguished carefully between the needs of those who intended to take degrees and those who did not. For the former he prescribed the study not only of rhetoric, logic, and philosophy but also of history, ancient literature, and "universal geography." For students not pursuing academic degrees, he recommended a more general syllabus of readings, including More's *Utopia,* the poetry of Herbert, Crashaw, and Buchanan, and Burton's massive *Anatomy of Melancholy,* which was first published in 1621.[14] That Holdsworth was elected to the presidency of Emmanuel College, Cambridge, in 1637 suggests that his teaching methods were not only admired but also frequently imitated by other Cambridge tutors of the era.

Although Holdsworth's strongly religious outlook caused him to ignore science, the latter subject was not neglected during the era. At both universities scientific and mathematical studies continued to flourish, but especially at Oxford, where the arrival of Henry Briggs in 1619 was a matter of considerable importance. Educated at St. John's College, Cambridge, where he received his A.B. and M.A. degrees in 1581 and 1585, respectively, Briggs was such an outstanding mathematician that no less a figure than William Oughtred praised him as "the English Archimedes." Between 1588 and 1597 Briggs was a fellow of St. John's College, where he often instructed undergraduates and served in 1592 as the university mathematical lecturer. But then, from 1597 until 1619 he resided in London, where he was the first Gresham professor of geometry and became a leading member of the distinguished circle that included William Gilbert and Edward

Wright. Briggs's greatest contribution was his energetic campaign to popularize logarithms, which had been developed by the Scottish mathematician John Napier. Deeply impressed by Napier's tables for rapid calculation, Briggs made the arduous journey to Scotland in 1616 and again in 1617 in order to converse directly with the man whose work he so admired. Because of the high esteem felt for Briggs himself, he was named in 1619 to the Savilian professorship of geometry, which had just been established at Oxford by Henry Savile, who, as warden of Merton College since 1585, had long championed mathematical and scientific studies at the older university. Until his death in 1630, Briggs served with distinction at Oxford and helped to win additional support for the "more modern subjects."[15]

Although Briggs left an important unfinished work, the *Trigonometria Britannica* (which was later completed by Henry Gellibrand), it might be objected that he had made his greatest contributions before assuming his Oxford professorship in 1619. Such a charge would be impossible to level against John Bainbridge, an even more important figure than Briggs and the first Savilian professor of astronomy from 1619 until his death in 1643. A man of exceptionally wide interests, Bainbridge gave numerous public lectures about his astronomical observations and discoveries, which he pursued with an eight-foot telescope that he himself began to make in 1626. He developed a fluent knowledge of Arabic in order to be able to read important mathematical works in that language. He also played a major role in establishing the Oxford Botanical Gardens, and he conducted a learned correspondence with several leading scientists on the continent, including Pierre Gassendi. Finally, he produced a band of dedicated disciples, the most important of whom were Henry Gellibrand of Trinity College and John Greaves of Merton. Both Gellibrand and Greaves were regular attenders at Bainbridge's public lectures during the early and mid 1620s, and Gellibrand is known to have met in conference with the older man on several occasions. Because of Bainbridge's high regard for both his disciples, he eventually helped to secure their appointments to be the Gresham professors of astronomy and geometry, respectively.[16] In that way Oxford repaid with interest—and in less than two decades—the favor that Gresham College had extended in 1619 when it sent Briggs to teach at the older university.

In several other ways Oxford and Cambridge continued to

show exceptional vitality during the generation preceding the Civil War. Although the Cambridge University Library attracted only a few gifts during those years, the Bodleian Library at Oxford registered steady growth as a result of truly munificent benefactions received from the earl of Pembroke, Archbishop Laud, and several other wealthy donors between 1629 and 1639. In fact, the Bodleian acquired so many valuable manuscripts during that decade that foreign scholars arrived in order to use them.[17] The collections of the various colleges also expanded at a steady rate, often receiving as many as 400 to 1,000 books through single bequests. At Oxford during the reign of James I, at least one new library of considerable importance was established. In 1613 Philip Bisse, rector of Batcome, Dorset, for nearly fifty years, made an interesting arrangement for the disposition of his outstanding collection of approximately 2,000 works. Because of his long friendship with Dorothy Wadham and her late husband Nicholas (d. 1609), Bisse agreed that Mrs. Wadham should receive all his books immediately after his death, so she could use them to found a college library at the large new academic society she was currently establishing in accordance with her husband's will.[18]

Because of the high popular regard they still commanded, both universities continued to receive large monetary gifts from time to time. For example, in 1610 a wealthy grazier of Abingdon, Berkshire, Thomas Tisdale, left £5,000 in a permanent trust, the recurring income from which was to be used to finance thirteen scholarships and fellowships at an unspecified Oxford college for the most promising graduates of the Abingdon Grammar School. Those prestigious awards, which paid larger stipends than most, were attached for more than a decade to Balliol College, but in 1623 the Tisdale Trust was almost doubled in value by funds contributed by Richard Wightwick. Thereupon the Tisdale trustees decided to purchase Broadgates Hall and convert it into a permanently endowed society known as Pembroke College. Once this was done, the thirteen Tisdale scholarships and fellowships were reassigned to the new institution, to the great dismay of the Balliol authorities, who did recover a part of their loss by appealing to the generosity of a former member, Archbishop Abbot.[19]

Another college of the period that greatly benefited from the benefactions of private donors was Sidney Sussex, Cambridge. Once it began its corporate life in 1598, Sidney Sussex received a stream of gifts and bequests for different purposes. In this way additional fellowships and scholarships were established, the stipends of the master and fellows increased, and a large number of books for the library purchased. Undoubtedly the most important boon to the college fortunes came in 1626, on the death of Sir John Brereton. One of the college's original fellows, Brereton had sought his fortune in Ireland, where he became both King's Sargeant and King's Remembrancer for that realm. In his will of 1626 Brereton left his old college the considerable sum of £2,600 for the purchase of the Yorkshire manor of Cridling Park, which was currently rented at £143 a year. Brereton did not specify how the college should use this large new source of recurring income, which was an unusual feature of such a generous bequest during that era.[20]

By the time Charles I's Personal Rule ended in 1640 after eleven years without a parliament, most of the colleges had ample sources of income. New College, Oxford, for example, received average rents of £2,970 from its various estates during the late 1630s, while nearby Christ Church is believed to have had a gross income of £6,000 in 1640.[21] As a consequence of such great wealth, the two universities were in a position to make large contributions to either side when the Civil War broke out in the summer of 1642. Unfortunately for their future wellbeing, most of the colleges were strongly royalist in sympathy and gave unwavering support to the side that lost. Even Richard Holdsworth, a determined puritan and the respected master of Emmanuel College, Cambridge, since 1637, was an ardent champion of Charles I against his parliamentary opponents. Had it not been for the vigilance of Oliver Cromwell, his brother-in-law Valentine Walton, and several other landowners who were equally ardent parliamentarians, large amounts of valuable plate would have been sent by the various Cambridge colleges to the king's original military capital at York. On 17 August 1642, parliament instructed Cromwell and four of the aldermen of Cambridge to maintain a state of martial law in the town with power to detain anyone on suspicion. Soon afterwards Cromwell took action against the college heads of Jesus, Queens', and St. John's, who were sent under armed guard to the Tower of London. In 1644 the master of Peterhouse, John Cosin, was similarly deprived for his "crime" of smuggling most of the college plate to the royal mint at York.[22]

Meanwhile at Oxford, where local support for the parliamentary cause was notably weaker, large sums were raised to assist

Charles I. The university itself advanced £860 out of its cash reserve of £922, while a further £500 was dispatched to York from the Bodleian Chest. The officials of Balliol College, one of the poorer academic societies, managed to collect £200 for the war effort, while Queen's College made the unexpectedly generous contribution of £2,881.[23] Further, during the second week of August 1642, Oxford began to raise an armed force with which to assist the crown, and during the winter of 1642–43 almost all university exercises were suspended so that able-bodied students could join Charles's regiments. Shortly thereafter the embattled monarch decided to make Oxford his headquarters for the remainder of the conflict. The buildings of New College, now emptied of its younger students, were converted into a major arsenal, with both the bell tower and the cloister being stocked with muskets and ammunition. As this happened, it became necessary to protect the university town from a likely parliamentary attack, and work began on a complex system of trenches and earthenworks. On 5 June 1643, all healthy adults less than sixty years of age were ordered to work at least one day each week on the fortifications or provide a substitute. Later, in January 1644, all the colleges and halls were directed to raise £800 each within the next five months in order to help finance the fortifications.[24] Because of Oxford's unswerving devotion to the royalist cause, the university had no right to expect lenient treatment when the Civil War ended in an overwhelming parliamentary triumph in June 1646.

Within a year the victorious parliamentarians established a special commission of twenty-five men to carry out full visitations of both universities. This commission began its work at Oxford in September 1647, and by 1650 it had purged most of the colleges of all men suspected of outright hostility towards the new regime. At Jesus College, the principal for the last eighteen years, Francis Mansell, was ejected, despite his proven record as an outstanding administrator, while almost all the college fellows were deprived during subsequent months. In June 1648 seventeen fellows of New College were expelled, and within another two months the warden of that society, Henry Stringer, who was also Regius professor of Greek, suffered the same punishment. About that time five fellows of nearby Lincoln College were removed, while in 1650 a sixth member of that society was ejected.[25] Yet these changes at Oxford did not have a detrimental effect on academic conditions, since capable men were usually named to replace those who were ousted. In

January 1649 George Marshall, a Cambridge M.A. and former parliamentary chaplain, was appointed to the wardenship of New College; while a few months earlier the exceptionally capable John Wilkins had accepted the mastership of nearby Wadham. As Wilkins' modern biographer has written, "Under his leadership Wadham attained its greatest influence and became one of the most popular colleges in the university."[26]

At Cambridge similar changes took place, and by 1649 the heads of thirteen colleges had been deprived, although their parliamentary replacements were for the most part men of considerable ability. Indeed, the new masters of Clare Hall and King's College, Ralph Cudworth and Benjamin Whichcote, respectively, were among "the most distinguished men, in intellect and character, who held such office in the 17th century."[27] Perhaps because the younger university had been unable to show its actual sympathy for the royalist cause, the parliamentary leaders made a conscious effort to help Cambridge in at least one important way.

By the mid 1640s the holdings of the Cambridge University Library had failed to keep pace with those of the Bodleian Library at Oxford, which had grown spectacularly since 1610. For over fifteen years the official Cambridge librarian had been Andrew Whelock, an outstanding linguist of Clare Hall and a man of unusual energy. Whelock had attempted to enlarge the collection, which had no more than a thousand volumes in 1629, into one more appropriate for a major university, but his efforts had achieved limited success. After 1646 several prominent parliamentarians led by the great lawyer John Selden, who was by chance one of the two M.P.s for Cambridge, sought to assist Whelock in whatever ways they could. It was probably at the suggestion of Selden and his associate John Lightfoot that parliament voted funds in 1648 for the purchase of an important collection of Hebrew books that the London book-dealer George Thomason had just acquired from Italy. This valuable collection was then added to the holdings of the Cambridge University Library, which were considerably strengthened thereby. During the next five years the Library continued to benefit from the generosity of parliament and its supporters. As a result the collection grew to approximately 12,000 volumes by the time of Whelock's death in 1653.[28]

Thus the universities suffered far less harm than they might have endured — and much less damage than had been inflicted on them during the religious upheavals of the mid Tudor period.

Nevertheless, both universities were dealt a serious psychological blow at the time of the Restoration from which they took over two centuries to recover.

After the death of Oliver Cromwell, who had been England's undisputed ruler for more than a decade, there was so much political turmoil throughout the country in 1658 and 1659 that the monarchical form of government was reestablished in 1660 to great popular rejoicing. The elder son of Charles I, who had been beheaded in 1649, was invited to take the throne as Charles II, and a determined effort was made to turn the hands of the clock back to the period just before the outbreak of the Civil War. In many cases men who had been expelled from Oxford and Cambridge fellowships between 1646 and 1650 were allowed to recover them, and in a few instances those who had been ejected from college headships were allowed to return.

For example, Thomas Marshall of Lincoln College, Oxford was allowed to reclaim the fellowship from which parliament had demanded his ouster in 1648. A brilliant student, Marshall had matriculated at Lincoln College in 1640 and been elected to a Trapps Scholarship the next year. In 1643 he volunteered to serve Charles I at his own expense and joined the regiment led by the earl of Dover. Four years later, after the conflict ended and the king was taken captive, Marshall fled into European exile, and shortly thereafter parliament ordered his expulsion from the fellowship to which he had recently been elected. Between 1648 and 1660, Marshall used his time on the continent to become one of the leading philologists of the seventeenth century, but as soon as the monarchy was restored in 1660, he returned to Oxford and recovered his fellowship. Because of his obvious ability, he was elected rector of Lincoln College in 1672 and served with great distinction in that position until his death thirteen years later.[29] A similar case involved Edward Martin, the principal of Queens' College, Cambridge, until Cromwell arrested him in August 1642 and sent him under armed guard to the Tower of London. A year later Martin was transferred to the bishop of Ely's mansion at Holborn, where he was held under detention until 1647. Subsequently Martin also fled to the continent and lived in dire poverty throughout the 1650s, parliament having confiscated all his Cambridge possessions as a result of his uncompromising royalism. In 1660 Martin returned in triumph to his old college, at which he served as chaplain until he died.[30]

These men who reappeared at the universities after a decade or more in continental exile tended to be more fervent royalists, and greater critics of parliament, than ever. Unwilling to compromise their principles under duress in 1646 or 1647, they refused to consider doing so once their hardships ended in seeming vindication. As a consequence, the universities became bastions of conservatism, narrower and more ideological than before 1642; and in some instances the doctrine of non-resistance to royal authority was publicly asserted. This was highly disturbing to the descendants of those who had risked their lives and property by fighting against Charles I in order to defend parliament's right to exist. Men of moderate and somewhat left-wing views, who subscribed to the majority opinion that there should be limits to the exercise of royal power, were dismayed by what was now being taught at the universities, and they increasingly refused to allow their sons to go and study there. During the first decade of the Restoration, as many as 460 new students still matriculated at Oxford each year, but by the 1750s the average number of entering freshmen had dropped to only 200.[31]

Thus it is obvious that the universities commanded considerably less popular support after the 1660s than they had during earlier periods. Not only did their enrollments decline in consequence, reversing an established trend that, except for the periods 1535-55 and 1590-1615, was now almost three centuries old, but financial gifts to Oxford and Cambridge also showed a marked tendency to contract. It is true that during the decades after 1660, almost all the colleges received generous bequests from aristocratic donors at one time or another. But these benefactions now came from a narrower circle of committed philanthropists; they occurred at longer and more irregular intervals; and they resulted in a much slower rate of educational expansion. For example, eight endowed professorships had been established between 1619 and 1636, a period of seventeen years. But it required another 140 years, lasting from 1660 until 1800, before eight additional professorships were founded. Similarly, whereas the Bodleian Library had expanded to 25,000 volumes between its establishment in 1598 and 1660, it acquired only 5,000 additional books during the half century after the Restoration.[32]

Just as the universities lost size and considerable popular support after 1660, so did the Inns of Court, although probably for a different reason. By the mid-seventeenth century, the Inns had become increasingly expensive to attend, since they collected steep entry fees from new students and imposed heavy payments on their residents whenever construction projects needed to be funded or the debts of the society reduced. Primarily for economic reasons, therefore, the Inns began to shrink in membership after the 1660s, and by the middle of the eighteenth century they were much smaller than they had been during their zenith between 1580 and 1640.[33]

It is possible of course that some measure of the Inns' contraction after 1660 was owing to the general disregard for higher education that had become evident in most places. Not only did the mainstream of English opinion now harbor suspicions of the universities because of their ultraroyalism, but the somewhat contradictory view had developed that advanced education had been a leading cause of the Civil War in the first place. After all, many college tutors of the 1620s and 1630s had directed their pupils to study the political treatises of ancient Rome, which had stressed the virtues of republican constitutions and upheld the citizen's right to resist the ungodly decrees of tyrannical rulers.[34] Although parliament in 1646 dismissed a few schoolmasters for their unflinchingly royalist views,[35] the philosopher Thomas Hobbes even denounced the grammar schools during the 1650s for the way they too had taught republican theories and thereby produced a stream of parliamentary leaders, including John Hampden, John Milton, and Oliver Cromwell. Two decades later Christopher Wase popularized this dubious opinion in his influential book, *Considerations Concerning the Free Schools as Settled in England.* Although the main royalist leaders had also attended them, Wase maintained that serious discord was as much a by-product of the grammar schools as of the universities, since all had promoted ideas that were inimical to safe, traditional values. As a consequence the grammar schools also suffered a serious setback in enrollment and popular esteem during the later seventeenth century.[36]

The new female academies of the early seventeenth century, which had rarely emphasized academic subjects, were not immune from the currents of stagnation and decay. Roger Thompson maintains in fact that from the 1660s the female academies "grew more and more like *debutante* factories, turning out mindless coquettes with no aim in life but to await proposals."[37] Perhaps Mr. Thompson's skillful writing exaggerates the situation a bit, but in his support, Bathusa Pell Makin published a small book in 1673 entitled *An Essay to Revive the Antient Education of Gentlewomen.* In that work, Mrs. Makin deplored the course of recent developments and searched for arguments to convince her readers that they ought to resume rigorous intellectual training for their daughters. In the end she took refuge in the impoverished theory that formal education would prepare girls for the mundane tasks of later married life.[38] Most revealing of all about the educational currents of Charles II's reign is the fact that, at almost the exact moment Mrs. Makin's book appeared, a serious decline in the level of popular literacy became evident enough to be measurable by modern historians.[39]

Thus, although other factors were involved, the Civil War of the 1640s and the later Restoration Settlement dealt a sharp blow to the educational movements that had begun many decades before as a result of the Black Death. For over a century after Charles I's execution in 1649, educational standards declined and less assistance was given to educational institutions than had been the case during earlier eras. Although literacy began to grow again as a consequence of the Industrial Revolution, it was not until after 1875 that education was again as widespread among the English people as it had been during the years 1580-1640. And only during the generation just prior to World War I did the universities admit proportionately as many students as they had accepted during early Stuart times.

Notes

Abbreviations

BJES	British Journal of Educational Studies
Cal. Pat. Rolls	Calendar of the Patent Rolls
Cal. S.P. Dom.	Calendar of State Papers Domestic
DNB	Dictionary of National Biography
EHR	English Historical Review
Hist. of Ed.	History of Education
HLQ	Huntington Library Quarterly
HMC	Historical Manuscripts Commission
J.Eccl.H.	Journal of Ecclesiastical History
JHI	Journal of the History of Ideas
JMH	Journal of Modern History
L & P Henry VIII	Letters & Papers, Foreign & Domestic, of the Reign of Henry VIII
LQR	Law Quarterly Review
P & P	Past & Present
TRHS	Transactions of the Royal Historical Society
VCH	Victoria History of the Counties of England

Introduction

1. See, for example, Lawrence Stone, "The Educational Revolution in England, 1580–1640," *P & P*, no. 28 (1964), and Louis Knafla, "The Matriculation Revolution and Education at the Inns of Court in Renaissance England," in A. J. Slavin, ed., *Tudor Men and Institutions* (Baton Rouge: Louisiana State University Press, 1972). For an early challenge to the Stone-Knafla view, see Elizabeth Russell, "The Influx

of Commoners into the University of Oxford before 1581: An Optical Illusion?" *EHR*, vol. 92, no. 345 (1977).

2. David Cressy, *Literacy and the Social Order: Reading and Writing in Tudor and Stuart England* (Cambridge: Cambridge University Press, 1980), 41, 80, and passim.

Chapter 1: The Black Death and the Crisis in Clerical Education

1. Quoted in R. Barrie Dobson, ed., *The Peasants' Revolt of 1381*, 2d ed. (London: Macmillan, 1981), 61–62. For a comparable modern view, see Emma Mason, "The Role of the English Parishoner," *J.Eccl.H.*, vol. 27, no. 1 (1976), 27.

2. H. E. Malden, *Trinity Hall* (London: Robinson Books, 1902), 18.

3. Hastings Rashdall, *The Universities of Europe in the Middle Ages*, new ed. (Oxford: Oxford University Press, 1936), III:309–10.

4. Quoted in Philip Ziegler, *The Black Death* (New York: Harper and Row, 1971), 263.

5. A. F. Leach, *A History of Winchester College* (London: Gerald Duckworth, 1899), 72.

6. R. L. Storey, "The Foundation of the Medieval College, 1379–1530," in John Buxton and Penry Williams, eds., *New College, Oxford* (Oxford: Oxprint, 1979), 3–4.

7. May McKisack, *The Fourteenth Century* (Oxford: Clarendon Press, 1959), 500.

8. E. F. Jacob, *The Fifteenth Century* (Oxford: Clarendon Press, 1961), 668–69.

9. Quoted in Leach, *A History of Winchester College*, 174–75.

10. Hugh Aveling and W. A. Pantin, eds., *The Letter Book of Robert Joseph* (Oxford: Oxford Historical Society, 1967), I:159–60.

11. James Heywood, ed., *Collection of Statutes for the University and Colleges of Cambridge* (London: Clowes and Sons, 1840), I:33–34.

12. Helen Jewell, "English Bishops as Educational Benefactors," in R. Barrie Dobson, ed., *The Church, Politics and Patronage in the Fifteenth Century* (Gloucester: Alan Sutton, 1985), 147.

13. F. M. Powicke, *The Medieval Books of Merton College* (Oxford: Clarendon Press, 1931), 29, 31; Ernest Savage, *Old English Libraries* (London: Methuen, 1911), 147, 193; J. W. Thompson, *The Medieval Library* (New York: Hafner, 1939), 398; C. H. Clough, ed., *Profession, Vocation and Culture* (Liverpool: Liverpool University Press, 1982), 171–72; Jacob, *The Fifteenth Century*, 666.

14. J. R. Lander, *Crown and Nobility, 1450–1509* (Montreal: McGill-Queen's University Press, 1976), 8.

15. Colin Richmond, *John Hopton* (Cambridge: Cambridge University Press, 1981), 134–35, 140–41; Jewell, "English Bishops as Educational Benefactors," 149.

16. Ralph A. Griffiths, ed., *Patronage: The Crown and the Provinces* (Gloucester: Alan Sutton, 1981), 175; M. A. Hicks, *False, Fleeting, Perjur'd Clarence* (Gloucester: Alan Sutton, 1980), 66.

17. Peter Heath, *The English Parish Clergy* (London: Routledge and Kegan Paul, 1969), 79; Rosemary O'Day, *The English Clergy* (Leicester: Leicester University Press, 1979), 233; Felicity Heal and Rosemary O'Day, eds., *Church and Society in England* (London: Macmillan, 1977), 72; Lander, *Crown and Nobility, 1450-1509*, 8; Norman P. Tanner, *The Church in Late Medieval Norwich* (Toronto: Pontifical Institute of Mediaeval Studies, 1984), 29; J. C. T. Oates, *Cambridge University Library* (Cambridge: Cambridge University Press, 1986), 25-27.

Chapter 2: Education and Literacy Among the Laity

1. Sir John Fortescue, *De Laudibus Legum Anglie*, ed. S. B. Chrimes (Cambridge: Cambridge University Press, 1949), 117, 119.

2. Ibid.

3. E. W. Ives, "The Common Lawyers in Pre-Reformation England," *TRHS*, 5th series, vol. 18 (1968), 146-47.

4. Fortescue, *De Laudibus Legum Anglie*, 116-17.

5. W. P. Baildon, ed., *Records of the Honorable Society of Lincoln's Inn: The Black Books* (London: Lincoln's Inn, 1897), I:1v, 103, 135, 177; R. J. Fletcher, ed., *The Pension Book of Gray's Inn*, 2 vols. (London: Chiswick, 1901-10), I:xlix; Ives, "The Common Lawyers," 185.

6. E. W. Ives, "A Lawyer's Library in 1500," *LQR*, vol. 85, no. 1 (1969), 105, 107.

7. Charles Sisson, "Marks as Signatures," *The Library*, 4th series, vol. 9, no. 1 (1928), 1.

8. W. A. Pantin, "Instructions for a Devout and Literate Layman," in J. J. G. Alexander and M. T. Gibson, eds., *Medieval Learning and Literature* (Oxford: Clarendon Press, 1976), 399.

9. Quoted in M. B. Parkes, "The Literacy of the Laity," in David Daiches and Anthony Thorlby, eds., *The Medieval World* (London: Aldus, 1973), 565.

10. Richard Bailey, "The Development of English," 147.

11. Anne Hudson, "Some Aspects of Lollard Book Production," in Derek Baker, ed., *Schism, Heresy, and Religious Protest* (Cambridge: Cambridge University Press, 1972), 148-49.

12. Quoted in John W. Adamson, *"The Illiterate Anglo-Saxon" and Other Essays* (Cambridge: Cambridge University Press, 1946), 40-41.

13. John W. Adamson, "The Extent of Literacy in England," *The Library*, 4th series, vol. 10, no. 2 (1929), 169-70.

14. Quoted in Albert C. Baugh, *A History of the English Language*, 2d ed. (Englewood Cliffs: Prentice-Hall, 1957), 241.

15. Margaret Aston, "Lollardy and Literacy," *History*, vol. 42, no. 206 (1977), 347; Parkes, "The Literacy of the Laity," 560.

16. Nicholas Orme, *From Childhood to Chivalry* (London: Methuen, 1973), 34; H. S. Bennett, *The Pastons and Their England*, 2d ed. (Cambridge: Cambridge University Press, 1970), 2, 105-7, 111, 261-62; Thomas A. Walker, *Peterhouse* (Cambridge: Heffer, 1935), 39.

17. Quoted in W. Claridge, *The Origin and History of the Bradford Grammar School* (Bradford: J. Green, 1882), 15. See also H. A. Landsberger, ed., *Rural Protest* (London: Macmillan, 1974), 137.

18. Lawrence Stone, ed., *Schooling and Society* (Baltimore: Johns Hopkins University Press, 1976), 5, 11; Nicholas Orme, *English Schools in the Middle Ages* (London: Methuen, 1973), 52.

19. Jacob, *The Fifteenth Century*, 664.

20. Quoted in Derek Pearsall, *John Lydgate* (London: Routledge and Kegan Paul, 1970), 74.

21. Sir Thomas More, "The History of King Richard the Third," in P. M. Kendall, ed., *Richard III: The Great Debate* (New York: W. W. Norton, 1965), 77.

22. K. B. McFarlane, *The Nobility of Later Medieval England* (Oxford: Clarendon Press, 1973), 236; Dorothy Gardiner, *English Girlhood at School* (Oxford: Oxford University Press, 1929), 107-8.

23. Ibid., 109-13, 131; Bennett, *The Pastors and Their England*, 110-12; Thompson, *The Medieval Library*, 402; Richmond, *John Hopton*, 131; C. A. J. Armstrong, *England, France, and Burgundy* (London: Hambledon, 1983), 141; E. M. G. Routh, *Lady Margaret* (London: Humphrey Milford, 1924), 30.

24. H. S. Bennett, *Six Medieval Men and Women* (Cambridge: Cambridge University Press, 1962), 94-99.

Chapter 3: Humanism, Monastic Conditions, and New Educational Institutions

1. W. H. Woodward, *Vittorino da Feltre and Other Humanist Educators* (Cambridge: Cambridge University Press, 1897), xvi. See also Hanna H. Gray, "Renaissance Humanism," *JHI*, vol. 24, no. 4 (1963), 498-99.

2. Roberto Weiss, *Humanism in England*, 2d ed. (Oxford: Basil Blackwell, 1957), 42-43, 46.

3. Ibid., 77-78; Buxton and Williams, eds., *New College, Oxford*, 28; Clough, ed., *Profession, Vocation and Culture*, 162-63; Josephine W. Bennett, "Andrew Holes," *Speculum*, vol. 19, no. 3 (1944), 322-23.

4. Kenneth Charlton, *Education in Renaissance England* (London: Routledge and Kegan Paul, 1965), 48, 50; Thompson, *The Medieval Library*, 397-98; H. W. C. Davis, *A History of Balliol College*, rev. ed. (Oxford: Basil Blackwell, 1963), 46-48.

5. Weiss, *Humanism in England*, 97-98, 100, 104, 106.

6. Ibid., 104; R. R. Bolgar, *The Classical Heritage and its Benefici-aries* (Cambridge: Cambridge University Press, 1963), 311.

7. Weiss, *Humanism in England,* 154–56, 159.

8. Ibid., 26, 31–4, 37–8; A. L. Poole, ed., *Medieval England* (Oxford: Clarendon Press, 1958), II:439.

9. David Knowles, *The Religious Orders in England* (Cambridge: Cambridge University Press, 1959), III:25.

10. *VCH Hampshire,* II:47; W. W. Capes, *The English Church in the XIV and XV Centuries* (London: Macmillan, 1900), 299–300.

11. *VCH Cambridgeshire,* II:219, and III:421; Arthur Gray and Frederick Brittain, *Jesus College, Cambridge* (London: Heinemann, 1979), 15–16, 23.

12. *VCH Oxfordshire,* III:173–4; E. F. Jacob, *Archbishop Henry Chichele* (London: Nelson, 1967), 77–78; W. H. Stevenson and H. E. Salter, *Early History of St. John's College, Oxford* (Oxford: Clarendon Press, 1939), 3–13.

13. A. G. Little, "The Educational Organization of the Mendicant Friars," *TRHS,* new series, vol. 8 (1894), 52, 55.

14. *VCH Chester,* III: 139; *VCH Worcester,* IV: 50; Savage, *Old English Libraries,* 61–62.

15. Ibid., 50–51; *VCH Hertfordshire,* IV:413; Thompson, *The Medieval Library,* 377–78.

16. Barbara Harvey, "The Monks of Westminster and the University of Oxford," in F. R. H. DuBoulay and Caroline Barron, eds., *The Reign of Richard II* (London: Athlone, 1971), 112, 115.

17. John Venn, *Caius College* (London: Robinson Books, 1901), 30–33.

18. James McConica, ed., *The Collegiate University* (Oxford: Clarendon Press, 1986), 130.

19. John Venn, *Early Collegiate Life* (Cambridge: Heffer, 1913), 71, 73; H. P. R. Finberg, *Tavistock Abbey* (Cambridge: Cambridge University Press, 1951), 224–25; Stevenson and Salter, *Early History of St. John's College, Oxford,* 38; Tanner, *The Church in Late Medieval Norwich,* 31.

20. *VCH Huntingdonshire,* I: 382; *VCH Hertfordshire,* IV: 411; Nicholas Orme, *Education in the West of England* (Exeter: University of Exeter Press, 1976), 210, 215.

21. A. W. Parry, *Education in England in the Middle Ages* (London: W. B. Clive, 1920), 178–79; A. F. Leach, ed., *Educational Charters and Documents* (Cambridge: Cambridge University Press, 1911), 445.

22. Ibid., 440. See also Harvey, "The Monks of Westminster," 126.

23. Nicholas Carlisle, *A Concise Description of the Endowed Grammar Schools in England and Wales* (hereafter cited as *The Endowed Grammar Schools*) (London: Bulmer, 1818), I:573.

24. Eileen Power, *Medieval English Nunneries* (Cambridge: Cambridge University Press, 1922), 245.

25. *VCH Warwickshire,* II:68–69.

26. *VCH Middlesex,* I:187. See also Geoffrey Baskerville, *English Monks and the Suppression of the Monasteries* (London: Jonathan Cape, 1937), 208.

27. Ibid.

28. Power, *Medieval English Nunneries*, 266, 272-73; Orme, *English Schools in the Middle Ages*, 53-54.

29. John Lawson, *Medieval Education and the Reformation* (London: Routledge and Kegan Paul, 1967), 62.

30. Gardiner, *English Girlhood at School*, 194; S. J. Curtis, *History of Education in Great Britain*, 3d ed. (London: University Tutorial Press, 1953), 53.

31. Leach, ed., *Educational Charters and Documents*, xxii.; Muriel St. Clare Byrne, ed., *The Lisle Letters* (Chicago: University of Chicago Press, 1981), IV: 468-69; V. J. Scattergood and J. W. Sherborne, eds., *English Court Culture* (London: Gerald Duckworth, 1983), 76; W. Gordon Zeeveld, *Foundations of Tudor Policy* (Cambridge, MA: Harvard University Press, 1948), 75.

32. Orme, *English Schools in the Middle Ages*, 158, 259-60; James McConica, *English Humanists and Reformation Politics* (Oxford: Clarendon Press, 1965), 120-21; Maria Dowling, *Humanism in the Age of Henry VIII* (London: Croom Helm, 1986), 152.

33. *VCH Staffordshire*, IV:154; John Garstang, *A History of the Blackburn Grammar School* (Blackburn: North-East Lancashire Press, 1897), 13-14, 19; Orme, *English Schools in the Middle Ages*, 248-49.

34. Ibid., 196; Joan Simon, "A. F. Leach on the Reformation, II," *BJES*, vol. 4, no. 1 (1955), 32.

35. Geoffrey Hindley, *England in the Age of Caxton* (New York: St. Martin's Press, 1979), 142-43; Jo Ann Moran, *The Growth of English Schooling* (Princeton: Princeton University Press, 1985), 90; Charlotte F. Smith, *John Dee* (London: Constable, 1909), 6.

36. Orme, *Education in the West of England*, 21.

37. A. F. Leach, *English Schools at the Reformation* (London: Gerald Duckworth, 1896), 6; Kathleen Edwards, *The English Secular Cathedrals in the Middle Ages*, 2d ed. (Manchester: Manchester University Press, 1967), 173-74, 194-95; Moran, *The Growth of English Schooling*, 54-55.

38. J. B. Oldham, *A History of Shrewsbury School* (Oxford: Basil Blackwell, 1952), 2; Orme, *English Schools in the Middle Ages*, 21; John Rodgers, *The Old Public Schools* (London: B. T. Batsford, 1938), 43.

39. Carlisle, *The Endowed Grammar Schools*, I:335; Jacob, *The Fifteenth Century*, 667; Curtis, *History of Education*, 39-40.

40. *VCH Oxfordshire*, I:472-73; Weiss, *Humanism in England*, 169-70; Simon, *Education and Society in Tudor England* (Cambridge: Cambridge University Press, 1967), 52; A. J. Fletcher, "The Expansion of Education in Berkshire and Oxfordshire," *BJES*, vol. 15, no. 1 (1967), 55.

41. Michael McDonnell, *The Annals of St. Paul's School* (London: Privately printed for the Governors, 1959), 34-40. For the school's statutes of 1512, see C. H. Williams, ed., *English Historical Documents, 1485-1558* (New York: Oxford University Press, 1967), 1039-45.

42. Charles E. Mallet, *A History of the University of Oxford* (London: Methuen, 1924), I:424.

43. *The New English Bible: The New Testament* (Cambridge: Cambridge University Press, 1972), 129.

44. McDonnell, *The Annals of St. Paul's School*, 66-68; Michael

McDonnell, *A History of St. Paul's School* (London: Chapman and Hall, 1909), 36–37; Joseph H. Lupton, *A Life of John Colet,* new ed. (London: G. Bell, 1909), 170–71.

45. P. L. Hughes and J. F. Larkin, eds., *Tudor Royal Proclamations* (New Haven: Yale University Press, 1964), I:317; Curtis, *History of Education,* 85–86; J. Howard Brown, *Elizabethan Schooldays* (Oxford: Basil Blackwell, 1933), 69–71.

46. For Jordan's views, see *The Charities of Rural England, 1480–1660* (London: Allen and Unwin, 1961), 301–4; and *The Forming of the Charitable Institutions in the West of England* (Philadelphia: Transactions of the American Philosophical Society), vol. 50, part 8, 1960, 61.

Chapter 4: Women and Education

1. Gardiner, *English Girlhood at School,* 85–86; Joseph and Frances Gies, *Women in the Middle Ages* (New York: Crowell, 1978), 178.

2. Clough, ed., *Profession, Vocation and Culture,* 145–46.

3. Orme, *Education in the West of England,* 175–77.

4. *VCH Sussex,* II:411; *VCH Nottinghamshire,* II:218; Moran, *The Growth of English Schooling,* 73, 166–68.

5. J. G. Gray, *The Queens' College* (London: Robinson, 1899); John Twigg, *A History of Queens' College* (Woodbridge: Boydell, 1987), 2–5.

6. Ibid., 11; Charles H. Cooper, *Memorials of Cambridge* (Cambridge: Macmillan, 1860), 288–89; Bryan D. G. Little, *The Colleges of Cambridge* (Bath: Adams and Dart, 1973), 68–69; Gray, *The Queens' College,* 18, 20, 24.

7. Ibid., 24, 27; *VCH Cambridgeshire,* III:409, 411; Cooper, *Memorials of Cambridge,* I:298–300.

8. G. F. Browne, *St. Catharine's College* (London: Robinson Books, 1902), 18, 27, 40–41, 45, 55.

9. Andrew Clark, ed., *The Colleges of Oxford* (London: Methuen, 1891), 269.

10. A. A. Mumford, *Hugh Oldham* (London: Faber and Faber, 1936), 46–47; Mary M. D. McElroy, "Literary Patronage of Margaret Beaufort and Henry VII" (Ph.D. dissertation, University of Texas, 1964), 99, 334–43, 350.

11. Polydore Vergil, *Anglica Historia,* ed. Denys Hay (London: Camden Society, 3d series, vol. 74, 1952), 7.

12. W. K. Jordan, *The Charities of London, 1480–1660* (London: Allen and Unwin, 1960), 30.

13. Carole Rawcliffe, *The Staffords* (Cambridge: Cambridge University Press, 1978), 94–95. See also M. V. C. Alexander, *The First of the Tudors* (Totowa: Rowman and Littlefield, 1980), 162–67.

14. Edward Surtz, *The Works and Days of John Fisher* (Cambridge, MA: Harvard University Press, 1967), 181; James B. Mullinger, *The University of Cambridge* (Cambridge: Cambridge University Press, 1873), I:423–24, 435.

15. *VCH Cambridgeshire,* III:164; J. W. Clark, ed., *Endowments of the University of Cambridge* (Cambridge: Cambridge University Press, 1904), 57; *VCH Oxfordshire,* III:17; Charles H. Cooper, *Memoir of Margaret, Countess of Richmond and Derby* (Cambridge: Cambridge University Press, 1874), 60.

16. Charles H. Cooper, *Annals of Cambridge* (Cambridge: Warwick and Company, 1842), I:271–72; W. A. Pantin, *Oxford Life in Oxford Archives* (Oxford: Clarendon Press, 1972), 34; Mallet, *A History of the University of Oxford,* I:409.

17. D. R. Leader, "Professorships and Academic Reform at Cambridge, 1488-1520," *The Sixteenth Century Journal,* vol. 14, no. 2 (1983), 215.

18. *VCH Cambridgeshire,* III:430; John Peile, *Christ's College* (London: Robinson Books, 1900), 25, 28, 34; H. C. Porter, *Reformation and Reaction in Tudor Cambridge* (Cambridge: Cambridge University Press, 1958), 16.

19. *Cal. Pat. Rolls, 1494–1509,* 433, 519, 522; Rawcliffe, *The Staffords,* 97; Peile, *Christ's College,* 103-4, 121.

20. Ibid., 34–35; Sears R. Jayne, *Library Catalogues of the English Renaissance* (Berkeley: University of California Press, 1956), 94.

21. Cooper, *Memoir of Margaret, Countess of Richmond,* 102-3; Simon, *Education and Society,* 81.

22. Ibid., 90; Cooper, *Memorials of Cambridge,* II:66–67.

23. *VCH Cambridgeshire,* III:438.

24. Cooper, *Memorials of Cambridge,* II:68–71; Mullinger, *The University of Cambridge,* I:464; Surtz, *The Works and Days of John Fisher,* 38.

25. Ibid., 143–44; Dowling, *Humanism in the Age of Henry VIII,* 151; J. E. B. Mayor, ed., *The Early Statutes of the College of St. John* (Cambridge: Cambridge University Press, 1859), xii–xiii.

26. Ibid., xvii–xviii; Cooper, *Memorials of Cambridge,* II:73, 81, 91–92, 154; Porter, *Reformation and Reaction,* 16.

27. Mullinger, *The University of Cambridge,* I:527; Arthur Tilley, "Greek Studies in Sixteenth-Century England," *EHR,* vol. 53, no. 211 (1938), 438–39.

28. Ascham to Brandesby, printed in Williams, ed., *English Historical Documents, 1485-1558,* 1070.

29. Quoted in Foster Watson, *The Old Grammar Schools* (Cambridge: Cambridge University Press, 1916), 66-67.

30. Richard Marius, *Thomas More* (New York: Albert A. Knopf, 1984), 9, 223.

31. Elizabeth Rogers, ed., *St. Thomas More: Selected Letters* (New Haven: Yale University Press, 1961), 104-5.

32. Lu Emily Pearson, *Elizabethans at Home* (Palo Alto: Stanford University Press, 1957), 173; F. R. Johnson, *Astronomical Thought in Renaissance England* (Baltimore: Johns Hopkins University Press, 1937), 43-44.

33. Quoted in Foster Watson, ed., *Vives and the Renascence Education of Women* (London: Educational Classics, 1912), 175.

34. Pearl Hogrefe, *Tudor Women* (Ames: Iowa State University Press, 1975), 147.

35. Pearson, *Elizabethans at Home,* 214.

36. Hastings Robinson, ed., *Original Letters Relative to the English Reformation* (Cambridge: Parker Society, 1846), I:79.

37. Carroll Camden, *The Elizabethan Woman,* rev. ed. (Mamaroneck: Appel, 1975), 57; Hogrefe, *Tudor Women,* 85, 109-11.

38. Doris M. Stenton, *The English Woman in History* (London: Allen and Unwin, 1957), 133-34; Pearson, *Elizabethans at Home,* 217-18; W. J. Jones, *The Elizabethan Court of Chancery* (Oxford: Clarendon Press, 1967), 93.

39. Byrne, ed., *The Lisle Letters,* I:31-32. See also F. J. Mozley, *Coverdale and His Bibles* (London: Lutterworth, 1953), 210.

40. Byrne, ed., *The Lisle Letters,* I:87, and III:9.

41. Robinson, ed., *Original Letters Relative to the English Reformation,* I:7; Charlton, *Education in Renaissance England,* 213; Camden, *The Elizabethan Woman,* 57.

42. Neville C. Williams, *Thomas Howard, Fourth Duke of Norfolk* (London: Barrie and Rockliff, 1964), 4-5; Stenton, *The English Woman in History,* 129-30.

43. Ibid., 130; Robinson, ed., *Original Letters Relative to the English Reformation,* I:2, and II:702-3; Gardiner, *English Girlhood at School,* 176-8.

44. Sears R. Jayne and F. R. Johnson, eds., *The Lumley Library* (London: Printed for the Governors of the British Museum, 1956), 3-4; Williams, *Thomas Howard, Fourth Duke of Norfolk,* 6-7; Stenton, *The English Woman in History,* 131.

Chapter 5: Printing, Books, and the Bible

1. Quoted in Rudolf Hirsch, *Printing, Selling, and Reading 1450-1550* (Wiesbaden: Harrassowitz, 1967), 1, 46.

2. Ives, "A Lawyer's Library in 1500," 106.

3. Quoted in H. S. Bennett, "Printers, Authors, and Readers," *The Library,* 5th series, no. 3 (1949), 163.

4. Lotte Hellinga, *Caxton in Focus* (London: British Library, 1982), 81, 83.

5. Thompson, *The Medieval Library,* 408; Alexander, *The First of the Tudors,* 170.

6. Hellinga, *Caxton in Focus,* 83, 95.

7. Ibid., 89.

8. H. S. Bennett, *English Books and Readers, 1475-1557,* 2d ed. (Cambridge: Cambridge University Press, 1965), 126-27, 183-91; Warren Chappell, *A Short History of the Printed Word* (New York: Alfred A. Knopf, 1970), 77; Bennett, "Printers, Authors, and Readers," 164.

9. Cooper, *Memoir of Margaret, Countess of Richmond,* 108-9; Bennett, *English Books and Readers,* 192; A. W. Pollard and G. R. Redgrave, eds., *A Short-Title Catalogue of Books* (London: The Bibliographical Society, 1926), no. 19, 166; Aston, "Lollardy and Literacy," 365.

10. Bennett, *English Books and Readers*, 195-96; A. G. Dickens, *The English Reformation* (London: B. T. Batsford, 1964), 310-11.

11. Helen C. White, *The Tudor Books of Private Devotion* (Madison: University of Wisconsin Press, 1951), 39, 43-44; Phoebe Sheavyn, *The Literary Profession in Elizabethan England*, 2d ed. (New York: Barnes and Noble, 1967), vii-viii.

12. F. F. Bruce, *History of the Bible in English*, 3d ed. (Oxford: Oxford University Press, 1978), 28-30; F. J. Mozley, *William Tyndale* (New York: Macmillan, 1937), 12-13, 17; C. H. Williams, *William Tyndale* (Palo Alto: Stanford University Press, 1969), 2-4.

13. Quoted in Bruce, *History of the Bible in English*, 23.

14. Hugh Pope, *English Versions of the Bible* (St. Louis: Herder, 1970), 64.

15. *VCH London*, I:253; Dickens, *The English Reformation*, 111; Williams, *William Tyndale*, 17.

16. Ibid., 17-19; Bruce, *History of the Bible in English*, 31; A. W. Pollard, ed., *Records of the English Bible* (Oxford: Oxford University Press, 1911), 4-6.

17. David Daiches, *The King James Version of the Bible* (Chicago: University of Chicago Press, 1941), 5-7; Claire Cross, *Church and People 1450-1660* (Hassocks: Harvester Press, 1976), 59; Dickens, *The English Reformation*, 113.

18. Mozley, *William Tyndale*, 145, 151; Mozley, *Coverdale and His Bibles*, 4-5, 226-27; Bruce, *History of the Bible in English*, 42.

19. William Neil, ed., *Harper's Bible Commentary* (New York: Harper and Row, 1962), 220.

20. Bruce, *History of the Bible in English*, 44. See also Charles C. Butterworth, *The Literary Lineage of the King James Bible* (Philadelphia: University of Pennsylvania Press, 1941), 80; Williams, *William Tyndale*, 112-13.

21. Ibid., 50-60; Neville C. Williams, *The Cardinal and the Secretary* (New York: Macmillan, 1975), 218; Dickens, *The English Reformation*, 109.

22. Ibid., 185; Henry W. Robinson, ed., *The Bible in Its Ancient and English Versions* (Oxford: Clarendon Press, 1940), 175; Mozley, *Coverdale and His Bibles*, 81-82, 107.

23. S. L. Greenslade, ed., *The Cambridge History of the Bible* (Cambridge: Cambridge University Press, 1963), 148-49.

24. Bruce, *History of the Bible in English*, 55; R. B. Merriman, *The Life and Letters of Thomas Cromwell* (Oxford: Clarendon Press, 1902), 184; A. G. Dickens, *Thomas Cromwell and the English Reformation* (London: English Universities Press, 1959), 184; E. W. Ives, *Anne Boleyn* (Oxford: Basil Blackwell, 1986), 314-15; Mozley, *Coverdale and His Bibles*, 119.

25. Ibid., 114-15, 174; Daiches, *The King James Version of the Bible*, 20.

26. Ibid., 177; *L & P Henry VIII*, XII, Pt. II:220; Byrne, ed., *The Lisle Letters*, V:606-7; Robinson, ed., *The Bible*, 172-75; Butterworth, *The Literary Lineage of the King James Bible*, 114-16.

27. Ibid., 125-28; Robinson, ed., *The Bible*, 180; Bruce, *History of the Bible in English*, 69.

28. Ibid., 67-70; Pope, *English Versions of the Bible*, 189; Robinson, ed., *The Bible*, 175, 178; Greenslade, ed., *The Cambridge History of the Bible*, 151-52.

29. Mozley, *Coverdale and His Bibles*, 221-22, 226-27, 270; Butterworth, *The Literary Lineage of the King James Bible*, 132, 134-35, 139-40, 143.

30. Hughes and Larkin, eds., *Tudor Royal Proclamations*, I:296-98; Byrne, ed., *The Lisle Letters*, V:607; Pollard, ed., *Records of the English Bible*, 65, 261-65.

31. Bruce, *History of the English Bible*, 67; Mozley, *Coverdale and His Bibles*, 168; Dickens, *Thomas Cromwell*, 115.

32. Hughes and Larkin, eds., *Tudor Royal Proclamations*, I:284-86.

33. Quoted in Adamson, "The Extent of Literacy in the Fifteenth and Sixteenth Centuries," 170. See also Heal and O'Day, eds., *Church and Society*, 74.

34. Bennett, *English Books and Readers*, 27; Greenslade, ed., *The Cambridge History of the Bible*, 153; David H. Pill, *The English Reformation* (London: University of London Press, 1973), 112.

35. Ibid.; *L & P Henry VIII*, XXI, Pt. I:611; Hughes and Larkin, eds., *Tudor Royal Proclamations*, I:373-76; Mozley, *Coverdale and His Bibles*, 286-87.

36. Ibid., 220; Robinson, ed., *The Bible*, 180; Dickens, *The English Reformation*, 265.

37. W. H. Frere, ed., *Visitation Articles and Injunctions of the Period of the Reformation* (London: Longmans, 1910), II:117-18; Mozley, *Coverdale and His Bibles*, 289-90; Daiches, *The King James Version of the Bible*, 46.

38. Ibid., 47; Robinson, ed., *The Bible*, 180; Mozley, *Coverdale and His Bibles*, 8; W. K. Jordan, *Edward VI: The Young King* (London: Allen and Unwin, 1968), 135; *DNB*, II:77-78.

39. Bruce, *History of the Bible in English*, 83.

40. Sir Thomas Elyot, *The Boke named the Governour*, ed. H. H. S. Crofts (London, 1883), I:94.

41. C. W. Blench, *Preaching in England in the late Fifteenth and Sixteenth Centuries* (Oxford: Basil Blackwell, 1964), 42.

42. Ibid., 50-51.

43. Quoted in Rachel Weighall, "An Elizabethan Gentlewoman," *The Quarterly Review*, no. 428 (1911), 127.

44. Lawrence Stone, "Literacy and Education in England, 1640-1900," *P & P*, no. 42 (1969), 77.

Chapter 6: Three Steps Forward, Two Steps Backward, 1529-1558

1. *VCH Buckinghamshire*, I:172-75.
2. Finberg, *Tavistock Abbey*, pp. 274-75.
3. *L & P Henry VIII*, II, Pt. II:1182.

5. Zeeveld, *Foundations of Tudor Policy,* 195.

6. N. H. Nicolas, ed., *The Privy Purse Expences of King Henry the Eighth* (London, 1827), 8, 13, 46, 73, 90.

7. *L & P Henry VIII,* V:22; Mallet, *History of the University of Oxford,* II:35–38; Knowles, *The Religious Orders in England,* III:162–63.

8. *VCH Suffolk,* II:329, 331; Leach, *The Schools of Medieval England,* 298; Dowling, *Humanism in the Age of Henry VIII,* 120–21.

9. See above, 77.

10. *L & P Henry VIII,* VII:37–38.

11. Ibid., 71.

12. Hugh F. Kearney, *Scholars and Gentlemen* (London: Faber and Faber, 1970), 19.

13. Ibid., 16, 20.

14. *L & P Henry VIII,* IX:208. See also D. F. S. Thomson and H. C. Porter, eds., *Erasmus and Cambridge* (Toronto: University of Toronto Press, 1963), 22.

15. Thomas Wright, ed., *Three Chapters of Letters relating to the Suppression of the Monasteries* (London: Camden Society), 1st series, vol. 26, 1843, 71.

16. Oates, *Cambridge University Library,* 350; Neil R. Ker, *Medieval Libraries in Great Britain* (London: Royal Historical Society, 1941), preface; Neil R. Ker, "Oxford College Libraries in the Sixteenth Century," *Bodleian Library Record,* vol. 6, no. 3 (1959), 459, 463.

17. Frere, ed., *Visitation Articles and Injunctions,* II:10–11; Henry Gee and W. J. Hardy, eds., *Documents Illustrative of English Church History* (London: Macmillan, 1896), 274; D. R. Leader, "Teaching in Tudor Cambridge," *Hist. of Ed.,* vol. 13, no. 2 (1984), 117.

18. G. R. Elton, *Reform & Renewal: Thomas Cromwell and the Common Weal* (Cambridge: Cambridge University Press, 1973), 29, 33; McConica, ed., *The Collegiate University,* 215; Simon, *Education and Society,* 201–2.

19. *L & P Henry VIII,* XIV, Pt. II:151.

20. Knowles, *The Religious Orders in England,* III: 247–48.

21. *L & P Henry VIII,* XIV, Pt. II:293; J. J. Scarisbrick, *The Reformation and the English People* (Oxford: Basil Blackwell, 1984), 87; Christopher Hill, *Puritanism & Revolution* (New York: Shocken Books, 1962), 33.

22. B. H. Newdigate, *Michael Drayton and His Circle* (Oxford: Basil Blackwell, 1961), 16–18.

23. Fletcher, "The Expansion of Education in Berkshire and Oxfordshire," 53–54.

24. Porter, *Reformation and Reaction,* 11–12; G. M. Edwards, *Sidney Sussex College* (London: Robinson Books, 1899), 5.

25. Simon, *Education and Society,* 203.

26. For Ascham's comments, see Edward Miller, *Portrait of a College* (Cambridge: Cambridge University Press, 1961), 32; for those of Latimer, see Mark Curtis, *Oxford and Cambridge in Transition* (Oxford: Clarendon Press, 1959), 69.

27. *VCH Cambridgeshire,* II:164, and III:177; Edward K. Purnell, *Magdalene College* (London: Robinson Books, 1904), 36, 43.

28. M. D. Forbes, ed., *Clare College* (Cambridge: Cambridge University Press, 1928), 75-76.

29. *VCH Cambridgeshire*, III:463; Cooper, *Memorials of Cambridge*, II:208.

30. Claire Cross, *The Puritan Earl* (London: Macmillan, 1966), 122.

31. Francis Wormald and C. E. Wright, eds., *The English Library before 1700* (London: Athlone, 1958), 152-53, 163-64; Seymour DeRicci, *English Collectors of Books and Manuscripts* (Cambridge: Cambridge University Press, 1930), 14-15; *DNB*, XIII:957.

32. *VCH Middlesex*, I:187; Marjorie Plant, *The English Book Trade*, 2d ed. (London: Allen and Unwin, 1965), 49; Wormald and Wright, eds., *The English Library before 1700*, 151.

33. Ibid., 163-64; Ker, *Medieval Libraries of Great Britain*, preface.

34. Jayne and Johnson, eds., *The Lumley Library*, 4, 10-11; Jayne, *Library Catalogues of the English Renaissance*, 106; A. N. L. Munby, *Cambridge College Libraries*, 2d ed. (Cambridge: Heffer, 1962), 47; Geoffrey Bill, "Lambeth Palace Library," *The Library*, 5th series, vol. 21, no. 3 (1966), 192.

35. Neil R. Ker, *Books, Collectors, and Libraries*, ed. by A. G. Watson (London: Hambledon, 1985), 472-82; May McKisack, *Medieval History in the Tudor Age* (Oxford: Clarendon Press, 1971), 23-24; T. D. Kendrick, *British Antiquity* (London: Methuen, 1950), 88, 90, 95.

36. A. H. Anderson, "The Books and Interests of Henry, Lord Stafford," *The Library*, 5th series, vol. 21, no. 2 (1966), 87.

37. Malcolm B. Parkes and A. B. Watson, eds., *Medieval Scribes, Manuscripts, and Libraries* (London: Scolar Press, 1978), 258-60, 281-86, 293.

38. *L & P Henry VIII*, XIII, Pt. II:212, 321, and XIV, Pt. II:212.

39. Norman Wood, *The Reformation and English Education* (London: Routledge and Sons, 1931), 20-21.

40. Mervyn E. James, *Family, Lineage, and Civil Society* (Oxford: Clarendon Press, 1974), 99.

41. Carlisle, *The Endowed Grammar Schools*, I:563.

42. *VCH Cheshire*, III:230.

43. *L & P Henry VIII*, XII, Pt. II:123-24.

44. Kearney, *Scholars and Gentlemen*, 21.

45. Bolgar, *The Classical Heritage*, 314; A. A. Leigh, *King's College* (London: Robinson, 1899), 39; Gray, *The Queens' College*, 70; McConica, ed., *The Collegiate University*, 230-31, 344-45, 359; Douglas Bush, "Tudor Humanism and Henry VIII," *University of Toronto Quarterly*, vol. 7, no. 2 (1938), 172.

46. F. D. Logan, "The Origins of the so-called regius professorships," in Derek Baker, ed., *Renaissance and Renewal* (Oxford: Basil Blackwell, 1977), 276-77. Perhaps it should be noted that the stipends of the four professors of law and medicine were paid out of the revenues of the Court of Augmentations from November 1546. On this point, see McConica, ed., *The Collegiate University*, 345.

47. Ibid., 32, 34, 105-6; *L & P Henry VIII*, XX, Pt. I:388; *VCH Oxfordshire*, III:235.

48. Mallet, *A History of the University of Oxford*, II:39-40; Penry

Williams, *The Tudor Regime* (New York: Oxford University Press, 1979), 296; Simon, *Education and Society,* 212; Clark, ed., *The Colleges of Oxford,* 347–48.

49. Ibid., 307; *VCH Oxfordshire,* III:235–36; Mallet, *A History of the University of Oxford,* II:40–41.

50. Cooper, *Memorials of Cambridge,* II:210, 227–29, 235, 237; Walter W. R. Ball, *Trinity College, Cambridge* (London: J. M. Dent and Sons, 1906), 41; Dowling, *Humanism in the Age of Henry VIII,* 106.

51. *L & P Henry VIII,* XXI, Pt. II: 342–43; *VCH Cambridgeshire,* III: 462–63; Mullinger, *The University of Cambridge,* I:132, and II:81; J. R. H. Moorman, *The Grey Friars in Cambridge* (Cambridge: Cambridge University Press, 1952); Kearney, *Scholars and Gentlemen,* 21.

52. Cooper, *Memorials of Cambridge,* II:340–41; Ball, *Trinity College, Cambridge,* 50.

Chapter 7: Developments During Two Reigns, 1547–1558

1. Clark, ed., *The Colleges of Oxford,* 218, 243; Buxton and Williams, eds., *New College, Oxford,* 48.

2. *Cal. S.P. Dom., 1547–1580,* 17; M. L. Bush, *The Government Policy of Protector Somerset* (London: Edward Arnold, 1975), 57; Curtis, *Oxford and Cambridge in Transition,* 158–59.

3. Ibid., 95–96; *VCH Cambridgeshire,* III:178; Simon, *Education and Society,* 252–53; Leigh, *King's College,* 92.

4. Phyllis Allen, "Medical Education in Seventeenth-Century England," *Journal of the History of Medicine,* vol. 1, no. 1 (1946), 118.

5. Davis, *History of Balliol College,* 48, 78; Thompson, *The Medieval Library,* 397, 411.

6. Ibid., 392–93, 399; B. H. Streeter, *The Chained Library* (London: Macmillan, 1931), 199; Wormald and Wright, eds., *The English Library before 1700,* 168–69, 213, 240; Oates, *Cambridge University Library,* 70; Ker, "Oxford College Libraries," 499.

7. Leach, *English Schools at the Reformation,* 1–7; R. H. Tawney, *Religion and the Rise of Capitalism* (London: John Murray, 1926), 143.

8. *L & P Henry VIII,* XIX, Pt. II:441; Leach, *A History of Winchester College,* 200–201; Alan Kreider, *English Chantries* (Cambridge, MA: Harvard University Press, 1979), 158, 160.

9. Ibid., 160, 185, 191; *Statutes of the Realm,* III:389–93; Leach, *The Schools of Medieval England,* 321; Scarisbrick, *The Reformation and the English People,* 9, 65–66.

10. Ibid., 66; *Statutes of the Realm,* IV, Pt. I:24–33; Gee and Hardy, eds., *Documents Illustrative of English Church History,* 328–57; Kreider, *English Chantries,* 191–92.

11. Ibid., 8–9, 14; *Cal. Pat. Rolls, 1548–1549,* 417–18; Orme, *English Schools in the Middle Ages,* 277.

12. *Cal. Pat. Rolls, 1548-1549,* 417.

13. Orme, *Education in the West of England,* 30-31. See also Stanford Lehmberg, *Sir Walter Mildmay and Tudor Government* (Austin: University of Texas Press, 1964), 21, 24.

14. *VCH Cheshire,* III:249; G. A. J. Hodgett, *Tudor Lincolnshire* (Lincoln: History of Lincolnshire Committee, 1975), 143-44; Simon, *Education and Society,* 227-28; A. E. Douglas-Smith, *The City of London School* (Oxford: Basil Blackwell, 1965), 27; Scarisbrick, *The Reformation and the English People,* 119-20; Orme, *English Schools in the Middle Ages,* 278.

15. Watson, *The Old Grammar Schools,* 5.

16. A. L. Rowse, *The England of Elizabeth* (New York: Macmillan, 1951), 494-95; Lehmberg, *Sir Walter Mildmay,* 23.

17. David M. Palliser, *The Age of Elizabeth* (London: Longmans, 1983), 361.

18. Simon, *Education and Society,* 238; Lehmberg, *Sir Walter Mildmay,* 23; Brian Gardner, *The Public Schools* (London: Hamish Hamilton, 1973), 68, 71.

19. Jordan, *The Charities of Rural England,* 315-16.

20. J. B. Oldham, *A History of Shrewsbury School 1552-1952* (Oxford: Basil Blackwell, 1952), 1-5ff.

21. Ibid.

22. *Cal. Pat. Rolls, Philip and Mary,* II:69, 152; Williams, ed., *English Historical Documents, 1485-1558,* 1076.

23. *VCH Cambridgeshire,* III:463, 466; Cooper, *Memorials of Cambridge,* II:241; Walter W. R. Ball and J. A. Venn, eds., *Admissions to Trinity College, Cambridge* (London: Macmillan, 1913), I:56; Mallet, *A History of the University of Oxford,* II:42.

24. Clark, ed., *The Colleges of Oxford,* 243-44; Buxton and Williams, eds., *New College, Oxford,* 48.

25. Wood, *The Reformation and English Education,* 127-29; Miller, *Portrait of a College,* 18; Charles Crawley, *Trinity Hall* (Cambridge: Printed for the College, 1977), 18; Henry P. Stokes, *Corpus Christi* (London: Robinson Books, 1898), 53, 64-65; Mullinger, *The University of Cambridge,* II:151.

26. Ibid., 153; Buxton and Williams, eds., *New College, Oxford,* 44; Venn, *Caius College,* 43; Bush, "Tudor Humanism and Henry VIII," 170.

27. *Cal. Pat. Rolls, Philip and Mary,* II:90; H. E. D. Blakiston, *Trinity College* (London: Robinson Books, 1898), 52.

28. Ibid., 44, 54-55; McConica, ed., *The Collegiate University,* 458-61; Jayne, *Library Catalogues of the English Renaissance,* 108; Mallet, *A History of the University of Oxford,* III:157.

29. Ibid.; Blakiston, *Trinity College,* 56, 63-64, 83; James McConica, "Scholars and Commoners in Renaissance Oxford," in Lawrence Stone, ed., *The University in Society* (Princeton: Princeton University Press, 1974), I:156.

30. Blakiston, *Trinity College,* 53, 65-66, 71.

31. W. H. Hutton, *St. John Baptist College* (London: Robinson Books, 1898), 11-13; Louis B. Wright, *Middle-Class Culture in Elizabethan England* (Chapel Hill: University of North Carolina Press, 1935), 54-55; Mallet, *A History of the University of Oxford,* II:175.

32. Ibid., 176, 190, 194; *Cal. Pat. Rolls, Philip and Mary*, II:322–23; Stevenson and Salter, *Early History of St. John's College*, 114, 141, 151.

33. Mallet, *A History of the University of Oxford*, II:179; Hutton, *St. John Baptist College*, 15, 41–42.

34. Ibid., 42; Stevenson and Salter, *Early History of St. John's College*, 129, 151.

35. Ibid., 122–23; Mallet, *A History of the University of Oxford*, II:193; McConica, ed., *The Collegiate University*, 458, 460; Ker, "Oxford College Libraries," 503.

36. For information in this and the next paragraph, see Venn, *John Caius*, 4–7, 10; John Venn, *Biographical History of Gonville and Caius College* (Cambridge: Cambridge University Press, 1897), II:30–33; Christopher Brooke, *History of Gonville and Caius College* (Woodbridge: Boydell, 1985), 57–59.

37. Gillian Lewis, "The Faculty of Medicine," in McConica, ed., *The Collegiate University*, 230.

38. *Cal. Pat. Rolls, Philip and Mary*, IV:160–62; Charles E. Raven, *English Naturalists from Neckham to Ray* (Cambridge: Cambridge University Press, 1927), 149; Venn, *John Caius*, 7–8.

39. Venn, *Caius College*, 50–53; Brooke, *History of Gonville and Caius College*, 62; Mullinger, *The University of Cambridge*, II: 160–63.

40. Gweneth Whitteridge, *William Harvey and the Circulation of the Blood* (New York: American Elsevier, 1971), 8–9.

41. Quoted in Venn, *John Caius*, p. 29.

42. Venn, *Caius College*, 54–55, 67–68; Venn, *Early Collegiate Life*, 105–6; Porter, *Reformation and Reaction*, 101–2.

43. Venn, *John Caius*, 28, 30, 35–36.

44. Jayne, *Library Catalogues of the English Renaissance*, 113, 120; Venn, *Biographical History of Gonville and Caius College*, III:228; Brooke, *History of Gonville and Caius College*, 62; Whitteridge, *William Harvey*, 5.

Chapter 8: Religion, Science, and Society: The Universities During the Elizabethan Period

1. E. G. Hardy, *Jesus College* (London: Robinson Books, 1899), 54–56.

2. Quoted in E. S. Shuckburgh, *Emmanuel College* (London: Robinson Books, 1904), 32.

3. G. M. Edwards, *Sidney Sussex College* (London: Robinson Books, 1899), 29–30; C. W. Scott-Giles, *Sidney Sussex College*, 2d ed. (Cambridge: Cambridge University Press, 1975), 27.

4. Curtis, *History of Education*, 138–41; Edward A. Tenney, *Thomas Lodge* (New York: Russell and Russell, 1969), 54–55.

5. A. O. Meyer, *England and the Catholic Church under Queen*

Elizabeth, ed. John Bossy (New York: Barnes and Noble, 1967), 9; J. R. Green, *History of the English People* (London, 1883), II:403; John Bossy, *The Catholic Community in England, 1570–1850* (New York: Oxford University Press, 1976), 183.

6. Mullinger, *The University of Cambridge,* II: 176–80; Porter, *Reformation and Reaction,* 101–7.

7. Mallet, *History of the University of Oxford,* I:369–70, and II:105–6; Hutton, *St. John Baptist College,* 18–20; C. M. Dent, *Protestant Reformers in Elizabethan Oxford* (Oxford: Oxford University Press, 1983), 19–22.

8. Quoted in Simon, *Education and Society,* 307.

9. Patrick Collinson, *The Elizabethan Puritan Movement* (Cambridge: Cambridge University Press, 1967), 129.

10. Curtis, *Oxford and Cambridge in Transition,* 195–96; Miller, *Portrait of a College,* 20.

11. Buxton and Williams, eds., *New College, Oxford,* 49, 51.

12. Ibid., 21–23; Stevenson and Salter, *Early History of St. John's College,* 394.

13. Patrick McGrath, *Papists and Puritans under Elizabeth I* (New York: Walker, 1967), 112–13; Adrian Morey, *The Catholic Subjects of Elizabeth I* (Totowa: Rowman and Littlefield, 1978), 107; Meyer, *England and the Catholic Church under Queen Elizabeth,* 89, 132.

14. Mallet, *History of the University of Oxford,* II:121–22.

15. Venn, *Caius College,* 82–83, 94, 96; McGrath, *Papists and Puritans,* 204.

16. Brooke, *History of Gonville and Caius College,* 77; Venn, *Early Collegiate Life,* 151, 153, 157; Mordechai Feingold, *The Mathematicians' Apprenticeship* (Cambridge: Cambridge University Press, 1984), 51–52.

17. E. G. R. Taylor, *Late Tudor and Early Stuart Geography* (London: Methuen, 1934), 73–77; E. G. R. Taylor, *The Haven-Finding Art* (London: Hollis and Carter, 1956), 215, 218; A. L. Rowse, *The Elizabethan Renaissance: The Cultural Achievement* (New York: Scribner's, 1972), 239.

18. Thomas A. Walker, *Peterhouse* (Cambridge: Heffer, 1935), 117; Jayne, *Library Catalogues of the English Renaissance,* 126–32; Ker, "Oxford College Libraries," 503–4.

19. E. G. R. Taylor, *The Mathematical Practitioners of Tudor & Stuart England* (Cambridge: Cambridge University Press, 1954), 40–41; Feingold, *The Mathematicians' Apprenticeship,* 39, 59, 77–78; F. R. Johnson, "Thomas Hood's Inaugural Address," *JHI,* vol. 3, no. 1 (1942), 98.

20. Feingold, *The Mathematicians' Apprenticeship,* 50–51.

21. Ibid., 37; Tenney, *Thomas Lodge,* 50; John W. Shirley, *Thomas Harriot* (Oxford: Clarendon Press, 1983), 34–35.

22. McConica, ed., *The Colegiate University,* 223, 696, 716; R. T. Gunther, *Early Science in Oxford* (Oxford: Privately printed, 1937), 146, 182; Foster Watson, *The Beginnings of the Teaching of Modern Subjects* (London: Pitman Books, 1909), 340; Curtis, *Oxford and Cambridge in Transition,* 340.

23. Ibid., 237; Feingold, *The Mathematicians' Apprenticeship,* 70–71, 101, 111–12.

24. Davis, *History of Balliol College,* 85; Curtis, *Oxford and Cambridge in Transition,* 237.

25. Ibid., 235-36; Oliver L. Dick, ed., *Aubrey's Brief Lives* (London: Secker and Warburg, 1950), 5; Richard Deacon, *John Dee* (London: Muller, Blond and White, 1968), 70; Michael Foster, "Thomas Allen," *Oxoniensia,* vol. 46 (1981), 102-4.

26. McConica, ed., *The Collegiate University,* 552.

27. Esther S. Cope, *The Life of a Public Man* (Philadelphia: Memoirs of the American Philosophical Society, vol. 142, 1981), 10, 13-15.

28. Lawrence Stone, *The Crisis of the Aristocracy, 1558-1641* (Oxford: Clarendon Press, 1965), 690.

29. W. H. G. Armytage, *Four Hundred Years of English Education,* 2d ed. (Cambridge: Cambridge University Press, 1920), 3; Rowse, *The England of Elizabeth,* 259-60; Miller, *Portrait of a College,* 32.

30. John Dover Wilson, ed., *Life in Shakespeare's England* (Cambridge: Cambridge University Press, 1911), 64-65.

31. Lawrence Stone, "The Size and Composition of the Oxford Student Body," in Lawrence Stone, ed., *The University in Society,* I:19.

32. Robert Tittler, "Education and the Gentleman in Tudor England," *Hist. of Ed.,* vol. 5, no. 1 (1976), 7.

33. William Harrison, *The Description of England,* ed. Georges Edelen (Ithaca: Cornell University Press, 1968), 129; Ian Green, "Career Prospects and Clerical Nonconformity," *P & P,* no. 90 (1981), 73.

34. Lehmberg, *Sir Walter Mildmay,* 227-28.

35. Scott-Giles, *Sidney Sussex College,* 26; Edwards, *Sidney Sussex College,* 33.

36. Venn, *Early Collegiate Life,* 131.

37. Alexander C. Judson, *Life of Edmund Spenser* (Baltimore: Johns Hopkins University Press, 1945), 39.

38. John Sargeaunt, *Annals of Westminster School* (London: Methuen, 1898), 11, 25.

39. Venn, *Early Collegiate Life,* 151, 153.

40. John Stow, *A Survey of London,* ed. Charles L. Kingford (Oxford: Clarendon Press, 1908), I:174; Wright, *Middle-Class Culture,* 57; Jordan, *The Charities of Rural England,* 43.

41. R. S. Paul and W. J. Smith, *History of Middleton Grammar School* (Manchester: Manchester University Press, 1965), 9; Cooper, *Memorials of Cambridge,* I: 8.

42. Ibid., II:263; *VCH Hertfordshire,* III:370.

43. Jordan, *The Charities of London,* 212; Cooper, *Memorials of Cambridge,* I:8, and II:94, 360; Mallet, *History of the University of Oxford,* II:2; Collinson, *The Elizabethan Puritan Movement,* 46; Rowse, *The England of Elizabeth,* 499-500.

44. Stokes, *Corpus Christi,* 73.

45. Lehmberg, *Sir Walter Mildmay,* 225.

46. Stevenson and Salter, *Early History of St. John's College,* 295-96; Strickland Gibson, *Some Oxford Libraries* (Oxford: Oxford University Press, 1914), 87.

47. Scott-Giles, *Sidney Sussex College,* 15.

48. Robert F. Scott, *St. John's College, Cambridge* (London: J. M. Dent, 1907), 5-6; Cooper, *Memorials of Cambridge,* I:95, 138-39.

49. Jayne, *Library Catalogues of the English Renaissance*, 17; McConica, ed., *The Collegiate University*, 448, 451; Ker, "Oxford College Libraries," 468, 480–82.

50. Ibid., 468, 480–82, 502; Munby, *Cambridge College Libraries*, 7–8; Wormald and Wright, eds., *The English Library before 1700*, 215; Ker, *Books, Collectors, and Libraries*, 468.

51. Cooper, *Memorials of Cambridge*, III:19; Savage, *Old English Libraries*, 69; Munby, *Cambridge College Libraries*, 32; Cross, *The Puritan Earl*, 33.

52. Charles Sayle, *Annals of the Cambridge University Library* (Cambridge: Heffer, 1916), 49, 51; Oates, *Cambridge University Library*, 85–87, 93–97, 139, 152.

53. Ibid., 117, 141, 152; Sayle, *Annals of the Cambridge University Library*, 57; Jayne and Johnson, eds., *The Lumley Library*, 12.

54. Ian Philip, *The Bodleian Library in the Seventeenth and Eighteenth Centuries* (Oxford: Clarendon Press, 1983), 4–10; Gibson, *Some Oxford Libraries*, 22–23.

55. Ibid., 23; Philip, *The Bodleian Library*, 18; Jayne and Johnson, eds., *The Lumley Library*, 12; Jayne, *Library Catalogues of the English Renaissance*, 133–36.

56. Ibid., 135; Shirley, *Thomas Harriot*, 63.

57. Feingold, *The Mathematicians' Apprenticeship*, 118; Jayne, *Library Catalogues of the English Renaissance*, 134–36.

58. Ibid., 133; Gibson, *Some Oxford Libraries*, 23–24; Savage, *Old English Libraries*, 113; Mallet, *A History of the University of Oxford*, II:215.

59. Ibid., 217–18.

60. Gibson, *Some Oxford Libraries*, 26.

Chapter 9: Society, Religion, and the Grammar Schools, 1558–1603

1. Jordan, *The Charities of Rural England*, 317–18, 320–21, 324, 333; Brown, *Elizabethan Schooldays*, 6; Rowse, *The England of Elizabeth*, 495–96; Margaret Spufford, *Contrasting Communities* (Cambridge: Cambridge University Press, 1974), 203.

2. Sargeaunt, *Annals of Westminster School*, 12, 20; Rodgers, *The Old Public Schools*, 27, 30.

3. Leach, ed., *Educational Charters and Documents*, 521, 523; T. W. Baldwin, *Shakespeare's Small Latine and Lesse Greek* (Urbana: University of Illinois Press, 1944), I:380; Sargeaunt, *Annals of Westminster School*, 10–11.

4. H. F. Fletcher, *The Intellectual Development of John Milton* (Urbana: University of Illinois Press, 1956), 245–46.

5. Leach, *The Schools of Medieval England*, 247; Wasey Sterry, ed., *Annals of the King's College of Our Lady of Eton beside Windsor* (London: Methuen, 1898), 69–78; Tilley, "Greek Studies in England," 229.

6. See above, 130.

7. Edward Cardwell, ed., *Synodalia: A Collection of Articles of Religion . . . from the Year 1547 to the Year 1717* (Oxford, 1842), I:128; Charlton, *Education in Renaissance England,* 101–2; Lawson, *Medieval Education and the Reformation,* 94–95.

8. Quoted in Frank Streatfeild, *An Account of the Grammar School in the King's Town and Parish of Maidstone in Kent* (Oxford: Rogers and Broome, 1915), 27–28.

9. Quoted in R. W. Elliott, *The Story of King Edward VI School, Bury St. Edmunds* (Bury: Published by the Foundation Governors of the School, 1963), 31–32.

10. Quoted in Lawson, *Medieval Education and the Reformation,* 90.

11. Quoted in W. E. Tate, "The Episcopal Licensing of Schoolmasters in England," *Church Quarterly Review,* vol. 157, no. 325 (1956), 436–37. See also Curtis, *History of Education,* 94.

12. Lawson, *Medieval Education and the Reformation,* 90.

13. Leach, ed., *Educational Charters and Documents,* 495.

14. A. M. Gibbon, *The Ancient Free Grammar School of Skipton in Craven* (London: Hodder and Stoughton, 1947), 28–29.

15. S. J. Purvis, ed., *Tudor Parish Documents of the Diocese of York* (Cambridge: Cambridge University Press, 1948), 103–9.

16. W. P. M. Kennedy, ed., *Elizabethan Episcopal Administration* (London: A. R. Mowbray, 1924), II:118.

17. Kenneth Charlton, "The Teaching Profession in Sixteenth- and Seventeenth-Century England," in Paul Nash, ed., *History and Education* (New York: Random House, 1970), 35.

18. David Cressy, *Education in Tudor and Stuart England* (New York: St. Martin's Press, 1975), 67; Morey, *The Catholic Subjects of Elizabeth I,* 112–13, 144.

19. Orme, *Education in the West of England,* 19.

20. Spufford, *Contrasting Communities,* 189.

21. Cressy, *Education in Tudor and Stuart England,* 10; Brian Simon, "Leicestershire Schools, 1625–1640," *BJES,* vol. 3, no. 1 (1954), 46.

22. David C. Somervell, *History of Tonbridge School* (London: Faber and Faber, 1947), 22–23.

23. Quoted in Carlisle, *The Endowed Grammar Schools,* II:35.

24. *Ibid.,* 8.

25. Gardner, *The Public Schools,* 120; John B. Whitehead, *The History of the Great Yarmouth Grammar School* (Great Yarmouth, 1951), 22; Somervell, *History of Tonbridge School,* 22–23.

26. Carlisle, *The Endowed Grammar Schools,* I:624; Baldwin, *Shakespeare's Small Latine and Lesse Greek,* I:441; Watson, *The Beginnings of the Teaching of Modern Subjects,* 308.

27. Ancel R. M. Stowe, *English Grammar Schools in the Reign of Queen Elizabeth* (New York: Columbia University Press, 1908), 56, 88–89; Jordan, *The Charities of Rural England,* 303; Hodgett, *Tudor Lincolnshire,* 142; Curtis, *History of Education,* 95.

28. Quoted in *ibid.,* 76.

29. Quoted in Arthur K. Cook, *About Winchester College* (London: Macmillan, 1917), 69.

30. Watson, *The Old Grammar Schools,* 122-23; Gardner, *The Public Schools,* 73; Brown, *Elizabethan Schooldays,* 25.

31. Malcolm Seaborne, *The English School* (Toronto: University of Toronto Press, 1971), 6, 54.

32. Charles Hoole, *A New Discovery of the Old Art of Teaching School* (Menston, Yorkshire: The Scolar Press, 1973), 223.

33. T. W. Bramston, ed., *The Autobiography of Sir John Bramston* (London: Camden Society, 1st series, vol. 32, 1845), 101; Watson, *The Old Grammar Schools,* 122.

34. Brown, *Elizabethan Schooldays,* 131.

35. John Lawson and Harold Silver, *A Social History of Education in England* (London: Methuen, 1973), 118.

36. Edmund Beevor, ed., *The History and Register of Aldenham School,* 8th ed. (London: Baylin, 1948), xxv-xxviii.

37. Quoted in McDonnell, *The Annals of St. Paul's School,* 165.

38. Henry Peacham, *The Complete Gentleman,* ed. V. B. Heltzel (Ithaca: Cornell University Press, 1962), 33.

39. Cook, *About Winchester College,* 5, 19, 60.

40. Richard Mulcaster, *Positions* (New York: DaCapo Press, 1971), 40-50. See also John Bruce, ed., *Liber Famelicus of Sir James Whitelocke* (London: Camden Society, 1st series, vol. 70, 1858), 12.

41. Mulcaster, *Positions,* 4.

42. Edmund Coote, *The Englische Scholmaister* (London, 1596), passim. See also Charlton, *Education in Renaissance England,* 104.

43. Watson, *The Beginnings of the Teaching of Modern Subjects,* 308; Baldwin, *Shakespeare's Small Latine and Lesse Greek,* I:441.

44. John Brinsley, *Ludus Literarius,* ed. E. T. Campagnac (London: Constable, 1917), 165, 172, 190, 214, 222.

45. John Brinsley, *A Consolation for our Grammar Schooles,* ed. T. C. Pollock (New York: Scholars' Facsimilies and Reprints, 1943), iii, v, 3, 5, 17.

46. Darwin Wilmot, *A Short History of the Grammar School, Macclesfield* (Macclesfield: Claye, Brown and Claye, 1910), 18-19.

47. Gibbon, *The Ancient Free Grammar School of Skipton in Craven,* 24-30.

48. Lawson, *A Town Grammar School,* 61-69.

49. Mallet, *History of the University of Oxford,* II:316; Kendrick, *British Antiquity,* 105-8.

50. A. J. Hawkes, "Peter Carter," *Notes and Queries,* vol. 196, no. 17 (1951), 356-57.

51. Dick, ed., *Aubrey's Brief Lives,* 188; Watson, *The Beginnings of the Teaching of Modern Subjects,* 61; J. R. Hale, ed., *The Evolution of British Historiography* (Cleveland: World Publishing Co., 1964), 23.

Chapter 10: Women, Lawyers, and Clerics

1. Jordan, *Philanthropy in England,* 25, 283.
2. See above, 80.
3. Gardiner, *English Girlhood at School,* 185-87; Stenton, *The English Woman in History,* 137; Hogrefe, *Tudor Women,* 134; Elizabeth Godfrey, *Home Life under the Stuarts* (New York: Stokes, 1926), 102-3.
4. Ibid., 99-100; Watson, *The Beginnings of the Teaching of Modern Subjects,* xlviii-xlix, 422.
5. Cressy, *Education in Tudor and Stuart England,* 112-13; Antonia Fraser, *The Weaker Vessel* (New York: Random House, 1984), 130-31, 323. See also the articles on Bathusa Pell Makin in *DNB* and the *Biographia Britannica.*
6. Gardiner, *English Girlhood at School,* 209-11, 217, 278; Godfrey, *Home Life under the Stuarts,* 99-100; Barbara Kanner, ed., *The Women of England* (Hamden: Archon Books, 1979), 165-66; Roger Thompson, *Women in Stuart England and America* (London: Routledge and Kegan Paul, 1974), 204.
7. Stenton, *The English Woman in History,* 147-49.
8. Hogrefe, *Tudor Women,* 115.
9. Alison Plowden, *Tudor Women* (London: Weidenfeld and Nicolson, 1979), 168.
10. Fraser, *The Weaker Vessel,* 129.
11. Joan Rees, *Samuel Daniel* (Liverpool: Liverpool University Press, 1964), 2; Pearson, *Elizabethans at Home,* 219; Stenton, *The English Woman in History,* 69-70.
12. Ibid., 137; Gardiner, *English Girlhood at School,* 185-87; Hogrefe, *Tudor Women,* 134; Godfrey, *Home Life under the Stuarts,* 102-3.
13. Quoted in Ivy Pinchbeck and Margaret Hewitt, eds., *Childhood in English Society* (London: Routledge and Kegan Paul, 1969), I:271.
14. Ibid., 271-72.
15. Stenton, *The English Woman in History,* 137.
16. James O. Halliwell, ed., *The Autobiography and Correspondence of Sir Simonds D'Ewes* (London: Richard Bentley, 1845), I:63.
17. Lawson and Silver, *A Social History of Education,* 317; Cressy, *Education in Tudor and Stuart England,* 112-13; Fraser, *The Weaker Vessel,* 324; Watson, *The Beginnings of the Teaching of Modern Subjects,* 420.
18. Ibid., xlviii-xlix, 16, 422; Kanner, ed., *The Women of England,* 155; Adamson, *"The Illiterate Anglo-Saxon" and Other Essays,* 60.
19. Gardiner, *English Girlhood at School,* 232; Pearson, *Elizabethans at Home,* 220.
20. W. S. Holdsworth, *A History of English Law,* 3d ed. (London: Methuen, 1936), V:34-55, 393-96; Charlton, *Education in Renaissance England,* 177-86. See also Michael Birks, *Gentlemen of the Law* (London: Stevens and Sons, 1960), 103-6.
21. Fletcher, ed., *The Pension Book of Gray's Inn,* I:xxxii.
22. A. W. B. Simpson, "The Early Constitution of Gray's Inn," *Cambridge Law Journal,* vol. 28, no. 2 (1975), 141.

23. Quoted in Wilfrid Prest, *The Inns of Court under Elizabeth I and the Early Stuarts* (Totowa: Rowman and Littlefield, 1972), 130.

24. HMC, *Finch MSS.*, I:39.

25. Louis Knafla, "The Law Studies of an Elizabethan Student," *HLQ*, vol. 32, no. 3 (1969), 221-40.

26. W. S. Holdsworth, *Some Makers of English Law* (Cambridge: Cambridge University Press, 1938), 100-101.

27. Louis Knafla, "The Matriculation Revolution and Education at the Inns of Court," in A. J. Slavin, ed., *Tudor Men and Institutions* (Baton Rouge: Louisiana State University Press, 1972), 242.

28. Heywood, ed., *Collection of Statutes for the University and Colleges of Cambridge*, I:264-65.

29. John P. Dawson, *The Oracles of the Law* (Ann Arbor: University of Michigan Press, 1968), 64-65; S. E. Thorne, *Essays in English Legal History* (London: Hambledon, 1985), 193.

30. W. S. Holdsworth, *Sources and Literature of English Law* (Oxford: Clarendon Press, 1925), 186, 188.

31. Ibid., 107, 125.

32. Quoted in Ives, "The Common Lawyers," 196.

33. Holdsworth, *Sources and Literature of English Law*, 138-39.

34. L. W. Abbott, *Law Reporting in England* (London: Athlone Press, 1973), 161-62, 207-9, 217; Dawson, *The Oracles of the Law*, 65-67.

35. Bertil Johannson, *Law and Lawyers in Elizabethan England* (Stockholm: Almquist and Wiksell, 1967), 24-25, 59.

36. Charles H. Hopwood, ed., *Middle Temple Records* (London: Selden Society, 1904-5), I:171, and II:449.

37. J. T. Cliffe, *The Yorkshire Gentry* (London: Athlone, 1969), 75-76; Elisabeth Bourcier, ed., *The Diary of Sir Simonds D'Ewes* (Paris: Publications de la Sorbonne, Litteratures 5, n.d.), 42.

38. Claire Cross, *The Royal Supremacy in the Elizabethan Church* (London: Allen and Unwin, 1969), 93-94.

39. Christopher Hill, *Economic Problems of the Church* (Oxford: Clarendon Press, 1956), 207; Hill, *Society and Puritanism in Pre-Revolutionary England* (London: Secker and Warburg, 1967), 60; Rosemary O'Day and Felicity Heal, eds., *Continuity and Change* (Leicester: Leicester University Press, 1976), 66; John H. Pruett, *The Parish Clergy under the Later Stuarts* (Urbana: University of Illinois Press, 1978), 42; Lawrence Stone, "The Educational Revolution in England, 1560-1640," *P & P*, no. 28 (1964), 47.

40. Rosemary O'Day, "The Ecclesiastical Patronage of the Lord Keeper," *TRHS*, 5th series, vol. 23 (1973), 90, 105.

41. *VCH Cambridgeshire*, III:474; Lehmberg, *Sir Walter Mildmay*, 227, 233; Shuckburgh, *Emmanuel College*, 36; Collinson, *The Elizabethan Puritan Movement*, 125.

42. Cooper, *Memorials of Cambridge*, III:15-16; Scott-Giles, *Sidney Sussex College*, 25-26; Simon, *Education and Society*, 239.

43. Venn, *Caius College*, 82-83, 94, 96; Joan Simon, "The Social Origins of Cambridge Students, 1603-1640," *P & P*, no 26 (1963), 60-61, 64.

44. Magrath, *The Queens' College*, I:ix, 182, 237; Dent, *Protestant Reformers in Elizabethan Oxford*, 172, 176, 196.

45. Harrison, *The Description of England*, 28; John Strype, *The Life and Acts of John Whitgift* (London, 1822), I:380-81; Hill, *Economic Problems of the Church*, 202-3.

46. Dick, ed., *Aubrey's Brief Lives*, 227.

47. On the various ways the clergy were helped, see especially Hill, *Economic Problems of the Church*, passim, and Phyllis Hembry, *The Bishops of Bath and Wells, 1540-1640* (London: Athlone Press, 1967), passim.

48. Richard Hooker, *The Laws of Ecclesiastical Polity* (London, 1598), 476; Armytage, *Four Hundred Years of English Education*, 18; Harrison, *The Description of England*, 129; F. J. Fisher, ed., "Wilson's State of England," *Camden Miscellany*, XVI (London: Camden Society, 1936), 23.

49. Gunther, *Early Science in Oxford*, 203; Taylor, *The Haven-Finding Art*, 218, 228-29; Dick, ed., *Aubrey's Brief Lives*, 116.

50. Ibid.

51. Taylor, *Late Tudor and Early Stuart Geography*, 53-56; J. N. D. Bush, *English Literature in the Earlier Seventeenth Century*, 2d ed., rev. (Oxford: Clarendon Press, 1966), 189.

52. George B. Parks, *Richard Hakluyt and the English Voyages*, 2d ed. (New York: Ungar, 1961), 226.

53. *Ibid.*, 228-29; E. W. Gilbert, *British Pioneers in Geography* (New York: Barnes and Noble, 1972), 41; A. W. Ward and A. R. Waller, eds., *The Cambridge History of English Literature* (Cambridge: Cambridge University Press, 1910), IV:106-8, 465.

54. Florian Cajori, *William Oughtred* (Chicago: Open Court Publishing, 1916), passim; Harold Hartley, ed., *The Royal Society* (London: The Royal Society, 1960), 6-7; Dorothy Stimson, *Scientists and Amateurs* (New York: Henry Schuman, 1946), 29; David E. Smith, *A History of Mathematics* (New York: Ginn, 1923), I:393-94; Phyllis Allen, "Scientific Studies in the English Universities of the Seventeenth Century," *JHI*, vol. 10, no. 2 (1949), 229-30, 233; A. J. Turner, "Mathematical Instruments and the Education of Gentlemen," *Annals of Science*, vol. 30, no. 1 (1973), 58-60, 68.

55. Dick, ed., *Aubrey's Brief Lives*, 222.

56. Ibid., 224-25. See also Cajori, *William Oughtred*, 15.

Chapter 11: Zenith and Decline

1. Nicholas Tyacke, "Popular Puritan Mentality in Late Elizabethan England," in Peter Clark and others, eds., *The English Commonwealth, 1547-1660* (Leicester: Leicester University Press, 1979), 89.

2. H. S. Bennett, *English Books and Readers, 1558-1603* (Cambridge: Cambridge University Press, 1965), 271; Bush, *English Literature in the Earlier Seventeenth Century*, 27.

3. Stone, ed., *Schooling and Society*, 97.

4. Lawrence Stone, "Literacy and Education in England 1640-1900," *P & P*, no. 42 (1969), 101.

5. John Milton, "Of Education," in *The Complete Prose Works of John Milton, Vol. 2: 1643-1648* (New Haven: Yale University Press, 1959), 379-80.

6. Bramston, ed., *The Autobiography of Sir John Bramston,* 101.

7. McDonnell, *The Annals of St. Paul's School,* 203-5; Brown, *Elizabethan Schooldays,* 131.

8. Peacham, *The Complete Gentleman,* 34-35.

9. Gardiner, *English Girlhood at School,* 237.

10. Hoole, *A New Discovery of the Old Art of Teaching School,* 235-36.

11. C. B. Freeman, "A Puritan Educator," *BJES,* vol. 9, no. 2 (1961), 136.

12. Stone, ed., *The University in Society,* I:17.

13. E. Hockliffe, ed., *The Diary of the Rev Ralph Josselin* (London: Camden Society, 3d series, vol. 15, 1908), 3-4.

14. Miller, *Portrait of a College,* 39-40.

15. Scott, *St. John's College,* 51; Dick, ed., *Aubrey's Brief Lives,* 38-39; F. R. Johnson, "Gresham College," *JHI,* vol. 1, no. 4 (1940), 427, 429; S. F. Mason, "Science and Religion in Seventeenth-Century England," in Charles Webster, ed., *The Intellectual Revolution of the Seventeenth Century* (London: Routledge and Kegan Paul, 1974), 199; Feingold, *The Mathematicians' Apprenticeship,* 50-51.

16. Ibid., 70, 144-46; Gunther, *Early Science in Oxford,* 229; Donald Pennington and Keith Thomas, eds., *Puritans and Revolutionaries* (Oxford: Clarendon Press, 1978), 77-82 and passim.

17. Mallet, *History of the University of Oxford,* II:222-23; Gibson, *Some Oxford Libraries,* pp. 30-31; Wormald and Wright, eds., *The English Library before 1700,* 9-10; Philip, *The Bodleian Library,* 35-36.

18. Jayne, *Library Catalogues of the English Renaissance,* 131-32; Paul Morgan, *Oxford Libraries outside the Bodleian* (Oxford: Oxford Bibliographical Society, 1973), 148.

19. Davis, *History of Balliol College,* 112-13.

20. Edwards, *Sidney Sussex College,* 49-50, 52-53; Scott-Giles, *Sidney Sussex College,* 44; Jordan, *The Charities of London,* 265-66.

21. Buxton and Williams, eds., *New College, Oxford,* 55; McConica, ed., *The Collegiate University,* 550.

22. Twigg, *History of Queens' College,* 48-49; Oates, *Cambridge University Library,* 169.

23. McConica, ed., *The Collegiate University,* 549, 551; V. H. H. Green, *The Commonwealth of Lincoln College* (Oxford: Oxford University Press, 1979), 236.

24. Ibid., 236-37; Buxton and Williams, ed., *New College, Oxford,* 55.

25. Ibid.; J. N. L. Baker, *Jesus College, Oxford* (Oxford: Printed for Jesus College, 1971), 15; Green, *The Commonwealth of Lincoln College,* 242-43, 276.

26. Barbara Shapiro, *John Wilkins 1614-1672* (Berkeley: University of California Press, 1969), p. 118.

27. Brooke, *History of Gonville and Caius College,* 128-29.

28. Oates, *Cambridge University Library,* 231.

29. Green, *The Commonwealth of Lincoln College,* 275-76, 278, 289.

30. Twigg, *History of Queens' College,* 48-50, 143.

31. Buxton and Williams, eds., *New College, Oxford,* 59.

32. McConica, ed., *The Collegiate University,* 551; Wormald and Wright, eds., *The English Library before 1700,* 14.

33. Prest, *The Inns of Court,* 237.

34. Kearney, *Scholars and Gentlemen,* 143, 149-50; Kevin Sharpe, "The Foundation of the Chairs of History at Oxford and Cambridge," in Charles Schmitt, ed., *History of Universities* (Amersham: Averbury, 1982), II:131-32; Mark Curtis, "The Alienated Intellectuals of Early Stuart England," *P & P,* no. 23 (1962), 25-26.

35. Henry L. Clarke and W. N. Weech, *History of Sedbergh School 1625-1925* (Sedbergh: Jackson and Son, 1925), 36.

36. Watson, *The Old Grammar Schools,* lv, 130; J. E. Stephens, ed., *Aubrey on Education* (London: Routledge and Kegan Paul, 1972), 1.

37. Thompson, *Women in Stuart England and America,* 201.

38. Watson, *The Beginnings of the Teaching of Modern Subjects,* li, 420, 422; Fraser, *The Weaker Vessel,* 324.

39. Stone, "Literacy and Education in England 1640-1900," 138.

Suggestions for Additional Reading

Those wishing to learn more about the educational developments discussed in this book are advised to begin with Joan Simon, *Education and Society in Tudor England* (Cambridge: Cambridge University Press, 1967), an outstanding work that is particularly good on the events of the mid-sixteenth century. Because Mrs. Simon's book contains an exhaustive bibliography of items published before 1966, there is no need here for a long list of works that appeared before that date. However, the general reader might wish some guidance in regard to more recent works, so I have compiled a short bibliography of what might be considered the most important studies of the last two decades or so.

Baker, John N. L. *Jesus College, Oxford 1571-1971.* Oxford: Printed for the College, 1971.
Brooke, Christopher. *A History of Gonville and Caius College, Cambridge.* Woodbridge: Boydell Press, 1985.
Buxton, John and Penry Williams, eds. *New College, Oxford 1379-1979.* Oxford: Oxprint, 1979.
Catto, J. I., ed. *The Early Oxford Schools.* Oxford: Clarendon Press, 1984.
Cobban, Alan B. *The King's Hall within the University of Cambridge in the Late Middle Ages.* Cambridge: Cambridge University Press, 1969.
——. *The Medieval Universities.* London: Methuen, 1975.
Crawley, Charles. *Trinity Hall: The History of a Cambridge College 1350-1975.* Cambridge: Printed for the College, 1977.
Dent, C. M. *Protestant Reformers in Elizabethan Oxford.* Oxford: Oxford University Press, 1983.
Feingold, Mordechai. *The Mathematicians' Apprenticeship.* Cambridge: Cambridge University Press, 1983.

Fox, Levi. *A Country Grammar School: A History of Ashby-de-la-Zouch Grammar School through Four Centuries 1567–1967.* Oxford: Oxford University Press, 1967.

Gray, Arthur and Frederick Brittain. *A History of Jesus College, Cambridge.* London: Heinemann, 1979.

Greaves, R. L. *The Puritan Revolution and Educational Thought.* New Brunswick: Rutgers University Press, 1969.

Green, V. H. H. *The Commonwealth of Lincoln College.* Oxford: Oxford University Press, 1979.

Kearney, Hugh F. *Scholars and Gentlemen: Universities and Society in Pre-Industrial Britain 1500–1970.* London: Faber and Faber, 1970.

Ker, Neil R. *Books, Collectors, and Libraries: Studies in the Medieval Heritage.* London: Hambledon Press, 1985.

———. *Records of All Souls College Library 1437–1600.* Oxford: Oxford University Press, 1971.

Lawson, John. *Medieval Education and the Reformation.* London: Routledge and Kegan Paul, 1967.

———. *A Town Grammar School Through Six Centuries: A History of Hull Grammar School Against its Local Background.* Oxford: Oxford University Press, 1963.

——— and Harold Silver. *A Social History of Education in England.* London: Methuen, 1973.

McConica, James, ed. *The Collegiate University.* Oxford: Clarendon Press, 1986.

Moran, Jo Ann Hoepner. *The Growth of English Schooling 1348–1548.* Princeton: Princeton University Press, 1985.

Oates, J. C. T. *Cambridge University Library.* Cambridge: Cambridge University Press, 1986.

O'Day, Rosemary. *Education and Society 1500–1800: The Social Foundations of Education in Early Modern Britain.* London: Longmans, 1982.

Orme, Nicholas. *Education in the West of England 1066–1548.* Exeter: University of Exeter Press, 1976.

———. *English Schools in the Middle Ages.* London: Methuen, 1973.

———. *From Childhood to Chivalry: The Education of the English Kings and Aristocracy 1066–1530.* London: Methuen, 1984.

Philip, Ian. *The Bodleian Library in the Seventeenth and Eighteenth Centuries.* Oxford: Clarendon Press, 1983.

Seaborne, Malcolm. *The English School: Its Architecture and Organization 1370–1870.* Toronto: University of Toronto Press, 1971.

Simon, Joan. *The Social Origins of English Education.* London: Routledge and Kegan Paul, 1970.

Stone, Lawrence, ed. *Schooling and Society: Studies in the History of Education.* Baltimore: Johns Hopkins University Press, 1976.

———, ed. *The University in Society. Volume I: Oxford and Cambridge from the 14th to the Early 19th Century.* Princeton: Princeton University Press, 1974.

Twigg, John. *A History of Queens' College, Cambridge 1448–1986.* Woodbridge: Boydell Press, 1987.

Index

Caxton, William, 42, 44–45, 48, 91–95
Cecil, Mildred, Lady Burghley. *See* Cooke, Mildred
Cecil, William, Lord Burghley, 84, 143, 161, 163–64, 173, 182
Cerne Abbey, 57
Chaderton, Laurence, 225
Chaderton, William, 182, 192
Chaldean, teaching of, 78
Chambre, John, 169
Chantries, dissolution of, 133, 140–42
Chantries, early history of, 59
Chantries, schools kept by, 59–61, 140
Charles I (of England), 211–12, 234, 240–41, 243–44, 246
Charles II (of England), 243, 246
Charles V (Holy Roman Emperor), 103
Charles the Bold (duke of Burgundy), 42, 91
Charlton, Kenneth, 218
Charterhouse School, London, 194
Chaucer, Geoffrey, 32, 71, 92
Cheadsey, William, 160
Cheke, John, 18, 79, 131
Chester Abbey, 50
Chichele, Henry, 20, 39, 51
Chichele, William, 39
Chipsey, Thomas, 115
Christ Church, Canterbury, abbey of, 10, 47, 50, 57, 126
Christ Church, Oxford, college of, 132–35, 146, 151, 160–61, 169–70, 172, 187, 228–29, 240
Christ's College, Cambridge, 75–78, 117, 147, 160, 171–72, 176, 225
Chrysostom, St. John, 47, 84, 152
Church canons (1571), 189
Church canons (1604), 193
Cicero, 45–46
Cistercian Order, 51
City of London School, 62, 143
Civil War, 184, 216, 218, 225, 232–33, 236, 240–41, 245–46
Clanbowe, Peryne, 41
Clare Hall, Cambridge, 125, 138, 140, 166, 179, 242
Clerical education
  improvements in, 20–22, 224–28, 232
  low quality of, 1, 3–4, 9, 20
  setbacks in, 113
Clerics, also schoolmasters, 195–96
Clerics, as educational donors, xi, 2, 9–15, 20, 113–14, 145, 180, 184
Clerics, as school trustees, 195
Clerics, books owned by, 20–22
Clerics, books written by, 229–31

Clerics, former schoolmasters, 192, 200–201
Clerics, percentage with university educations, 21, 225
Clifford, Anne, 213
Clifford, George, earl of Cumberland, 166, 213
Clifford, Lucy, 118
Clothworkers' Company, 196
Cobham Library, Oxford, 27–28
Coke, Edward, 219–20, 222–23
Cole, Henry, 138, 151
Cole, William, 161
Coleridge, Samuel Taylor, 207
Colet, John, 64–66
Colleges, changing social composition of, 172–74
Colleges, libraries of, 7, 9, 14, 20, 46, 76, 114, 120–21, 127, 139–40, 149, 151, 155–56, 167, 179–82, 239
Colleges, religious practices of, 158, 161
Colleges, rise of, 74, 120
Colleges, rights of appointment of, 196
Complutensian Polyglot, 106
Constable, Marmaduke, 30
Constable, Robert, 30
Constantine, Donation of, 48
Cooke, Anne, 84
Cooke, Anthony, 83, 160
Cooke, Catherine, 84
Cooke, Elizabeth, 84
Cooke, Mildred, 84, 176, 178
Coote, Edmund, 204, 233
Cope, Walter, 183
Cornwall, John, 31
Corpus Christi College, Cambridge, 6 n., 8–9, 71, 83, 127, 147, 174, 178, 180
Corpus Christi College, Oxford, 140, 160, 184, 196
Cosin, Edmund, 155, 160
Cosin, John, 240
Coventry, Sir Thomas the Elder, 221
Coventry, Sir Thomas the Younger, 225
Coverdale, Miles, 101, 203–6, 110, 112
Cowper, Robert, 18
Cox, Leonard, 58
Cox, Richard, 133, 160
Cranmer, Thomas, 104, 126, 141–42, 163
Craven, William, 179
Cresacre, Anne, 82
Cressy, David, ix–x
Croke, John, 183
Croke, Richard, 78–79, 95, 118
Crome, Walter, 22